MOTHER OF ORPHANS

MOTHER OF ORPHANS

**The True and Curious Story of Irish Alice,
A Colored Man's Widow**

DEDRIA HUMPHRIES BARKER

FLORIDA ■ NEW YORK
www.2leafpress.org

2LEAF✦PRESS

2LEAF PRESS INC.
New York Offices
P.O. Box 4378
Grand Central Station
New York, New York 10163-4378
editor@2leafpress.org

2LEAF PRESS INC. is a
nonprofit 501(c)(3) organization that promotes
multicultural literature and literacy.
www.2lpinc.org

Edited by: Phyllis Huang

Copy edited by: Ben Lafferty

Layout and design: Gabrielle David

Library of Congress Control Number: 2017963326

ISBN-13: 978-1-940939-78-0 (Paperback)
ISBN-13: 978-1-940939-87-2 (eBook)

10   9   8   7   6   5   4   3   2   1

Published in the United States of America

First Edition | First Printing

2Leaf Press trade distribution is handled by University of Chicago Press / Chicago Distribution Center (www.press.uchicago.edu) 773.702.7010. Titles are also available for corporate, premium, and special sales. Please direct inquiries to the UCP Sales Department, 773.702.7248.

For my mother, Mary Jane and
my sister, Marcia and all the
Mamas and Little Mamas.

CONTENTS

ACKNOWLEDGMENTS

HAVE SO MANY PEOPLE to thank for their support over nearly two decades.

David Simmons built my confidence with his editing of the first story about Alice for the Ohio Historical Society's *Timeline* magazine.

Much appreciation of my husband, Michael D. Barker, for his unconditional support for more than three decades, and in raising three children, Diallo, Terri and David. To my siblings for their support and interest as I resurrected an important relative nobody knew much about, and to my uncle, James W. Leigh Jr., who encouraged finding this story. I miss you, Sonny.

What would I have done without my friends who read or heard this book in various forms, Linda Peckham, and Linda Chadderdon, Vic Rauch, Ellen DeRosia, Lisa Findley, Theresa Vann, and my Sistalocks writing group: Landis Lain, Karen Williams, Lisa Bond Brewer and Robin Pizzo. I could not have done this without those hours and hours of discussion with you all. Love you.

What awesome librarians at Michigan State University, The Library of Michigan, Clark County Library and Archives at Springfield, Ohio; the Public Library of Cincinnati and Hamilton County, Ohio; Library of Lawrenceburg, Indiana, Dearborn County; the Ohio Historical Society, and The National Archives. Thank you to Phyllis Huang, my editor at 2Leaf Press, for her generosity. This book had a second mama and her name is Cathy J. Schlund-Vials. A deep bow of respect to her. These professionals gave me their best help. Any errors of fact are entirely my own.

I'm indebted to my brother and sister-in-law, Derrick A. Humphries and Jonca Bull, for the use of their third floor garret while I researched in The National Archives. My gratitude to Lansing Community College, and LCC English professor Teresa Purvis, coordinator of the annual Women's Literature Read-In, where I read a piece of this book for five years straight.

Thanks to All Saints Episcopal Church where my friend, Nancy Spates, hosted the first reading from this book, with dessert. And, to Steve Findley, and The Coffeehouse at ASEC, where I read chapters of this story.

Finally, to my mother, Mary Jane, who is a mother extraordinaire.

And my grandmother, Pauline Lucy, who let me gaze into her life. ⌘

CHAPTER 1

The Women

I N AUGUST 2011, Kim Kardashian married my nephew — NBA player Kris Humphries — but she was not the first white woman to marry into my large African American family.[*] The first white woman to marry into our family was born over a hundred years ago and became the matriarch of my maternal family line. She had fair skin but was not considered "white." She was Irish, and in the nineteenth century, there was a difference between the two. This woman's name was Alice Donlan. She was my maternal great-grandmother. In 1899, Alice crossed the color line

Alice
ALICE WAS A SECOND-GENERATION Irish woman born in Lawrenceburg, Indiana, a German-American riverfront town on the border of Ohio and Indiana in 1875. It was the Gilded Age, but Alice grew up under less than glittering circumstances. At the age of twenty-three and on the verge of spinsterhood, Alice left Lawrenceburg and eventually met and married a colored man, John Henry Lewis Preston Taylor Johnson, in 1899. She knew little about what she was getting herself into, and had not considered the very real possibility that they would not be granted a license to marry. Nevertheless, they forged ahead and relocated to Springfield, Ohio, where his

---

* Dedria A. Humphries, "How I Ended Up at Kim Kardashian's Wedding," Salon.com, October 8 2011. https://www.salon.com/2011/10/08/how_i_ended_up_at_kim_kardashians_wedding/. Accessed January 17, 2019.

family lived. Alice became the mother of four children, and raised her three surviving children with traditions from both sides of the family. Having been abandoned by her Irish family for marrying a black man, Alice proved her ability to manage life with her new African American relations. This lasted until her husband's death. As a widow, her efforts to care for and support her three children within the social mores of two different cultures proved impossible. One year after her husband died, Alice surrendered custody of her children to the Clark County Children's Home in Springfield, Ohio. This book is about my journey of ing the reasons why. Was it a power play designed to keep her children from their black relatives? Was it a chance to ditch her children and cross back over the color line? Ultimately, it is a story about a poor young white woman widowed by a black man who became the sole supporter of their children. Learning about my great-grandmother meant weaving her story with the stories of the lives of four generations of women in her black family. It is these women who represent the five chapters in this book: great-grandmother Alice, great-aunt Pauline, grandmother Polly, my mother Mary Jane, and a chapter about me, Dedria.

Pauline

PAULINE WAS THE YOUNGER SISTER of Alice's husband, John Henry. She was born and raised in Kentucky. A transplant to Ohio, Pauline lived for her family. After her mother passed away after a long illness, she turned her attention to her beloved and sole surviving brother, John Henry. Pauline had the distinct honor of having her name bestowed upon her only brother's first child, an act tantamount to appointing her guardian should something happen to the child's parents. Pauline adored her brother. After he died, the disagreement between her and Alice set in motion a conflict that escalated into what everyone saw as Alice's incomprehensible act: surrendering her children to an orphanage. Through Pauline, I also explored other members of John Henry's family: his father who was my second-great-grandfather, Isaac, a Maryland brick mason who had been enslaved and a Civil War soldier; and his niece Laura, orphaned as an infant and raised by her aunt Pauline. I go into as much detail as possible about John Henry's life to bring to light why his family was enamored with him, and what attracted Alice to him.

Polly

POLLY WAS ALICE'S DAUGHTER. Named Pauline Lucy after her aunt, she was called by the Irish nickname, Polly. She was her mother's lovechild, the oldest daughter, and the first of four children, born in 1902. She had a brother, Elmer, called Bud, born in 1904; a brother Levy, born in 1906 and lost to whooping cough at age three in ; and a sister, Elizabeth, born in 1910 and who was barely two years old when their father passed away. Polly was ten years old when her father died, and soon after, her mother surrendered her and her siblings to a public orphanage. She eventually was taken in by a white couple that later became the comedian Jonathan Winters' grandparents. Polly graduated from high school in 1920 but remained agonized throughout most of her life by a family situation she was never able to reconcile. She left Ohio for Detroit in 1920, and two years later married a man who would become a Detroit police officer.

Mary Jane

MARY JANE IS POLLY'S oldest daughter, the first of six children born in Detroit. A light-skinned elite of the West Side, Mary Jane grew up going to the best public schools, with little knowledge of what had happened to her mother's family. She loved the women who remained at odds with one another, Alice and Pauline. Like her mother, Mary Jane became the wife of a Detroit police officer and the mother of thirteen children. All of us went to college, helped by a family of women who valued education and by a civil rights movement that focused on it, and the landmark success of the U.S. Supreme Court decision in *Brown v. The Board of Education.*

Dedria

In the chapter Dedria, I chronicled my evolution as an African American woman of mixed-race ancestry and the profound impact it has had on my life. I am the third child and second daughter of Mary Jane's brood of thirteen. I was saved by my older sister from overwhelming family responsibilities during the 1960s, an era of economic struggle. I started working in schools at fifteen, employed through the Model Cities program, a part of President Lyndon Baines Johnson's Great Society and War on Poverty. I came of age during the 1970s, an era famous for free love, bell-bottoms, and disco. Although my academic strengths in reading and writing generated interest from small liberal arts colleges, I matriculated at one of Michigan's largest universities, Wayne State University in Detroit, in part because I gave birth to my first child soon after high school graduation. With my mother's support, my education continued with an ease unheard of for working mothers during Alice's day. Later, I became a professional journalist, writer, and teacher.

My search for my family history was inspired by Alex Haley's *Roots,* a fictionalized account of the seven-generation history of his family. It was published in 1976 and adapted into a television series in 1977.

$$\wp \quad \text{CS} \quad \text{CR}$$

IN 1966 AS I EMBARKED on what became a twenty-year task, I thought my great-grandmother Alice was a curious being. Initially, I could not see our connection and thought she was "a mystery wrapped inside an enigma," to mangle a quote from Winston Churchill. To better understand both my black and white ancestors, I had to re-learn history against the backdrop that shaped them.

There were three significant events that directly or indirectly affected Ohio, my family's starting point. Before the Civil War, Ohio had declared slavery illegal in 1787. With strong abolitionist sentiment throughout the state, Ohio played an essential role in the Underground Railroad. During the war, Ohio played a crucial role in providing troops, military officers, and supplies to the Union Army. After the war, Ohio had a profound effect on Reconstruction. Ohio residents, including my second great-grandfather, helped in earnest. Elected officials administered the Congressional Reconstruction of the Southern States armed with ideals they fought hard for in the war. Those same veterans formed the Grand Army of the Republic

(GAR), an advocacy group. With the support of black Republicans, the GAR not only sent five white men to the White House, but also supported voting rights for black veterans, promoted patriotic education, helped make Memorial Day a national holiday, and lobbied the United States Congress to establish regular veterans' pensions. In this heady time, these progressives believed in freedom and that hard work could result in advancement.

While the 1890s has been referred to as the "Gay Nineties" (during the Gilded Age) and defined as an era full of merriment, optimism, and prosperous comfort, but for most Americans, nothing could be further from the truth. It was a decade marked by wars (including internal conflicts in the U.S.), economic depression, and strikes in the industrial workforce. What is worth noting, however, is that during the Gay Nineties, a period often called "The Progressive Era" brought forth widespread social activism and political reform across the United States. The seeds of the suffrage movement, which took root well before the Civil War, gained momentum with reform groups such as temperance leagues, religious movements, women's clubs, and moral reform societies that proliferated across the U.S. after Reconstruction. Many American women were beginning to chafe against what historians termed the "cult of true womanhood," that is, the idea that the only "true" woman was a pious and submissive wife and mother concerned exclusively with home and family. Even today, the question of whether women can "have it all" is, in many ways, no different from the central question being asked by the cult of domesticity: What is a woman's role? During my research, as I learned more about the women in my family, I was pleasantly surprised by what I ed.

Finally, and as it pertained to my great-grandparent Alice and John Henry, the state of Ohio had passed an anti-miscegenation law in 1861 and repealed it in 1887. The simultaneous repeal of this law against race-mixing and Ohio's other remaining racially discriminatory legislation marked the state's transition into a society in which people of color could — and did — take their rightful place in Ohio's civic and political processes. It was these three factors that helped create a path for my great-grandparents to come together and begin our maternal family.

I reviewed personal documents and memorabilia, did research at libraries, examined census documents for Ohio, Kentucky, and Michigan, and interviewed surviving family members. U.S. Census records were invaluable. However, the accuracy of the census, especially on black people, remains a topic of debate. I showed my mother, Mary Jane, a government document whose information ran counter to what she believed about her people. She said, "Maybe."

My maternal family's women's history began well before the #Metoo movement. It caps decades of women who have made contributions in their communities and families. It was easy to overlook their contributions because we thought we were a patriarchal family while in fact we were very much a matriarchal one. It was Alice's driving determination that her children receive a formal education, even if it meant surrendering her children to an orphanage, that set the precedent. Her strong will has become a cornerstone of my family. Struggling to raise productive people in a family such as ours has often been intense, especially in an era when women were subjected to second-class citizenship. This book looks at the tangled roots of the start of my family. It began with this Irish woman, Alice, who made choices against social expectations.

Alice actually reminds me of some of the women described in recently published books about race-mixing in families. James McBride shares in *The Color of Water: A Black Man's Tribute to His White Mother* (1995) how only through research was he able to solve the mystery of his mother's racial identity (she would not tell him) and she was Jewish. Lalita Tademy's *Cane River* (2001) traces generations of her female ancestors in Louisiana to explore how her French forebears mixed their blood line with black women and maintained their family's fair skin color. Other books, notably Kathryn Stockett's *The Help* (2009) tells a familiar story of the relationship between a black maid and white mistress, a negative dynamic that made black and white women need, yet resent each other. This was Alice's story in reverse. She was an Irish maid in a

Cincinnati Great House (a mansion owned by new monied people, the *nouveau riche*), which would now be known as a McMansion. She suffered insults from white women of means, just as black maids did. Denied the respect of being called by her proper, given names, the Irish maid was expected to answer to a generic name that deprived her of individuality. She was treated like a child. The workplace intensity between black and white women followed Alice into her husband's family of sisters.

Alice's image in our family was further tarnished because she gave up her children. Nevertheless, I soon realized that she had many admirable qualities. She was thought of as "a tough old bird" by her grandchildren, though my mother, her granddaughter, remembered her simply as "Grandma," whose sporadic visits nevertheless had a sense of regularity when she visited her home in Detroit. She was loved and recognized for the kindness she showed in support of her granddaughter's education. Ultimately, this is a story of a woman who was set adrift from a path of expectations of nineteenth-century women who refused to be discouraged by social discrimination. Determined to bequeath her children an anchor from her Irish heritage and upbringing with access and better opportunities through education, she utilized the resources available to her. Given the circumstances, perhaps she was being reasonable. At least Alice was forgiven by at least one of her children for crossing the color line and then crossing back without her.

Learning about Alice helped me gain a better understanding of the challenges she faced. It inspired greater love and compassion for her flaws and mistakes. Alice's story is reminiscent of mine. In the end, love works and families often forgive. Our family history goes beyond the names and dates I found in our tree; it is about what makes us who we are. It is about people who lived and breathed and suffered and triumphed. It is about roots and branches and leaves and entire forests. *Mother of Orphans* is a story about all of us. ⌘

CHAPTER 2

Alice

THERE WAS NO WAY for me to have known what happened to my great-grandmother Alice because my family never told us kids anything about her. In 1961, when a purse snatcher knocked her down on the street in Detroit's West Side, I was two miles away, a nine-year-old girl learning, reluctantly, about how to become a house slave. Later I learned Alice was on her one-mile trek to church services, walking from her daughter and son-in-law's house to St. Cecilia's Catholic Church. She must have been a sight: a little, old, frail white lady creeping through a black neighborhood with a proper leather pocketbook dangling from her arm, the kind of handbag containing more handkerchiefs than dollar bills. Hunchbacked, Alice was so bent over that her head seemed stuck to the front of her chest. Her skin color and shape rendered her an easy mark. When some black guy tried to snatch her purse, he knocked her down onto the pavement and broke her hip. That was the touch of death; she died soon thereafter.

The place of Alice's death could not have been more different than that of her birth, and where her thirteen years of married life played out to the moment that would forever define her in my eyes. She was born in Lawrenceburg, Indiana, a riverfront town. She lived all her life in the American Midwest, a neighborhood of eight northern industrial states — Michigan, Ohio, Illinois, Minnesota, Wisconsin, Indiana, and Iowa — boxed-in by the Atlantic seaboard, the Plains, the Southern states, and Canada. Alice's hometown sits on the bank of the Ohio River.

In 1884, the year Alice turned nine years old, there was an epic flood, a Great Flood (the greatest flood until 1937). It was greater than the floods of previous years, 1882 and 1883. The Great Flood of 1884 came on like a drag queen fashion show: one sparkly dress after the other. For Christmas 1883, a sequined cape of fine hail fell to a ground covered with gossamer snow that was already several inches thick. By January, silky snow had been whipped into chiffon by the gale. In February 1884, the soft air of spring melted the snow into a runway stretching to the river, pumping up the volume. Every historical source reported, and every street light pole along the bank was marked to show that the Ohio River crested at nearly seventy-two feet. The levee, built to hold the river back, was breached, reducing Lawrenceburg to mud as the water rolled over the land.

On February 28, 1884, *The Register Weekly* newspaper's headline reminded Lawrenceburgians their struggle had lasted "Forty days and forty nights." C. B. Miller, secretary of the relief committee, reported that the schools opened doors to 3,000 people whose houses were uninhabitable: fifty-four shifted off their foundations, fourteen fell, and eleven vanished.[1] Clean-up crews employed every man, and boy twelve years of age and older. The earnings were lucrative and many students preferred to work rather than take their final school examinations. That meant next fall the seventh and eighth grade classes contained no male students. Those grades were considered to be wiped out. Frustrated, school and civic officials issued a city proclamation and declared that henceforth school attendance would be "to ninth grade, at least."[2] Alice attended school, where she learned math and bookkeeping. But for most girls, school was dispensable because family duties took precedence.

The Ohio River is well-known among black people to deliver not destruction but freedom. The Underground Railroad, a clandestine overland escape from slavery, operated for decades across the Ohio River. It tripped the throbbing hearts of enslaved black people who planned to use it as a bridge to freedom. When they sang, "Wade in the water/wade in the water, children," they were serenading the

Ohio River, that watery cleft between the free and the slave states, telling her they trusted her to deliver them, body and soul. Thomas Jefferson wrote in his *Notes on the State of Virginia* that the Ohio River was the "most beautiful on earth. Its current gentle, waters clear, and bosom smooth and unbroken by rocks and rapids."[3] Along many points on its banks, the Ohio River was a beautiful freedom giver but not in Lawrenceburg, Indiana.

The 1870 U.S. Census counted just twenty-six blacks among Lawrenceburg's 5,000 population, including in the hills where Alice's grandparents lived. This lack of colored citizenry existed even though around the bend, there was a thriving black community in Cincinnati. The state of Indiana went on to become an outpost for the Ku Klux Klan, a white supremacist group terrorizing black people starting in the early 1920s. So Alice, born and baptized in Lawrenceburg, was not a woman raised to live in 1960s Detroit. Although her people, the Irish, knew what it was like to be persecuted for just being who they are, they had little sympathy for black people.

She came from immigrant stock. Or were they refugees? They were actually both: refugees forced into exile in the United States by a humanitarian and political disaster, having suffered English persecution in Ireland for over eight centuries. Certainly, the maltreatment of newcomers to the United States was hardly a cross for the Irish to bear on their own. However, they were particularly vilified by the country's Anglo-Saxon Protestants whose ancestors had explicitly made their exodus across the ocean to find a refuge from papism and ensure their worship was cleansed of any remaining Catholic vestiges. It was only during my adult lifetime that the English and the Irish had more or less reached a resolution. But then came Brexit, and now it seems the Irish are back to the drawing board to prevent their two Irelands from careening into the collective Irish Catholic's face. I suspect my maternal great-grandmother's people had a different experience than my paternal great-grandfather's people, who were captured and sold out of their country to become slaves in America.

There has been a lot written about the Irish-American experience in books, magazines, and periodicals. Interest intensified with the election of John F. Kennedy when he became the first Catholic president of the United States in 1961. In the nineteenth century, from 1820 to 1850, however, the Irish were hardly considered American citizens, let alone presidential material. They were a starving people. The potato famine drove them onto ocean-going ships, some not at all ocean-worthy, bound for New York. Once they landed, the Irish filled the most menial and dangerous jobs around the country, often at low pay. Some men, including Alice's people, cut canals. They dug trenches for water and sewer pipes. They laid rail lines. They cleaned houses. They slaved in textile mills. They worked as stevedores, stable workers, and blacksmiths. My family members worked riverfront Indiana, fed by the Ohio River, in all its verdant splendor, which reminded them of home. Indiana expert Mona Robinson wrote that these "refugees" "settled in almost every other smaller city or town."[4]

Most Irish brought little or nothing to America, but their intense interest in education. In his bestselling memoir, *Angela's Ashes* (1996), Irish-American Frank McCourt, chronicled years of family impoverishment caused by his father's alcoholism. When they could not make it in the U.S., his parents took their children back to Ireland, and poverty followed them. Nevertheless, McCourt's mother had high expectations for her son, the scholar, even as her baby girl died of starvation. McCourt describes with humor his family's life in abject educated poverty. Eventually, he migrated to the United States, where he attended public college and went on to teach in a premier New York City high school.[5]

"Choosing a school for their children was a major concern for parents," wrote Marie Davis in "Child-rearing in Ireland 1700-1830: An Exploration." The "major concern" was attempts by academics to convert Catholic children to Protestanism. To avoid that, Irish Catholic parents paid to send their children to "hedge school" which was held outside or in roofless buildings and instructed by Catholic-friendly academics. Hedge school was against the law, but Davis wrote, risking legal penalty reflected, "the determination of poor Catholic parents to... obtain an education for their children by any available means."[6] More than a century later Alice showed the same determination when she sent Polly to an orphanage. Her action stemmed from centuries of persecution and oppression of the Irish

Maureen Murphy noted that "having arrived in America with a good basic education and the social graces natural to people in the Irish countryside, [the women] realized that education, a good appearance and social graces would carry their children a long way."[7] Alice went to school. She was in a good position to do well by her children.

In 2000, I went to Lawrenceburg to begin my research. On a Saturday in May, after I had spent a week at a writers' conference in New Harmony, Indiana, I sped east to get to the library before it closed. I rode alongside the Ohio River as much as I could and stole glances of it as I approached. As a Detroiter, I thought I knew what a waterfront town should look like, but all I could think was: dingy. All that silt the floods washed up from the riverbed, I imagined clinging to the buildings, even tinting the air. One author wrote that Lawrenceburg had "the unkempt aspect so common to the small river places."[8]

At 4:30 in the afternoon, I ran from my car through the front door of the library and headed straight for the sign "GENEALOGY." The lady at the desk called out, "Who are you looking for?" and then she was by my side, matching my pace. She was the local genealogist Chris McHenry, and my research had started. "Donlan," I told her. She said, "The Squire." I did not know what a squire was, and she said, "justice of the peace." I nodded, yes. "That makes sense. My sister is a judge." Those who dig and explore the records quickly learn that occupations can run in families, even among relatives separated by time and space, or benign contempt, as such was the case with Alice's family because she became a colored man's wife.

McHenry introduced me to the Squire and every other one of Alice's forebears in the faded census records. She copied the information I needed and promised to send me additional materials. I went back another time, but never saw her again. The rest of the information she sent was general histories that let me know what forces had shaped my great-grandmother.

℘ ☙ ❧

THE DONLANS FIRST APPEARED in the 1840 U.S. Census of Kelso, a farming community in the hills above Lawrenceburg. In Alice's time, Lawrenceburg was a prosperous little town, with people making things from the commodities delivered via the Ohio River, like furniture, coffins, and liquor. Her grandfather, the Squire, and grandmother, Mary Curley, born in Ireland, lived in the hills above the city. William B. Donlan, the Squire, was well-known for his jail adjacent to his courtroom, the cost of bail ("a vote for Democrats"), the physical punishment he sometimes gave his recalcitrant prisoners, and the marital advice given to couples seeking a divorce ("stay together"). The newspapers called him "peculiar."[9] Maybe he did seem strange to Lawrenceburg's precise Germans, but not so much to Irish Catholics. He was a Famine Irish, straight from Cork. He was used to institutions, notably the Catholic Church, providing correction, schooling, and cures the Irish needed. That continued when they immigrated to the U.S. By 1870, the Squire was well-off with an estimated net worth of $800 and three parcels of real estate he farmed. The only thing I found out about Alice's grandmother is her name. I spotted it in the St. John's registry: "February 9, 1845 Baptized, Winford Donelon, son of William Donlan and Mary Curley, his wife." The couple had seven daughters and two sons. Winford was the older son. He became Alice's father. The 1860 U.S. Census showed Alice's father (his name now spelled Wilfried) was in school in Dover when he was fifteen years old, and that his older sister was in school at age seventeen.

Alice's maternal grandparents had once lived in Dover. But early on in their marriage, John and Ellen Starke moved to Lawrenceburg. The 1860 U.S. Census shows that John was born in Maryland in 1810 to Irish parents. He became the father of six children. The oldest was a son born in Maryland; then John Starke moved to Indiana, where he married Ellen, who was ten years younger. Their other five children were born in Indiana. John worked as a laborer, and his net worth was fifty dollars. The children included a daughter named after her mother, who would become Alice's mother. On April 4, 1874, at age twenty-three, Ellen Starke Jr., married

Winford Donlan, age twenty-nine. On the occasion of their marriage, Ellen received a Catholic prayer book called a missal. "To Ellie," the inscription on the inside cover said, "from Florence," whose last name had faded beyond recognition. This book, which is in my possession, is one of the few Donlan family keepsakes Alice was able to pass down to her black family. I do not think she had many. Alice's parents began their married life in Lawrenceburg, where Ellen recorded her first child's birth on her missal's back cover, "Alice Donlon [sic] born April 1, 1875 Lawrenceburgh, Ind."[10]

My great-grandmother Alice was named after one of her father's sisters, and baptized with Robert and Mary Starke standing as god-parents. The Reverend P. P. B. Duddenhausen, a German priest, baptized Alice at Lawrenceburg's St. Lawrence Church. A German Catholic church, St. Lawrence was organized in 1840 by the Kimmel, Schwartz, Meier and Crusart families. In 1867, the second St. Lawrence Church was built and became the tallest structure in town. Not only did it have a 145-foot high steeple, but the building also sat on land that was the highest point in town, at that time the only flood insurance available. As Alice's baptism registration was written in Latin and difficult to read, the church secretary wrote when she sent it to me. She was right. In contrast, up in the hills at St. John's where the Squire and his family worshiped, Catholic activity was registered in English, at least as far back as 1845 when Winford was baptized. Reverend Joseph Merkl recorded on October 12, 1894 that the eighty-nine-year-old William Donlan was "refreshed again with the most holy sacraments." It meant he was dead and buried.

James Baldwin had something to say about the power of language. In his essay, "If Black English Isn't A Language, I Do not Know What Is," he wrote:

> "It goes without saying, then, that language is also a political instrument, means, and proof of power. It is the most vivid and crucial key to identity: It reveals the private identity, and connects one with, or divorces one from, the larger, public, or communal identity."[11]

Baldwin proved that to me when he signed books at Wayne State University. His personal appearance was memorable because I sat next to him as he signed his books. His use of common language was a profoundly penetrating tool that connected people. Inherently, the domination of one culture is not a bad thing, if it is your culture. The culture in Lawrenceburg was German. Alice was Irish.

A disconnect would exist no matter what. Alice was the second-generation of her family born in the United States; and the third-generation on her mother's side. Back in the Gilded Age, a person's ethnic background mattered a lot. It was a stain no ambition could bleach; and in the case of Alice, it was a time when the Irish were called "niggers turned inside-out," and considered "smoked Irish."[12] Noel Ignatiev asked in his *How the Irish Became White* (1995), "how the Catholic Irish, an oppressed race in Ireland, became part of an oppressing race in America?"[13] He studied the Irish in Philadelphia and concluded that they became white by their steadfast refusal to be black. They did it by demeaning black people and violently creating a space between them. And given the slur, they re-invented themselves as the antithesis of black people. Ignatiev wrote that the Irish took the worst jobs and performed them as if they were paid top dollar when they were actually low bidders. Once the Irish pushed the blacks out, they refused to let them back in by establishing unions.[14] But the title of Angela F. Murphy's book, *American Slavery, Irish Freedom: Abolition, Immigrant Citizenship and the Transatlantic Movement for Irish Repeal* (2010), illustrates how the two groups shared similar struggles.[15]

At the inception of this country, the English defined themselves as white people and everyone else "other." They used race to justify limiting opportunities for others that included those who immigrated to America. Thomas N. Brown wrote that "nativism is primarily an extension of English hatred for the Irish." But it was "the realities of loneliness and alienation, and of poverty and prejudice" from which Irish-American nationalism "derived its most distinctive attitudes: a pervasive sense of inferiority, intense longing for acceptance and respect, and an acute sensitivity to criticism."[16] It is a fight that black people continue to engage in against racism and white privilege. Although German immigrants were not ostracized as the Irish, they would eventually bear the brunt of anti-German hysteria during World War I. While Alice was raised among Germans, she was still Irish. Her name was Irish. So were her customs, food, attitudes, and accent, but after English subjugation, the Irish language was in sharp decline.

If Alice had been German, she might have had a chance with one of the Fitch brothers of Lawrenceburg, identical twins whose father was the president of First National Bank. The brothers opened a hotel by the train station. Thomas Fitch was elected Mayor of Lawrenceburg and became a mortician. Along with the other girls, pretty Alice might have dreamt about these brothers, but would their German mother, any German mother, even a German Catholic mother, welcome an Irish girl as a daughter-in-law in her family? Nearly impossible. Alice had no prospects in Lawrenceburg. Unmarried at age twenty-three, she was on the threshold of becoming a spinster. If she wanted to marry and have children, she needed to go elsewhere.

ℰ ℭ ℛ

Alice arrived in the Queen City.

IN 1898, AT AGE TWENTY-THREE, Alice left Lawrenceburg in search of her future. She could have gone up to the hills to search for a husband where her parents had been born and raised, and where the Irish still lived, but she was a city girl. So instead of getting on a buckboard wagon seat, she took her carpetbag to the train depot in downtown Lawrenceburg. It had a fine oak door with a beveled glass window like any other train depot. But it was strange because it crouched a few blocks up from the riverbank on William Street, half on the sidewalk, half in the roadway. In front of it, silver streaks of steel rail created a street meridian, on which passing horses tap-danced. She boarded the train headed east. Those black iron horses of the Gilded Age seemed straight out of a Western movie, trumpet chimneys letting out clouds of white steam, with curving cowcatchers at the front fender. It would take her one state east, just around the bend of the Ohio River, twenty-one miles to Cincinnati, a powerhouse city of 300,000 residents.[17] People commuted from towns like Lawrenceburg all up and down the shoreline to work in Cincinnati. The mecca of the region, Cincinnati offered something for everyone. Southerners crowned it "The Queen City." Revelers dubbed it "The Big, Sinful City." The urbane hailed it, "The London of North America." And for the stylish it was "The Paris of America."[18] If Alice was going to find a husband, it would be there, in the city in the bowl of the Ohio River Valley.

Her journey ended in a barn of a station. It was the Little Miami Railroad depot, a transportation palace more than five hundred feet long that opened overhead to a very high ceiling that looked like an inside sky. It had more arches than a church and stained glass windows in the shape of peacock tail feathers.[19] Cincinnati's Little Miami Railroad station was as fancy as the city was daring. When Alice arrived, she more than likely wore the style of the day: a dark blue dress hemmed short to the ankle. Alice took note of the latest fashions because the husband she sought was someone who would want a modern woman who knew how to dress, read, write and count money. When she left Lawrenceburg, a depression that had started in 1893 when she was eighteen years old, seemed never-ending. But as she descended into Cincinnati's Little Miami Railroad depot, the recession was beginning to break. But how could anyone know that? The downturn crippled small places like Lawrenceburg, but Cincinnati was a major city, the headquarters of Procter & Gamble (P&G). In 1898, P&G was riding the huge success of Ivory, the soap "So pure it floats—99 and 44/100% pure."

If Alice was to catch a husband in Cincinnati, she needed to look desirable. She needed new clothes, shoes, hats, gloves, and the money to buy them. She needed a job. But by the turn of the twentieth century, not only was the country in a recession, it was in the throes of nativism. White people boiled with an anti-Irish and anti-Catholic sentiment that could be traced back to the British Isles. The English hated the Irish. And in America, the WASPs kept the Irish lower than second-class, and made them compete with blacks for the lowest-paying jobs.

Alice's only option was to be a maid and provide menial labor in a white person's house. The English liked their "Bridgets," the catch-all name for an Irish maid. To replace the term "maid" with the name "Bridget" was an insult that denied Irish women their individuality and dignity in America.

Alice had to know the servant hierarchy. There were chamber-maids, parlor maids, scullery maids, and laundry maids (laundress), the worst of the maid jobs. Jo Baker's novel, *Longborn* (2013), appreciated that job from the point of view of a laundress employed in the Bennett household, the family at the center of Jane Austen's novel, *Pride and Prejudice* (1813). The laundress worked with her hands in water and lye soap most hours of the day. Her hands became rough, blistered, chapped, chafed, and in winter, stricken with chilblains. Most laundresses were widows with children who did the work because it provided a steady income. Well over twenty years old when she arrived in Cincinnati, Alice could not be a laun-dress marked by rough hands. She did not have enough time to raise the money for her accouterments by washing clothes then setting aside time to let her hands heal—there were no rubber gloves in 1898—before she went looking for a man.

If Alice wanted to be a wife, her hands needed to stay soft and supple for a man to hold. She required work that would not impede on her value as a potential wife. Laundry was a separate job, not one added to the numerous tasks of "a maid of all work."[20] But being a maid was not so bad. In an upper-class house, an Irish maid was exposed to the more beautiful things of life, and spent time among quality people. She learned how to dress and speak correctly, how to gauge quality linen and the lines of good furniture, and how to set a beautiful table.[21] She learned how to become more acceptable in the real world, and more impor-tantly, was able to avoid poverty. To further her cause, Alice sought work in the Cincinnati hills where the exclusive homes were. Alice went to work in a Cincinnati Great House; which one was too fine a detail to . Many early Irish immigrants to America were indentured, and their names might be found in account books. An enslaved woman warranted a brief description in a last will and testament with instructions for her disposition, along with other property, but Alice was a free woman, so there was no need to keep a record on her. I tried to determine which hill—Mount Airy, Mount Adams, Price Hill, Clifton, Mount Lookout, Mount Washington, or Mount Auburn that Alice worked.

Mount Auburn was already in decline by the late nineteenth century. The Taft House, the family home of President William Howard Taft, had been broken up into apartments. Mount Adams was posh, offering the most dramatic valley view. After its incline opened in 1876, people who neither resided nor worked on the hill waited in long lines to ride to its top. The "incline" was the newest thing: a funicular railway that used traction for movement on steeply inclined slopes. It worked by the principle of counterbalance; one streetcar lowered from the hilltop lifted another car from the valley floor below. Passengers waved as the cars passed each other on the tracks. People were in awe of the view, which rivaled that of the spectacular view of Cincinnati from the Kentucky highland. Atop Mount Adams, people enjoyed attractions such as Highland House resort. Its pavilion offered dining, bowling, opera, concerts under the stars, and strolling along garden paths.

Mount Adams also offered the Church of Immaculate Conception, where any self-respecting or socially-conscious Catholic living on that hill attended. Its Good Friday praying-up-the-steps event was legendary. Penitents climbed 111 steps and stepped across seven platforms while offering adoration, confession, thanksgiving, offering supplication, and intercession. Alice could not have worked or lived on Mount Adams because Immaculate Conception was strictly German Catholic. Her life on Mount Adams at Immaculate Conception would be the same as in Lawrenceburg at St. Lawrence Church. She would stand out as the Irish girl. So she did not work in a Great House on Mount Adams, or Mount Auburn. None of the other hills mattered, except Clifton.

One of the most magnificent of Cincinnati's Great Houses was "Brightside" on Clifton Hill, owned by Charles Herbet Duhme, the well-known jeweler. Duhme's was known as the Tiffany's of Cincinnati and the West. Architect H.E. Siler of Newport, Rhode Island designed Brightside, and it was described in Walter E. Langsam's *Great Houses of The Queen City* (1997) as a "simple cube, with a low-hipped roof."[22] That simplicity included an arch portico, a bowed front porch, second-story bay windows under a round window at the base of the third-story set off by inscribed or embossed small-scale Adamesque pilasters, swags, garlands, ribbons, and rosettes. Photographs show an interior with furnishings of dark wood and gilt, reflecting mirrors, chairs and divans, wood-trim on every edge, baseboards and chair rails. Oriental rugs needed to be swept and beaten. Delicate, precious things like crystal required constant cleaning to gleam. All of these things called for servants with rags and soap. *Ivory Soap.*

Since there was no record, I could only assume that Alice went to work in Clifton. Later in Alice's life, Clifton showed up consistently in odd places. For instance, she enrolled her oldest child in a school named Clifton even though it was out of their neighborhood, and involved walking past the Catholic school. Later, Alice took her children on vacation to a town called Clifton. This was not a major destination. There may have been a financial reason; for example, it was cheap. But I believe there was a compelling emotional reason for Clifton, like when mothers name their child for a favorite singer, politician, or a legend. My granddaughter Madison is named for the street where her parents met.

I can see it now: Alice presents herself for an interview at a Great House on Clifton Hill. She is standing while her prospective mistress, a society lady gives her the once over. The lady has taken a day off from church or other charitable work to conduct this interview because her husband, an executive at a bank or a factory, must sustain live-in help like his peers. After examining Alice from head to toe, at the conclusion of the interview, she tells Alice she will do. Alice was small, less than five feet in height, economically depressed and malnourished. Her consciousness about style kept her waist tiny and neat. A live-in maid must present well, for she reflected on her employers. The lady of the house was hiring the whole person, even if this was the only time she showed interest in Alice's real name. The job was to impart status, though the work, she says, is to polish the silver, keep the crystal gleaming, and wax the wood to glow. Alice thought about her knees getting rough from scrubbing floors, but her skirt is long. The expression on her mistress's face asked, "Who will know the condition of the knees of a virtuous maid? Be grateful you are spared the more difficult work of being a laundress." Alice took the job and she was on her way.

$$\mathcal{EO} \; \mathcal{C8} \; \mathcal{QR}$$

Meeting people, that is, men.

NOW INSTALLED in a reputable house, Alice was ready to set out to fulfill her goal. Church was a way to meet men because the Irish church watched courting-age people closely. An Irish woman told *National Geographic* that when the priest ed a young woman was stepping out, he asked with narrowed eyes, "And what did you do?"[23] Being a maid was a good job for an Irish Catholic marriage-seeker like Alice, for her situation can be literally described as "when opportunity knocks." "Opportunity," Lucy Lethbridge informs us, "in the men who came to the house regularly." An Irish Catholic maid being courted by a man at work, could, in all honesty, report to her inquiring priest, "What did I do? I received a package."[24]

And so it was with Alice, who met her future husband at work, which was confirmed by her daughter. One day Alice answered a knock at the rear door of the house on Clifton. She expected to find one of the regular porters, a man delivering meat, ice, coal, milk, fish and more. But when she pulled it open she found in the door frame a black man. She had not seen a black man up close until after she arrived in Cincinnati. Lawrenceburg's black population – an estimated two-tenths of one percent – was not enough for her to ever run into one on the street downtown. But Cincinnati had a black community of 14,000 and they worked like everyone else in town.[25] What a surprise for Alice. "Name's John Henry Johnson," he announced.

He was named after a bona fide working-class hero, a laboring man, whose last feat in life made him a legend and his story a

folktale. As the story goes, John Henry was a late nineteenth-century black man driving steel on the railroads after the Civil War. He
blasted rivets into rails with his huge sledgehammer to stick tracks
to the ground. He was the fastest worker around the Big Bend.
What a blow to the pride and the purse of the working man, when
the railroad companies put in a machine to drive the rivets. John
Henry challenged the machine to a contest. Many other men who
worked the rails, just like John Henry, were not as strong of back or
heart, so they gathered to watch. With biceps bulging, John Henry
pounded the rivets. He beat the machine but wore out his heart.
Parents who admired strength, spirit, and pride named their baby
boys after John Henry.

So common was the name "John Henry" that in city directories
and the census the name was often abbreviated to John H., or "J.
H." There should have been more John Henrys in Cincinnati, but I
found only eleven John Johnsons, eight with the middle initial "H."
Their occupations were also listed: cooks, laborers, so many porters,
a hod carrier, and two coachmen. Directories from 1898 to 1903,
show the following:

1898　Johnson John H., cook, boards 1005 Foraker
　　　　John H., laborer, h 662 W. 5th

1899　Johnson, John, coachman, 3016 Stanton Avenue
　　　　John, driver, 1137 Plum
　　　　John H., porter, 414 Oliver

1900　Johnson, John H., porter, h 1206 Whitlow

1901　Johnson John H., coachman, h 731 W. 7th Street
　　　　between Cutter & Linn
　　　　John H. hod carrier, h 7 Crippen Alley+

1902　Johnson, John H., porter, h 412 Oliver
　　　　John porter, rooms 33 E. Carter Alley

For Alice's beau, I picked John H. Johnson, coachman. My mother
pegged John Henry's specific occupation from her mother. My
mother said, "She told me he was a jockey." What jockey says to
me is that our John Henry worked with horses. At the turn of the

twentieth century, a horse and buggy were still the luxurious way to get around, so John H. Johnson, coachman, fits the jockey story. It makes so much sense that Alice's beau worked with horses because she was Irish and the Irish love horses. *National Geographic* called it "an infatuation" that stems from a *Ben-Hur* era of Celtic warriors who let their horses eat from "the emerald pastures."[26]

Alice opened the door to a man who was single, and worked with horses in her neighborhood. The city directory said he lived elsewhere, but in those days, the household staff was awarded living space as a part of their pay. He lived close to the coach house. So close, he heard the horses whinny in the stable, and smelled the leather in the tack room. He was a member of the Great House staff who held him in high esteem because the most valuable property of the household, aside from the house, was entrusted to him. He cared for the horses.

Before her stood a small man, firm, and sturdy. His stable coat was covered with horsehair. He was about her age; no, a bit older, might have been her second thought. He was a man from Lexington, Kentucky, which was especially attractive, as he was "marked by enthusiasm, freedom of speech, independence of action, and superlatively flamboyant conduct."[27] He was birthed and bred for equine acumen, which Alice found appealing. But starry eyes aside, it was the end of the Gilded Age, and Jim Crow was coming on fast with new laws regulating relationships between black and white people. States that had allowed race-mixing were targeted with new and restrictive laws. It mirrored the Republican party efforts in the twenty-first century with their treatment toward women (scheming to overturn *Roe v. Wade*) and immigrants (building a wall to keep out brown people).

One place where John and Alice were likely welcomed as a couple was the sociable Vine Street in downtown Cincinnati, also known as the "Big Sinful City." Ohio essayist David D. Anderson wrote in "Ohio and The Demon" that Cincinnati was "intransient" about drinking. In 1874, the year before Alice was born, 3,000 saloons, breweries, and distilleries operated in Cincinnati. Although the temperance movement was in its heyday, in 1874 imbibers still spent

$33 million on liquor. Neither the praying Mother Stewart in 1874, nor the hatchet wielding Carrie Nation in 1900 succeeded in closing down the bars.[28] Vine Street was part of the drinking district called Over-the-Rhine, at the time a German working-class neighborhood which catered to all. Vine Street seemed all sin and sensation: block after block, there were saloons next to taverns next to bars next to beer gardens next to pubs next to roadhouses, and on and on with betting parlors thrown in for good measure. Tom Bullock, a black man known for his book, *The Ideal Bartender* (1917), poured more than one drink in the big, sinful city on his travels between St. Louis, Louisville, Chicago, and Cincinnati. *The St. Louis Dispatch* described Bullock's drinks as "the liquefied soul of a southern moonbeam falling aslant the dewy slopes of the Cumberland Mountains."[29]

More than just a raucous northern French Quarter, Vine Street hosted the inner-workings of the community. *The Cincinnati Enquirer's* offices were there. So was the Yeatsman's Tavern, where four men gathered to dream about loaning books and founded a new library. People of different races mixed on Vine and Race streets because here they were allowed to lower their inhibitions. While the bulk of the nation's wealth was in the hands of a few, others were willing to gamble, take a chance and even bet with their lives to earn economic freedom, regardless of how elusive it may have been. How bold did Alice have to be to step out with John Henry, a colored man? And was the gamble worth it?

John Henry Preston Louis Taylor Johnson was a Kentuckian, chivalrous, cool as bluegrass, full of Derby talk, and as lucky as a horseshoe. Without being too stereotypical about it, he favored bourbon, and Alice liked gin. John Henry and Alice fell in love during an age when people reveled in drinking. They sat in cafés, placing bets on the horses and the dogs, spinning tall tales, while defying the racists who supported Jim Crow laws. People smelled change in the air of a new century.

This was Cincinnati, 1899. John Henry was a "hail fellow well met." I heard my grandmother Polly use this now archaic phrase several times to describe her father. It roughly means everything is going his way. With John Henry, as he was called by family members, Alice enjoyed presumably an open courtship, which is why her family abandoned her. No doubt her family planned for their daughter to marry a German. Alice's father had moved from the hills above Lawrenceburg to riverfront Lawrenceburg where Germans were dominant. Moving up the socioeconomic ladder was his plan. Attending the German Catholic church was his plan. Alice marrying a German boy or returning to the hills to marry an Irish boy was his plan. None of this happened. When Alice left Lawrenceburg and its prejudices behind, she found herself a man that she really liked, who happened to be black. She did not hide him. And she refused to settle for anything less than full disclosure about the man that she loved.

Like many other women, Alice needed a man to provide her with a house of her own, but the money John made at the Great House was not enough. He had other streams of iffy income from gambling: horse- and dog-betting. However, marriage required stability, and he had to get a real job. His father was a brick mason, so around 1900 or 1901, John Henry decided to get into construction. He became a hod carrier, masonry's entry-level position. A hod carrier carried trays of materials, mortar, and brick to the masons on a construction site. John Henry's father no doubt had required him to do that before he taught him how to plaster and lay bricks. But in Cincinnati, Ohio, there were trade unions that kept black men down or out.

There was more than one type of hod carrier device. The hod was a tray or trough where bricks and mortar were loaded. A hod could be attached to a pole that the laborer used to lift the tray to one shoulder and steady it with the pole. Then he walked to where the mason was working and delivered the construction materials. The most dramatic hod, the one John Henry most likely operated was a yoke like oxen wear. Wooden and fitted across the shoulders and around the neck, a slat fastened the yoke along the man's spine, making him stand taller and straighter. Three, four deep, on three sides of his head, the surrounding brick muted his hearing, and cut his side vision. It looked like it weighed a ton, but in truth, the yoke balanced the load evenly across both shoulders. By the end of the day, carrying brick to the mason tightened his arms, back and shoulders. His skin was salty from sweat, wet from cleaning the tools, ashy from dried mortar, his hands bloodied and nicked from hitting against the brick. It was hard work for strong young men. Who knows how long John Henry lasted as a hod carrier? The unions were in the hands of the Irish, so steady work was not guaranteed. When he got kicked out of that work, he would become a porter. Now that John Henry acquired steady work, there was only one problem: no one would marry them.

I looked for a marriage certificate. I asked the Catholic Diocese of Cincinnati and looked in the Church of Latter-Day Saint's genealogy database. I asked Hamilton County and the City of Cincinnati, Ohio. No record of a marriage. So Alice and John Henry were in love but had difficulty getting a marriage license. My first thought was that because interracial marriage, also called miscegenation, was illegal in the state of Indiana from 1818 to 1965, and in Kentucky from 1792 until the 1967 *Loving v. Virginia* ruling, it was illegal in Ohio. But the state of Ohio had repealed its 1861 anti-miscegenation law in 1887.[30] Sociologist Albert E. Jenks concurred that around 1910, Ohio resisted Jim Crow and the attempts to reinstate the hate law. Ohio, Jenks wrote, was one of a dozen states pressured to pass anti-miscegenation legislation, and only one state, Nebraska, caved-in.[31]

Alice and John ran into a brick wall because ideas against mixed-race marriages were in the hearts and minds of regular folk. They might have been able to court each other on Vine Street, but obstacles abounded to making their relationship legal. When they went to the church, the priest was on a sick call, or perhaps he pointed out that as important as it was that John Henry was a child of God, he was also a Baptist, and that type of mixed marriage was above his pay grade. Or when the hopeful couple went to the county or city clerk's office—surprise!—no more applications, or their application was lost. The bureaucrats went to lunch, or on break, or called in sick when the Irish lass and the black man showed up asking for their license to marry. They were frustrated by the influence of up-south states because Cincinnati is closer to Lexington than Cleveland.

I never found a marriage license for John Henry and Alice. Theirs apparently was a common law marriage, a situation almost as scandalous in 1899, turn of the twentieth century Christian Midwest America, as a mixed religion and mixed race union. It was called "living in sin." Children were considered illegitimate. No marriage license was likely the reason it took so long for their first child to be born. Alice gave birth to her and John's first child in 1902 at Cincinnati General Hospital. It was a girl they named for two of John's younger sisters, Pauline and Lucy. Alice called her daughter "Polly." The hospital registered their baby's birth certificate with an error that troubled Alice, but not so much that she rushed to correct it. As the Jim Crow era was building steam, someone at Cincinnati General Hospital—a clerk, a nurse, or a doctor—did not want it documented that on their watch, a white woman had delivered a black man's baby. As a result, the race box "Black," "colored" or "Negro" was checked to identify Alice. I saw Polly's birth certificate once at my aunt's house in Detroit. When I asked why it had not been corrected, my aunt just shrugged. The erroneous birth certificate was still in my aunt's house when she died. But when her husband, my uncle, died soon after, the record was lost.

In Cincinnati history books, a photograph of the pediatric ward showed white children sitting on a hospital bed with a brown child. Each one's race well defined, unlike Alice's child. Ray Stannard Baker was a famous muckraking journalist who investigated the attitudes of early twentieth-century Americans on race-mixing. He reported in his 1908 book, *Following the Color Line*, "In the majority of intermarriage, the white women belonged to the lower walks of life. They were German, Irish, or other foreign women, respectable, but ignorant."[32] John Henry did not seem like a man who tolerated stupid women. For Alice's part, her stolen identity on the certificate may have seemed a small thing compared to the swaddled infant in her arms.

The place to record her child's birth was in her mother's prayer book. She had it. The book was palm-sized and incredibly fragile with sheets of onion skin paper covered by the dense prayers and instructions for Mass, with illustrations of how to drape the altar and where to place the priest. On what occasion did she receive It? A holy book is a heavenly gift, but this one looked like it went through hell. Someone tried to destroy it. The pages are ripped out, torn roughly in half, stuck together, and water damaged. It rippled with Old Testament anger though no Old Testament verses appear in the volume. A religious book rent with anger that wounded and harmed. Did Alice's mother leave it in shreds, her passion ignited by her daughter marrying a black man?

Written at the top of page 160 in blue ink was "Pauline borned Feb. 7, 1902." It sounds like John Henry writing with a Kentucky twang, found a special place for his and Alice's first child. It was not the traditional place for the family genealogy; it is usually found on the inside front and back covers. Ellen recorded her children's births and her infant son's death there. And then she passed it on to her oldest child and only daughter who had done the unforgivable by marrying a black man, and was abandoned for it. The record of Alice's child joining the Donlan family sat alone among the scriptures and the rituals, unattached to the rest of the family and their lineage, all by itself. The Gospel of St. John is on the facing page:

> "In the beginning was the word, and the word was with God, and the Word was God. He was in the beginning with God. All things were made by him, and without him was made nothing that was made. In him was life, and the life was the light of men. And the light shineth in darkness, and the darkness did not comprehend" (John 1:1).

This was the new beginning that John Henry and Alice created when life came from light. It is what Alice thought of her children: light in a dark world, a world that legally separated the light and the dark, a world that shunned Alice. Even as a curtain fell between light and dark, Alice helped birthed a different kind of black person.

Alice moved with her baby and husband to Springfield, north of Cincinnati. After the Civil War, industry had begun to flourish in Springfield. In celebrating the one-hundredth anniversary of its founding, Springfield had sought to create itself anew. By 1900, Springfield became a train hub with thirty-eight locomotives aimed in all directions chugging through downtown every day. It had become an agricultural center and a place where other cities came to hew limestone. Many of Springfield's earliest industries were in some way related to agriculture. Factories produced threshers, reapers, mowers, and other agricultural implements. Both woolen and cotton textile mills also employed large numbers of local residents. Among Springfield's largest manufacturing interests were the Standard Manufacturing Company, the Lagonda Agricultural Works, and Champion Machine Company, an agricultural brand co-owned by Asa Bushnell. Lagonda and Champion would eventually merge into a bigger company called International Harvester. The Kelly-Springfield Tire Company, founded by Edwin Kelly and Arthur Grant in Springfield, Ohio in 1894 was sold to the McMillin group in 1899 for $1 million. Crowell Publishing, which had offices in Springfield and New York, published a chain of magazines, including *Collier's, Farm and Fireside,* and *Women's Home Companion.* They were all printed in Springfield by Crowell Publishing, which owned plants that operated three shifts a day. Thousands of magazines were mailed from their in-house post office every week. Springfield was the place to be.

It was a town where rich men sent their sons east to Ivy League schools. Upon graduation, they returned and became bank presidents and factory superintendents. They started new businesses that had a big future, such as the telephone company. The forefathers of the city built a new high school to look just like the Library of Congress, which Congress itself could barely afford, but Springfield did it with pocket change. Springfield was undergoing a make-over, and in time it boasted it was "Second only to Chicago."[33] In fact, the town name Springfield is still around in popular culture; it is where *The Simpsons* live.

The couple moved to Springfield in 1903 to join John Henry's father and two sisters. Alice had no family to speak to, which must have made leaving the Ohio Valley area where she had spent her early life, difficult. But there would be no reason for her to return since she did not have family in Cincinnati and could not see her family in Lawrenceburg. So they moved in with her father-in-law, Isaac, in the black neighborhood. It was from that house that Alice and John's second child and first son, Elmer, was born in June 2, 1904. They called him Bud. Evidence of Springfield's tolerance of interracial couples and acknowledgment that Alice and John's union was legal was the note on Bud's birth certificate. In the slot for race, a Springfield General Hospital clerk typed "Mulatto" and at the bottom explained, "Father is black; mother is white." This was so unlike Polly's birth certificate issued by the City of Cincinnati.

Alice was pregnant again in 1906, and ready to move out of her father-in-law's house in the neighborhood called The Jungles. John Henry worked as a bartender while Alice stayed home with the children. She might have been content living as a black woman, but the riots – two in four years – were more than she could bear. By the mid-century, black people would rebel in America's major cities such as Detroit and Newark, but the race riots of the early twentieth century, specifically the race riots of 1904 and 1906 in Springfield, were the work of white men who extracted vigilante justice. Lives were lost, and dozens of black homes and businesses were destroyed. It was quite extraordinary even in the emergent Jim Crow atmosphere of turn-of-the-twentieth century America. Even *The New York Times* scolded the town on its editorial pages.[34] As a result of the rioting, a number of blacks left Springfield for good. For her part, Alice told her husband they needed to leave the black neighborhood.

The family relocated to Irish Hill, a working class neighborhood located in the southeast section of Springfield proper. By the time they moved into their own home, while some of the neighbors were Italians, and Russians, the bar on the corner was still the Shamrock, and there was still the requisite Catholic church. John Henry and his father built Alice's house themselves. It was a frame "shotgun" style house, so-called because if a person shot a shotgun at the front door, the bullet would travel through every room before exiting out the back. It had a second floor and a front door indented from the front wall to form a shaded porch. Around the porch ceiling, John Henry hung fancy bric-a-brac wood trim, called lace. Isaac dug the cistern in the backyard. And true to the town's name, the first time he pitched his shovel into the earth, a spring gushed up.

Alice and John Henry loved picture-taking except of themselves. No photos of them together exist. The white picket fence that corralled the small front yard served as a backdrop when the traveling photographer came around in warm weather. They set their two children in front of the fence for a photo. In a tintype taken in Cincinnati, baby Polly wore only a diaper with a bow, and her hair parted down the middle. The hassock she was perched on was the one in Alice's new front room. Another photo shows John Henry's magnificent dog, Spot. Spot was a terrier, a pit bull, covered by a smooth, white coat blackened on his left eye. He was a fighting dog, which demanded respect, but he was not vicious. Terriers had been mascots for many kid-centered products, like Buster Brown shoes, and programs like *Our Gang*. But toward the end of the century, they were being trained with a viciousness now seen today. At the front of the house, John Henry placed Spot on his haunches between Polly and Bud. The dog was as tall as the little girl. Another photo shows Alice and John Henry's two children with a pony. Polly wore a somber face under a cowgirl hat, and Bud a ten-gallon Stetson and a pair of chaps, perched on the back of the pony.

By this time, Alice was wearing her hair in the cloud hairstyle of the Gibson girl, and scouting the newspaper ads for sales. She was happy with her black family. She and John Henry had built a bridge between at least one Irish and one black person. Whoever thought those two would be holding hands behind a white picket fence?

℘ ℭ ℘

1908

IN SEPTEMBER 1908, Alice was excited, even giddy on her daughter's first day of school. She bought Polly new shoes and book straps. Alice was hard-wired about education and believed it was her child's birthright to attend school to get a good education. Alice went to school. So did her father and his sister, who attended school until she was seventeen. Alice wanted the best schools for her children but still held a grudge against the Catholic Church for shunning her and John Henry. So she marched past St. Joseph's Church and its parochial school on Irish Hill, past the neighborhood public school and the black school to the Clifton school. It was a new school with the best teachers, but then there was the matter of Polly's birth certificate.

Hatred toward black school children existed in Springfield, concluded Springfield attorney Darnell Carter who studied the cause of the 1904 and 1906 riots in his hometown. White people in Springfield still held "grudges" against school desegregation "that were never resolved locally, but were quieted by state legislation. The fact that their children were compelled to attend school with blacks was irritating to many local whites."[35] By the turn of the century, the grudge was a decade old. Desegregation was court-ordered in the late nineteenth century after two lawsuits, the first settled by the building of a school for black students. Like a smoldering fire, resentments often fed gossip and fear-mongering that could erupt into violence. It was this resentment that fanned the flames during the riots of 1904 and 1906.

But the reality of school segregation in Springfield, Ohio, was that black children were enrolled in every one of the city's eighteen public schools with a higher number in some schools than in others. This was commonly referred to as "de facto segregation," the separation of groups as a result of custom, circumstance, or personal choice, that is not required or sanctioned by law. What made things more complicated was the status of Polly's race. According to Cincinnati General Hospital, Polly's father was black. That was enough to make his daughter black, but her race was sealed because, on paper, her mother was black as well. Would Alice need to show her daughter's birth certificate to enroll her in school? Which Springfield school? Not the Bushnell school named for the former state governor. There were only eight black students enrolled among four hundred students.[36]

At the Dibert School, blacks were welcome, so much so that 54 percent of the student body was black. Perhaps that was why Dibert students were beaten more than those at other schools. The 1911 school report showed frequent incidents of corporal punishment. Also, Dibert parents who wanted their child to attend school more than three or four short years were frustrated because the school stopped at fourth grade.[37] After that, they had to enroll their child in a second elementary school. If Alice's daughter was known to be black or, worse yet, mulatto, she would be rejected and relegated to the black school. While a single-race child would be subject to a quota, mulatto children were not even considered because of the stigma attached. A light-skinned Negro child with a white mother; everyone knew what that meant. Eyes narrowed and preconceived notions abounded. This was Alice's fear. She just wanted the best for her child.

Indeed, this desire brought increasing pressure on the mother of a school-age black child, which still exists today. Parents register their child with a suburban address to escape the decimated public schools in Detroit with the hope no one finds out. How would Alice get her daughter into the Clifton School, which was considered the best? It was just in the next neighborhood, close enough to walk. How would she provide proof of age without showing Polly's birth certificate?

Like her mother, Polly was small. She did not look like she was almost six years old. School teachers wanted to teach and not babysit underage students. In that regard, the birth certificate was needed to dispel the notion that Polly was not of age. Would they suspect Alice of fraud? How to reconcile the white woman in person with the birth certificate issued to a black mother? How does a mother prove a child is hers? Could John Henry enroll their daughter in the new school, and make up some story about her mother? Would the presence of a black father make Polly more acceptable to the principal of the new school? Could one of Alice's sisters-in-law (two of John Henry's sisters lived in Springfield) enroll Polly in school? If John Henry's sister Pauline claimed little Polly as her own, even with her light skin, maybe she could get in. Or could her aunt pose as her nursemaid?

Miscegenation laws and the social mores they reflected failed to protect black women. When W. E. B. DuBois and Booker T. Washington discussed the laws, sociologist Albert Jenks noted, they objected to the legal language that outlawed a black man and a white woman together, versus a white man committed to a relationship with a colored woman. The law, as it stood, allowed any man, black or white, to take advantage of a black woman and then forget about her. [38] Ohio had no such miscegenation law after 1887, but the social mores, which changed from north to south, from Lake Erie to the Ohio River, prevailed.

Beset by all of this including the fears inflamed by the Springfield zealots who attacked black people every other year, Alice, who agonized, finally enrolled her daughter Polly in Clifton. It was a big school that had fifteen rooms and enrolled nearly 700 pupils. It was a new facility with all the new school accouterments: experienced senior teachers, ambitious young teachers, desks with no scratches, chalk by the boxful and new books, including the *McGuffey Reader.* Who knows how she got her daughter in? All that mattered was that she did.

℘ C3 Q

The census taker calls in Springfield.

B. H. ANDROUS WALKED ONTO Irish Hill's Harrison Street and stopped at the door of the house numbered 606—Alice and John's home—to record information for the 1910 U.S. Census. According to census archivist Bill Creech, the purpose of the census is to collect information for the apportionment of seats in the Congress.[39] But census information can also open a window to valuable information. Family genealogists use census reports to find information about relatives they never knew, or never knew enough about, to complete their family trees. It was from the 1910 U.S. Census that I learned Alice and John Henry had been married for eleven years, dating their marriage to 1899. Despite the founding fathers' initial raison d'etre for the census, it has always asked about race. Unlike today, where

Americans can fill out their own census, at the turn of the twentieth century, the census taker, known formally as the enumerator, filled out the census and determined what people were, just like the Cincinnati General Hospital clerk who filled out Polly's birth certificate.

Every person living in the house got a line on the form, but the census probed deeper with women. They wanted to know, how many children did she give birth to? What number lived? It threw a pall over census taking, asking that question. On Harrison Street, most families had lost at least one child. For Alice, the answer was, "Three born, two live." They had lost their baby just five months earlier in November . A boy named Levy was born in 1906 and died in . Levy was sick for ten days with whooping cough when grippe, also called the croup, set in. The croup causes the affected body to produce a sticky phlegm that settles in the throat and strangles its victim. Just three years old, Levy was dead.

The death haunted Alice. When she left home, she had one brother, Elmer Donlon, three years younger than she was. Another brother, William B. Donlon, named after Wilfried's father had died. Their names and birth dates are inscribed in Alice's mother's prayer book, but a newspaper notice is also pasted there:

> "In this city, Ju th [sic] 1880, of whooping cough and flu, Willie, infant son of Wilford and Ella Donland, aged nine months and seventeen days."

Alice's pain when her baby son died must have multiplied with the pain she suffered as a five-year-old girl when her brother died.

But the census was more concerned with the men. In 1910, when the census taker asked about occupations, it was a less sensitive topic and a source of pride. John Henry was now a building contractor in the construction trades, and Alice stayed home. No doubt, he could have gotten a job at the foundry. His next door neighbors, Russian Lithuanians, worked there. But it was dangerous work being a molder, pouring liquid steel into containers, and for that reason, it was a job reserved for Negroes and those who did not speak English. Literacy was another census concern. Alice and

John Henry could read and write English. Polly could read because she was in school, but Bud could not because he had not yet started school. He was only five years old, and children entered the first grade at age six. Kindergarten? It was an invention of the Germans, and I doubt Alice would participate.

Queries about the financials were at the end of a long line of social questions. "Was the house owned free and clear or mortgaged?" Androus wrote "F" for the free. Alice did not have to worry about her husband earning enough money to make a payment every month. Satisfied with the information he had collected, the census taker left 606 Harrison Street, then he completed the race column: Alice "W" and John Henry "B." The children were a cross between; they were called "Mulatto," abbreviated to "Mu."

So the family moved forward with their lives. Alice quieted her grief over the loss of their baby boy Levy by turning her full attention to her children Polly and Bud, and a new pregnancy. She had a girl on September 13, 1910, who was named Elizabeth Loretta. John Henry continued supporting his wife and children with the jobs he could find. His Kentucky style proved attractive to men of substance. He took what he learned from his father about construction trades to the next level as a contractor. John Henry also found himself again in the stable, which, next to home, he loved the best. He spent time with the horses he adored. Alice was happy until the doctor's black buggy pulled up to her fence.

§Ɔ Cȣ Cȣ

John Henry's sickness.
DR. CHARLES HAMMER saw patients in his medical office in downtown Springfield's King Building, but on Tuesday, May 28, 1912, he made a house call. Dr. Hammer took his black bag to his horse and buggy hitched in the back of the building, and with the snap of the reins put his horse in motion to Irish Hill. For this visit, the second in as many days, Dr. Hammer charged a pittance if he charged at all. It would be well for the doctor to be able to report with authority on the case of Mr. Bushnell's horseman.

John L. Bushnell was Springfield's golden-haired boy. The town scion, he was the son of industrialist and former governor Asa Bushnell. John L. Bushnell graduated from Princeton class of 1894 as a mathematics major and returned home to Springfield to work in his father's many businesses. Of course, John L. Bushnell married a socialite, lived in a mansion, and they attended Christ Episcopal Church. When Asa Bushnell died in 1904, Bushnell inherited his companies and executive positions. But his great love was his award-winning show horses, a taste of luxury he acquired on the east coast. He trusted them to the only Kentucky horseman in Springfield, John Henry Johnson.

When Dr. Hammer pulled his buggy up to the Johnson home on Harrison street and entered the house, he immediately smelled the eucalyptus he had ordered, on advice from the big medical reference book by Dr. Osler. On the second floor, John Henry laid in bed eyes shut, breathing laboriously as the white-ghost odor of steaming eucalyptus swirled about like fog. On his chest, where his wife had so often rested her head, were hot water bags. Though his face was still tree-bark brown on the surface, its paleness defied belief that no black man could be without color.

John Henry's complexion was a problem because his heart was failing. Symptoms had come on slowly as heart conditions often did. At first, he grew tired and became easily spiritless. It had been difficult to separate his grief over the loss of his baby boy from his illness. His heavy-laden heart had turned into a slack organ incapable of pumping blood into his form. Without sufficient pressure, blood pooled at his feet, causing swelling around his ankles, which became elephantine. This frail, bedridden figure bore little resemblance to the husband Alice knew. John Henry came to her as a vibrant, robust young man from Bucktown, in Winchester, Kentucky. He had given her respect and love, made her his wife, and had given her a home and children.

Dr. Osler's medical book, a thick volume with his name printed in gold on the spine, said cardiac trouble afflicted manual laborers. Dr. Hammer had already told John Henry to quit his laboring work and anything else that could cause exertion. It meant giving up construction. It meant giving up the dog fights. It meant giving up loving his wife, and he felt like most thirty something-year-old men that life without sex was not worth living.

Yet John Henry acquiesced to these demands and adopted the gentleman's life. He made contracts with laboring men, with Alice keeping the books, but he continued working with the horses. Horses allowed him a slower lifestyle for a man with a weak heart. Bushnell's horses were Hackneys, a high stepping breed of little use except for shows. They competed at coliseums back east against horses owned by his Princeton friends, which was worthy of a report in *The New York Times*. Bushnell's horses, the newspaper reported, won equine honors. Training them was the last job John Henry held as he succumbed to his faltering heart. The only photo in existence of John Henry was taken of him sitting in a fancy driving carriage called a phaeton. He was driving Irvington Nelly, one of Bushnell's horses, named after one of John Henry's sisters. The photo would later be published in the *Dayton Daily News* to advertise the local competitors in a Dayton horse show in 1915. That was three years after John Henry's death. The publication of his photo showed the respect Bushnell had for his horseman, John Henry Johnson.

John Henry passed away in his bed on Wednesday, May 29, 1912. The next day, Thursday, May 30, was Decoration Day. Polly was to receive an attendance award, but she was absent. In his office, Dr. Hammer met with the undertaker to sign the death certificate.

John Henry's death certificate said he died of exhaustion, which is known today as cardiac disease.

John Henry was a gambler at his core. He had married a white woman, lived in the white part of town, let his wife send their kids to the white school, shunned the vocations set aside for colored men, and supported his family doing what he liked to do, and did it well.

During the first year of her widowhood, Alice understood bone-tired weariness, from dealing with her children and the housework, including cleaning, cooking, and doing laundry, because she could no longer pay a woman to help her. She had to save her money. She was wrung out, and financially on edge. Her house was free and clear, but like death, taxes were inevitable. She must keep the house; otherwise, she would have had nothing for herself and her children. Despite her deep sorrow, she was determined to take care of her children. She had three now, two juveniles and on her hip dark-eyed Elizabeth, one and a half years old. She was a comfort baby, conceived amid their grieving Levy, and now she continued in that role, clinging to her mother. Alice's children were growing and needed food and shelter, clothes and shoes, and school supplies. But supporting three young children and a household was demanding. In a moment of frustration, Polly remembered her mother saying, "I am glad Levy died because I would not have been able to raise four children by myself."

She was consumed with grief and weariness. She was distressed and needed help. Most widows either married for security or went back to work.

Although Alice still looked good, no white man would accept a white woman with black children. Even if she found another man of any color, her primary fear was he might mistreat her kids. He might beat Bud, accost Polly, or reject Elizabeth. He might want Alice to bear another child. That child might die as Levy had, and she did not want to risk it. Unless she married a rich man (and how would that happen?), she would have to work to support her three children.

Caring for the baby stopped her from getting a job. Polly and Bud, who were ten and eight, could watch themselves at home, but childcare was hard to come by. Women who needed that generally stayed home themselves. They took in laundry or sewing, whatever they could do at home while watching their babies too young for school.

In most American families, the oldest daughter stayed home from school to watch the baby. It was a given: children were a mother's responsibility, and in her absence, childcare was girl's work. It had been so in John Henry's family, but in Alice's family, the children went to school. How does an Irish woman let her daughter leave school in the fifth grade? How to explain that? In her mind, there was no excuse. Alice attended school up to the ninth grade. Her father went to school until he was fifteen years old. Her father's sister, Jane went until she was seventeen years old. The Squire was a learned man, a justice of the peace. He went to school. Everyone Irish went to school. School was all the Irish had going for themselves in their eternal fight with the English. It was a fight to keep their culture intact, and school was the way. Her Irish family might have thrown Alice out, but the Irish stayed in her. But there were no Irish to help. There was only John Henry's family, his father, and his sisters.

Alice was left to raise their three biracial children with the help of John Henry's six black sisters. Two of them lived in Springfield, two in Detroit, one in Milwaukee and one in Florida. The only time she met three of them was in 1908 when they all gathered in Springfield for the Christmas holidays. The two in Springfield, Pauline and Nellie, and the one from Detroit, Lucy, were nice enough, but Alice never believed they liked her. And then there was Laura, who Alice knew but did not like. The daughter of John Henry's dead sister, Laura was a goose of a woman, six years older than Polly, but she left school in the fourth grade. Alice thought so differently from her sisters-in-law. They differed in school, church, food, and even what to call Polly, who they insisted on calling "Little Pauline." With John Henry gone, the question of who would care for baby Elizabeth seemed obvious to Alice: an arrangement between her and her sisters-in-law, but they did not think so. They wanted Polly to stay home from school to watch the baby.

There is no right time to be widowed with children, but 1912 in Ohio had its advantages because of Abraham Lincoln. He had let Americans know he cared about widows and orphans, especially the children of dead soldiers from the Civil War. On the day of his second inauguration on March 4, 1865, Lincoln could see the end of the Civil War and the healing yet to come. People stood in ankle-deep mud in front of the Capitol, now complete, to hear their president speak. As always, it was poetry:

> "With malice toward none, with charity for all, with firmness in the right as God gives us to see the right, let us strive on to finish the work we are in, to bind up the nation's wounds, to care for him who shall have borne the battle and for his widow and his orphan..."[40]

Lincoln drove home the point that caring for a dead soldier's loved ones is echoed in the Biblical definition of an orphan: "We have become orphans, fatherless" (Lamentations 5:3).

No one heard Lincoln's cry ring louder than Ohio's Union Army veterans. By the tens of thousands, they returned home bolstered by their president's call for the humane treatment of the poor and unfortunate; to stop warehousing the maimed, sick, infirmed, crazy, and poor, men, women and children all together in one place. His assassination only strengthened their resolve to care for soldiers, their widows, and his orphans. They organized the Grand Army of the Republic, also known as the GAR, to tackle social problems through a progressive social program grounded in politics.[41] They constructed the Old Soldiers' Home and the Orphan's Home. It was the GAR's social agenda in 1887 that did away with laws against mixed-race marriage when an effort was underway to reinstitute such laws. Few states resisted, but Ohio did. They represented the party of Lincoln, the Republicans, who at that time were forward-thinking. They certainly were not the Republicans of the twenty-first century.

As industrialization came to Ohio, the Old Soldiers' Homes found a new use for injured workers and their families. Children still needed to be taken care of, especially when parents were unable to. The GAR backed politicians, many of whom were their members. Once elected, they followed the example of the GAR. Ohio built a county system of children's homes for dependent children, those who had one parent, usually a widowed mother. Private organizations such as The Odd Fellows built their own homes as insurance for their members' children. The Catholic Church provided "cradle-to-grave" services. These homes were options to state-constructed facilities for the incorrigible. With the private homes and the county system of children's homes, children were not thrown to the streets. They had a place to sleep, food to eat, and were able to attend school. Widowed mothers had a place to go to for help.

Nearly fifty years after Lincoln's call for empathy and action, President Teddy Roosevelt hosted the White House Conference on Care of Dependent Children in . He was convinced by sociologists that there was more that could be done to help widows and their children. Invitees ranged from judges, social services administrators, and religious people to a stellar cast of historically significant figures such as industrialist Andrew Carnegie, Negro educator Booker T. Washington, sociologists Jane Hull Adams, Homer Folks, and Jacob Riis. There was much debate about the horrors of orphanages versus the self-serving motives of care in a private family. Well-meaning men discussed the issue of impoverished families with a passion that nonetheless enjoyed a certain distance. These were professionals. They would never have direct custody and care of children even if the gravity of life forced their fortunes into a sudden collapse. Still, they were the ones in charge of institutions charged with the care of women and children.

Frank Loomis, the General Secretary of the Children's Bureau of Newark, New Jersey, summed up the arguments. "Orphanages can maintain any kind of school and send the child according to its own convenience. It reports only to itself." On the other hand, he said of foster care, "While a parent may send his own boys to school, he keeps the strange boy at home to help with the chores."[42]

Catholic Bishop McMahon, Supervisor of Catholic Charities in New York City, blasted industrial labor practices that robbed a family of their husband and father through death, disease or injury. Juvenile court Judge Ben B. Lindsey of Denver, said "This nation had never yet awakened up to the heroism of its women,...enduring hardships, privation, and struggles every day of their lives as great as that endured by any soldiery in the darkest days of a nation's war."[43] But it took one of the few women invited, Martha Falconer, superintendent of the girls' division of Philadelphia's House of Refuge, to call attention to the plight of girls. She urged a closer look at foster families who claimed to treat girls like one of their own. "What does it really mean?" she asked. "It usually means they want cheap labor."[44]

Politics swirled around the issue at the state and federal levels. For his part, President Roosevelt promised to send a special message to the Congress to ask for a Federal Children's Bureau to oversee the work recommended by the Conference. He asked for the Conference's support in writing the recommendations into law by lobbying their congressional representatives.[45] All of this was happening in Washington, D.C. Alice was in Springfield, where the state of Ohio had built a county-by-county system of orphanages. That word, "orphanage," reeked with the longing of a mother's love. That word inspired my quest to confront my great-grandmother's life and how her Irish ancestry shaped my African American reality.

℘ ⅋ ℞

1912

SCHOOL HAD TWO WEEKS to go when John Henry died in 1912, but Alice kept Polly and Bud close by for those sorrowful days. In the fall, Polly was in fifth grade and Bud in third. The days when Alice was the cupcake lady of Irish Hill had vanished.

Her last paid work was as a maid in Cincinnati. She could do that again. At thirty-seven years old, her figure was slender, and her hair lustrous and thick as a Gibson Girl, a style she liked even though it was a bit dated by 1912. Still, she looked first-class vintage as she traveled downtown to Springfield's leading hotel, the Arcade. Located on Washington Street and Fountain Avenue, the Arcade's entrance shared prime street-level space with various other businesses vying for the heavy foot traffic downtown. The Arcade was located across the street from Springfield's Penn station. Even though the Arcade had no kitchen, restaurant or room service, their one hundred and fifteen sleeping rooms were full most days with passengers, not just from Pennsylvania Railroad, but the Springfield and Xenia Railroad, which also stopped at Springfield's Penn station. And, with the Big Four depot – the Vanderbilt line, Cleveland, Cincinnati, Chicago and St. Louis Railway—two blocks east on Washington Street, the Arcade Hotel maids stayed busy making beds, earning wages and tips.

Getting a paying job was supposed to solve her problems, but only made her life harder. Alice needed someone to watch her baby while she was at work. Her sisters-in-law chipped-in to help, but since every one of them was also maid, Alice could not rely on them.

Watching children was a non-paying job that fell in the realm of doing a favor, truly a labor of love. Most women did not work, and those who did, did not earn enough to pay for childcare. If a woman had children at home and needed to earn money, she did so by taking in sewing or laundry. Alice did not. She did not want to be a seamstress or a laundress. Moreover, a laundress's daughter usually ended up helping her mother. Could Alice see her precious Polly, who she had schemed to get into a good school be reduced to a laundress? *No.*

Alice had neighbors who agreed to help with childcare, but that arrangement did not last. Alice's daughter Polly said the neighbor lady, a Mrs. Leoni, had children too, but her boys fought with her brother Bud. If all else failed, Alice stayed home from work, or Polly stayed home from school. Alice cobbled together childcare, day-to-day. At first, Alice just wanted to get through the school year. If she worked the day shift, her two older children would be in school while she worked. Working the night shift, they would all be asleep while she was away. But these plans failed because Alice needed to sleep too.

Alice and her sisters-in-law had a pow-wow over this. I knew John Henry's sisters, and I knew Pauline well, and they were not the most forthcoming with their thoughts. They communicated in the tradition of our family in Detroit, with one- and two-sentence conversations. This was how I envisioned their conversation in 1913: one-word answers, shrugs, or sidelong glances in response to intense questioning. Alice needed to know if her sisters-in-law would be willing to help. She wanted her children raised together. She wanted them to know each other. She wanted them to know they were family; she wanted them to be family with all the love a family could offer. Her priority was keeping her family together. However, for Alice, the idea of taking Polly out of school, apparently suggested by her sisters-in-law, crossed the line.

If marrying a colored man shamed her family, not educating her children shamed her, for it was an Irish mother's duty to educate her children. Very much like in the twenty-first century, one had only to open a book, or magazine, or newspaper to know that the uneducated or the poorly educated children had no future. Alice was haunted by an image, as were all Americans who read or heard about the best-selling book, *How the Other Half Lives: Studies Among the Tenements of New York* (1890).[46]

The author, Jacob A. Riis, was invited to President Theodore Roosevelt's White House Conference on Dependent Children. The photographs in his book were taken on his many visits to the European immigrant ghettos in New York City. An immigrant from Denmark, sociologist, and journalist, Riis' book became a bestseller when it published in 1890. It can still be found on library book-shelves and online bookstores. *How the Other Half Lives* provides a graphic illustration of a persistent American social problem. Riis documented children being treated as if they were grown men and women. Boys sold newspapers to help support their families. If they had no family home, they lived at the newsboys' lodge, where they gambled and drank. They did whatever they could to earn their keep. And the girls' situation was a sure dead-end. They worked long hours in factories, kept house, and took care of the babies who lived in them. One photograph, "Minding the Baby: Little Mother," shows two girls in a street doorway, unkempt, dirty, with desolation ringing their eyes. The older girl holds a toddler almost as large as she is. They were just the age of Alice's daughters. But was this a true comparison?

Riis captured big city life while Alice lived in a prosperous town in Ohio. His photos came from the late nineteenth century, the Gilded Age, while Alice lived in the industrial twentieth century. His subjects were immigrants while she was a third-generation American. Yet, all of that melted away in the face of a startling image of a pitiful, dirty little girl embracing a toddler. Alice had that image in her head. It could happen to them. It still happens to families in America. Girls are pressed into service in their family home because their work-ing mother or father need help. Alice's fear was reasonable. She was widowed. There was no end to how far a widow of no means could fall in the United States. People passed judgment but provided precious little help. They wanted to know why her family did not help, and seeing no rescue assumed it was she who had failed her family. What it also meant was that the men—father, uncle, brother, cousin—who controlled the resources in most families—did not approve of something she had done.

Alice's fear and her Irish heritage pushed her to reject the idea of taking Polly out of school to stay home to care for baby Elizabeth. There had to be another way.

80 CB CR

JUDGING BY THE DELIBERATIONS of the Clark County Children's Home Board of Trustees, the endeavor to provide a humane way forward for destitute families was outstripped by its ability to pay for an altruistic effort. Still, they tried month after month; the meeting minutes showed.[47] Two weeks and three days after Alice made her decision, the Clark County Children's Home Board of Trustees gathered for their monthly meeting on June 3, 1913. A. H. Drayer, the president, was presiding. Acting Home Superintendent, Belinda Brubaker was also present.

The agenda contained the usual items—children and money. They discussed the "inmates"—as the children who lived at the Home were often referred to—operating expenses, building and grounds maintenance, and personnel wages. At this particular board meeting, when Miss Brubaker provided her monthly report about the recently admitted inmates, she said, "Mother is a domestic, now. Her husband died last spring." This was the sad case of the Johnson children: Pauline Johnson, age eleven, Elmer Johnson, age nine, and Elizabeth Johnson, aged two and one half years old.

My great-grandmother Alice put her three children in an orphanage. The day, Friday, May 16, 1913, started out under a cloudy sky.[48] It had been a wet spring of rain and tears, but she was faring well enough. She had a job to work, and children to raise, but could not do both. Finally, it was time to make a decision. Alice shepherded her children from Irish Hill up to High Street. There they boarded the streetcar headed downtown. After that, she shooed them onto the Limestone Avenue streetcar going north. It crossed the bridge over Buck Creek. Along the way, the buildings outside the window helped her to see how times had changed. For one, the large red frame Victorian house had a huge stable and carriage house in the rear, which had been converted into a dairy delivery center.

Who knew why she picked Friday, May 16, 1913, to ride the streetcar north to Home Road and get off there to walk? It was far away from the city and watered by the rain. Perhaps a note earlier in the week from Polly's fifth-grade teacher, Miss Glenn, questioned her daughter's absences. It was thirteen days before the school's Decoration Day, which was also the one-year anniversary of John Henry's passing. The day loomed large, as despair threatened to descend on his widow. At the end of the country path, Alice was someplace new when she climbed the creaky front steps to the Clark County Children's Home. Only those in the superintendent's office knew for sure what happened.

The acting superintendent at the Children's Home, Miss Brubaker, was on loan from the county health department. On her desk were legal forms: Application and Surrender of Child, Physician's Certificate, and internal forms, namely, the Record of Inmates from Clark County Children's Home. Miss Brubaker asked Alice the questions on the Application and Surrender and decided the reason for taking in Alice's children was due to the "inability of the parent to provide." There were just enough spaces for the three children's names. Alice's occupation was "domestic," a catch-all term for women's menial labor. Her employer was not recorded on this form though the Arcade Hotel was listed on other official records. John Henry was listed as American. Parents were married. Mother and father's habits? "Good." (This was the "worthiness" that the White House Conference experts, and so many from the church looked for before awarding help.) She was not a drunk, or a slob, or a whore. The children were called inmates because they lived inside the institution. On the Record of Inmates form, the children were assigned numbers in order of their ages: 327 for Polly, 328 for Bud, and 329 for Elizabeth.

Alice pointed out an error in Polly's birth date; it should have been February 7, 1902. The superintendent made the correction, but the date was still wrong. It was a small matter compared to the next words in the first daunting graph of legalese that said:

> "...do hereby, for that purpose voluntarily surrender and entrust to the Trustees of said Children's Home or to such persons as they may select as their assignee, the entire charge, custody, management and control of the above-named children until they become of legal age, and do hereby invest the said Trustees and their assignee with the same power and control over the aforesaid children as those of which Mrs. Johnson possessed."

This meant that the children could be adopted, sent to a foster home or even worse, split up at the discretion of the Home.

"But I want them here together," Alice cried. "I want Polly and Bud to go to school. I want to know they are all safe." She repeated all the words she had already said to her sisters-in-law, as if those had been a rehearsal for this moment. Miss Brubaker listened and reassured anxious Alice that the Children's Home was there to help. They were close to the end: all that remained was Alice's signature. Upon seeing her distress, Miss Brubaker hesitantly wrote on the front of the Application: "Not to be put out." It meant Alice's children would not be pushed out of the Home to live with one family and then another.

Alice signed neatly, which belied her storming soul. She held baby Elizabeth close, buried her face in the child's soft black hair. Then she put the baby in Polly's arms. Everyone was crying now; Bud cried like his papa, sniffling, and Alice sobbed. She was the mother of orphans.

One need only read the story of Moses in the Bible to know that dire circumstances alone could force a woman to abandon her child. When Moses' mother put him in a basket in the bulrushes, she saved him from being slaughtered. Hidden, she watched until the handmaiden of the Pharaoh's daughter plucked him out from the water. Later she hired herself out as a nurse to the rich woman who became her son's guardian. Surrendering one's child remains a desperate last act. It was for Alice Donlan Johnson in 1913. She left the Clark County Children's Home alone and returned to work as a hotel maid.

The Record of Inmates documented Alice's despair. Her desire to keep her children together lasted for two weeks. A mother can change her mind; many did. With full knowledge of the Children's Home Board of Trustees, some mothers retraced their steps and took their children back in an attempt to make another go of family life. Older children's distress could be reconciled with explanations about the reality of life, and the despair their mothers faced, but toddlers could not. They cried for their mothers and when they were worn out, they finally surrendered, though never entirely. A mother's heart weeps and bursts. So, Alice went back. On Elizabeth's inmate record for May 30, 1913, a note of just four small words, "Taken out by mother."

No one really knew what happened, but this second attempt only lasted a month. Maybe Alice was able to arrange for childcare, but it fell through. Or maybe her job was in jeopardy, and she had no choice but to send Elizabeth back. We do know that the entry on Elizabeth's inmate record states: "Returned July 5, 1913." After that, Alice never took back custody of her children again. The Clark County Children's Home ensured her children had a safe place to live, and access to a guaranteed education.

Alice did not abandon her children, though. She visited them, took them out to lunch, and bought their clothes. She took them on vacation to Clifton, a resort close to Springfield. When the superintendent asked, she paid fees to help with their expenses. When her house needed repairs, when she needed clothes, when she needed food, she sacrificed. She was a mother who never planned to lose her children, never intended to orphan her children, but it happened. On this, the rest of her life pivoted.

In January 1920, the census taker knocked on the door of 830 N. Limestone Avenue, the home of Robert Rodgers, a wealthy industrialist from one of Springfield's old monied families. He, his wife and two daughters lived in the mansion. It was one of his relatives,

Dr. Rodgers, who gave the county the land for the Children's Home. Beginning in summer 1917, fifteen year old Polly, a Springfield High School student, lived with and worked for the family. The Clark County Children's Home put her out because of the pressing need for her bed.

The Rodgers' oldest daughter Alice was failing school. She was known to be the class clown, and for good reason. She was funny and later would become the mother of comedian Jonathan Winters. However, in 1917, Alice's parents were worried about her graduating eighth grade. Because of their connection to the Children's Home and the need for Polly to find a place to live, the Rodgers took her in as a live-in maid. Polly worked along with two other live-in servants, a housekeeper/cook, and a driver who slept in the carriage house where there was an automobile. Polly's job was to set the table and wash the dishes, but what the Rodgers really wanted her to do was set an excellent academic example for their daughter Alice.

In 1920, the entire Rodgers' household assembled for the census taker. It was a woman census taker named Margaret M. Wingate. Wingate must have assumed that the two female servants sharing the same last name were related, but they were not. The housekeeper/cook was a brown-skinned woman named Mae Johnson. The young maid was Pauline "Polly" Johnson. The census taker recorded both as "black" because she had the duty to record race but not the obligation to ask if she was correct. Polly's small circle of school chums were black, and as a high school senior, her thoughts were centered on Lincoln University, the Negro college. Alice's daughter had chosen to be black.

Meanwhile, across town, when census taker Harry A. Barnd knocked at 606 N. Harrison Street, Alice answered. She was forty-two-years-old, still employed as a hotel maid. She told him her daughter, Pauline, lived in the Irish Hill house with her. She may have told him about the daughter she was so proud of. She was going to be eighteen years old on her next birthday in February, and graduate from high school in June. Barnd recorded the mother and daughter as white. It was his duty to do so.

There was no way Polly lived with her mother, however much her mother yearned for it. She traveled by herself from the Rodgers' home on the streetcar to high school. From there, she could walk to her mother's house to visit. Whether she had a close relationship with her mother remains to be seen. The reason Polly could not live with Alice was that she attended school every morning, and worked at the Rodgers from afternoon into the early evening. After graduation, perhaps Polly could work at the Rodgers and live with her mother, until college. Alice's daughter was doing the Irish thing, pursuing her education.

In the late summer, at the end of the graduation party season, the *Springfield Daily News* society editor printed a brief story: "Miss Pauline Johnson entertained a few of her friends at the home of her aunt." The party was at the Buxton Avenue house where so much of the Johnson family life had happened under the care of its mistress, John Henry's sister Pauline. When Pauline moved to Detroit, her sister Nellie moved into the Springfield house with her family. Polly's party featured pink decorations. The young people danced and enjoyed "at a late hour, dainty refreshments." Alice was also in attendance as her name appeared among the other guests' names printed on the newspaper's society page.

While Polly was recorded in the 1920 U.S. Census with the Rodgers family, Bud was documented in South Charleston, a suburb of Springfield. It was a country neighborhood about twelve miles away with wide streets well-shaded during the summer and large houses on lots big enough for farming. It was mainly a German neighborhood, where Springfield Gas Company office manager Elmer Abbott, age fifty-seven, lived at 245 South Charleston with his wife, Ollie, age fifty-three. A childless couple, the Abbotts took in fifteen-year-old Elmer "Bud" Johnson. He was a foster child who worked for the Abbotts as a farmhand. Theirs was the ideal foster home, as envisioned by some of the men at the White House Conference on Care of Dependent Children. Bud had been put out of the Children's Home when he refused to continue his first year in high school in 1919. Bud dropped out of school because Polly, who was in her junior year, was firmly ensconced with the black kids. This caused problems for Bud, who found it easier to be with the white boys, so he stopped going to school altogether, to his mother's dismay.

Sociologists say color is a social construct, so one can never tell if a person is colorblind or sees Technicolor when they gaze upon a person. Somehow the census taker knew the problem with Bud was color. First recording Bud as white, something made him write over the "W," and turn it into a "B," for black.

It took census taker James E. Reynolds some time to record the one hundred people who lived at the Clark County Children's Home. Reynolds recorded eighty-seven children, filling three census forms. Ten-year-old Elizabeth Johnson was the ninth child recorded.

She was not in the Children's Home after that. When Polly graduated from high school, she wanted more than anything to get her sister out. It was not clear why Alice did not bring her youngest daughter home, but Polly was determined to do so. She enlisted the aid of her father's sister, Lucy and her husband, Ray Culberson, in Detroit. Uncle Ray was the key to this arrangement. By law, only a married woman could provide a foster home. The Culbersons signed Elizabeth out of the Children's Home on August 31, 1920. They kept her for the school year but returned the almost eleven-year-old girl back to the Children's Home on August 5, 1921. It is not clear why, and Home officials cited no reason. My family never talked about it except to say the girl was a "pistol," meaning difficult to handle.

Polly tried to get her sister out of the Children's Home a second time by using her status as the orphanage's first high school graduate to override the law, but there was now a new superintendent who did not know her well enough to help her.

When Polly married in 1922, she and her husband came for Elizabeth and took her to Detroit to live with them. But Elizabeth went to live with John Henry's sister, Pauline, the guardian of their family's orphans. Elizabeth enrolled in Detroit's Northwestern High School, dropped out, and eventually received her General Equivalancy Diploma. Elizabeth trained as a licensed practical nurse, married, birthed a son, divorced and left her son with his father, and went to work in Sitak, Alaska. She went far away from her birth family and the family she made. What I remember about her was that when I was a kid, she sent me several wristwatches for gifts. I lost or broke every one of them. In the late 1950s, she visited Detroit every Christmas. She was fun. She was a mystery.

Alice was the only member of her family that was still in Springfield. She finally left in 1929 after the stock market crashed. She sold her house to Will Browning, John Henry's sister's Nellie's husband. Alice moved, for reasons unknown, to the city of Canton, Ohio. She was hired as a housekeeper for the Aultman Hospital and worked there from 1929 to 1961. She had some good times: There is a 1950-ish color photograph of her with a white man named Don, leaning against an automobile during a stop on a road trip to California. She is smiling. Another photo shows her in a speedboat with a white man and a young white boy. When she retired in 1961, Alice came to live with Polly and her husband in Detroit. That year she was age eighty-six. Later that year, she died in Detroit, the kiss of death being the broken hip she suffered when a purse snatcher knocked her to the ground.

Alice was funeralized on November 22, 1961 at St. Cecilia's Catholic Church in Detroit. My mother was not allowed to attend her grandmother's funeral because she was pregnant with her tenth child. None of the great grandchildren, including nine-year-old me, was invited. Everyone in attendance noticed the deep anger Elizabeth harbored against her mother. The anger erupted when she almost yanked her mother's body out of the casket and screamed at the corpse, "Why didn't you take me out of there?" Her anger fanned to blue fire, perhaps because she did not know how her mother had tried. This was witnessed and reported by Elizabeth's son, who called his Irish grandmother, "a tough old bird." ⌘

NOTES

1. *Report of Lawrenceburg, Indiana Relief Committee of 1884,* (Lawrence burgh Press print, 1884).

2. *The History of Dearborn and Ohio Counties, Indiana; from their earliest settlement.* (1885; repr., Evansville, Ind: Unigraphic, 1970), 280.

3. *Thomas Jefferson, Writings : Autobiography / Notes on the State of Virginia / Public and Private Papers / Addresses / Letters* (New York: Library of America, 1984).

4. Mona Robinson, *Who's Your Favorite Hoosier?: Genealogy for Beginners* (Bloomington, IN: Indiana University Press) 55.

5. Frank McCourt, *Angela's Ashes* (New York: Scribner's, 1996).

6. Marie Davis, "Child-rearing in Ireland 1700-1830: An Exploration." *Ireland: Art into History,* eds. Raymond Gillespie and Brian P. Kennedy (Niwot, Colorado: Roberts Rinehart Publisher, 1994), 171-176.

7. Maureen Murphy, "Birdie, We Hardly Knew Ye: The Irish Domestics," Chapter 4, The Work: Where the Irish Did Apply," ed. Michael Coffey, and Terry Golway. *The Irish in America,* (New York: Hyperion, 1997), 144.

8. Reuben Gold Thwaites, *Afloat on the Ohio: An Historical Pilgrimage of a Thousand Miles in a Skiff from Redstone to Cairo* (New York, Doubleday, 1900), 186.

9. "News of Ye Olden Time" (1888; repr., Lawrenceburg, Indiana: *The Register,* May 15, 1919) np.

10 The spelling of names, people and places in Alice's story can be confusing because the spelling was not standardized, and over the century spelling has changed. And some institutions, such as the Catholic Church had rituals where they gave a person another name, like baptism. For example, The town, Lawrenceburg, was initially spelled "Lawrenceburgh."

11. James Baldwin, "If Black English Isn't a Language, Then Tell Me, What Is?" *The New York Times,* July 29, 1979. http://movies2.nytimes.com/books/98/03/29/specials/baldwin-english.html.

12. Noel Ignatiev, *How the Irish Became White* (London: Routledge, 1995), 41.

13. Ignatiev, 1.

14 Ignatiev, 117.

15. Angela F. Murphy, *American Slavery, Irish Freedom: Abolition, Immigrant Citizenship and the Transatlantic Movement for Irish Repeal,* (Baton Rouge, LA: Louisiana State University Press, 2010), 23.

16. Thomas N. Brown, *Irish-American Nationalism 1870-1890* (Philadelphia & New York: Lippincott, 1966), 23.

17. "History of Cincinnati," Ohio History Central, https://ohiohistorycentral.org/w/Cincinnati,_Ohio.

18. Sue Ann Painter, *Architecture in Cincinnati: An Illustrated History of Designing and Building an American City.* (Athens, Ohio: Ohio University Press, 2006), 89.

19. Carroll L.V. Meeks, *The Railroad Station: An Architectural History,* (New Haven: Yale University Press, 1956), Plate 77.

20. Lucy Leftbridge, "Visible And Invisible: 'Servants' Looks At Life Downstairs," *Fresh Air* interview by Terry Gross, WHYY, interview Philadelphia, PA: WHYY, January 2, 2014. .

21. Murphy, "Birdie, We Hardly Knew Ye," 144.

22. Walter E. Langsam, *Great Houses of The Queen City: Two Hundred Years of Historic and Contemporary Architecture and Interiors in Cincinnati and Northern Kentucky* (Cincinnati: The Cincinnati History Society and Cincinnati Museum Center at Union Terminal, 1997), 100.

23. Richard Conniff, "Ireland on Fast Forward," *National Geographic,* September 1994, 23.

24. Leftbridge.

25. Charles Theodore Greve, *Centennial History of Cincinnati and Representative Citizens* (Chicago: Biographical Pub. Co, 1904), 1016.

26. Conniff, "Ireland on Fast Forward," 10-11.

27. Hambleton Tapp & James C. Klotter, *Kentucky: Decades of Discord, 1865-1900* (Frankfort: Kentucky Historical Society, 1977) 94.

28. David D. Anderson, *Ohio in Myth, Memory, and Imagination* (East Lansing, Michigan: The Midwestern Press The Center for the Study of Midwestern Literature and Culture, 2004), 105.

29. Tom Bullock, *The Ideal Bartender* (1917; repr., East Lansing, Michigan: Michigan State University Library Digital & Multimedia Center, 2004), 3.

30. Metapedia, s.v. "Anti-miscegenation Law", Nordisk.nu, accessed August 29, 2016, https://www.metapedia.org/wiki/anti-miscegenation_law.

31. "Fourth Annual Report to the Board of Directors of the National Association for the Advancement of Colored People" (New York City: NAACP, 1913), quoted in Albert E. Jenks, "The Legal Status of Negro-White Amalgamation," *American Journal of Sociology, 21* (March 1916), 670.

32. Ray Stannard Baker, *Following the Color Line: An Account of Negro Citizenship in American Democracy* (1908; repr., New York: Harper & Row,, 1964), 172-173.

33. Benjamin F. Prince, ed. *The Centennial Celebration of Springfield, Ohio, held August 4th to 10th, 1901* (Springfield: Springfield Publishing Co., 1901), 108.

34. Darnell Edward Carter, *1904, 1906 and 1921 Race Riots in Springfield, Ohio, and the Hoodlum Theory* (Master's Thesis, The Ohio State University, 1993), 49.

35. Carter, 1.

36. *Annual Report of the Board of Education Springfield, Ohio, 1911.* (Springfield: The Lagonda Publishing Co.), 33.

37. *Annual Report,* 59.

38. Jenks, "The Legal Status," 672-73.

39. William Creech, conversation with the author at the National Archives, June 7, 2016.

40. Abraham Lincoln delivered his second inaugural address on March 4, 1865, during his second inauguration as President of the United States.

41. Wikipedia contributors, "Grand Army of the Republic," *Wikipedia, The Free Encyclopedia,* https://en.wikipedia.org/w/index.php?title=Grand_Army_of_the_Republic&oldid=926161091 (accessed December 26, 2019)..

42. "Proceedings of the Conference on the Care of Dependent Children Held at Washington, D.C., January 25, 26, " Second Session of the Sixtieth Congress (Washington, DC: U.S. Government Printing Office,), 69.

43. Proceedings, 219.

44. Proceedings, 130.

45. Proceedings, 214.

46. Jacob Riis, *How the Other Half Lives: Studies Among The Tenements Of New York* (Eastford, CT: Martino Fine Books, 2018).

47. Clark County Children's Home, *Minutes 1878-1891, 1902-1920* (Springfield, Ohio: June 3, 1913).

48. *Ohio Monthly Local Climatological data,* March 1921 report. National Climatic Data Center (U.S.) 1921 (Asheville, N.C.) DOC,NOAA, NESDICS, NCDC.

St. Lawrence Church, circa 1866. *Courtesy of St. Lawrence Catholic Church.*

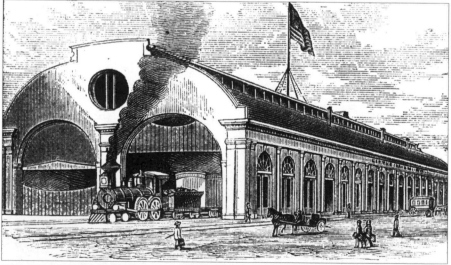

Little Miami Railroad Depot was one of the train companies that replaced the steamboats docking in Cincinnati on the Ohio River in 1900. *Courtesy of the Collection of The Public Library of Cincinnati and Hamilton County.*

Alice's mother, Ellen Stark Donlan, could have never dreamt that her only daughter's children would be black. *Courtesy of The Andrew J. and Mary Jane Humphries Foundation. Image by David R. Barker, The Ohio Historical Society.*

Alice Donlan Johnson, circa 1940. *Courtesy of The Andrew J. and Mary Jane Humphries Foundation. Image by David R. Barker, The Ohio Historical Society.*

"IRVINGTON NELLY" - JOHN L. BUSHNEL SPRINGFIELD, O.

The only photo of John Henry Johnson riding Irvington Nelly, a prize show horse owned by industrialist, John L. Bushnell. The horse was named after Johnson's youngest sister. *Springfield News* June 13, 1915. *Courtesy of the Archives of the Clark County Historical Society, Springfield, Ohio.*

Alice's mother's Catholic prayer book recorded births of Alice's mulatto children and a new chapter in the Donlan family. *Courtesy of The Andrew J. and Mary Jane Humphries Foundation.*

Pauline Lucy Johnson (Polly), born February 7, 1902, in Cincinnati, Ohio, daughter of John Henry and Alice Johnson. *Courtesy of The Andrew J. and Mary Jane Humphries Foundation. Image by David R. Barker, The Ohio Historical Society.*

Siblings Polly (l) and Elmer (called Bud) (r) with Spot, their father, John Henry's pit bull, circa 1906. *Courtesy of The Andrew J. and Mary Jane Humphries Foundation. Image by David R. Barker, The Ohio Historical Society.*

Polly (l) and Bud (r) on horse, circa 1910, Springfield, Ohio. *Courtesy of Andrew J. and Mary Jane Humphries Foundation. Image by David R. Barker, The Ohio Historical Society.*

Elmer "Bud" Johnson, circa 1913, age nine. *Courtesy of The Andrew J. and Mary Jane Humphries Foundation. Image by David R. Barker, The Ohio Historical Society.*

John Henry Johnson's widow, Alice, and children with his sisters on June 3, 1912, the day he was buried in Springfield, Ohio. Front row (l-r): Elmer "Bud" and Pauline "Polly" Johnson. Back row (l-r): Nellie, Lucy, Pauline, Effie, Esther, Lena; Alice holding her baby Elizabeth. *Courtesy of Andrew J. and Mary Jane Humphries Foundation. Image by David R. Barker, The Ohio Historical Society.*

Sociologist Jacob Riis' haunting photograph, "Minding the Baby: "a little mother" in his best-selling books told the story of girls kept out of school to help at home. *Photo by Jacob August Riis (1849–1914). Courtesy of the Museum of the City of New York.*

That the undersigned *Alice Johnson*

of *Springfield* County of *Clark* and State

of Ohio, of the minor children

described as follows, to-wit:

Pauline Johnson born on *2nd* day of *Feb*

1861, in *Limangali* Township,

County, and State of *Ohio* ; and *Elmer Johnson*

born on *2* day of *June* *1904*, in *Springfield*

Township, *Springfield* County, and State of *Clark* ; and

Elizabeth Johnson born on *13* day of *Sept*

1906, in *Springfield* Township *Springfield*

County, and State of *Ohio* ; desire that said children be admitted

to the Children's Home of *Clark* County, in accordance with

the laws of Ohio, and the regulations of said Children's Home, and do hereby, for

that purpose, voluntarily surrender and entrust to the Trustees of said Children's

Home or to such persons as they may select as their assignee, the entire charge,

custody, management and control of the above named children until they become of

legal age, and do hereby invest the said Trustees and their assignee with the same

power and control over the aforesaid children as those of which *Alice Johnson*

possessed.

Father's name in full *John Johnson* Nationality *Am*

If living, where If dead, when *May 30. 1912*

Father's habits *Good* Occupation *Laborer*

Mother's maiden name in full *Alice Johnson* Nationality *Am*

If living, where *606 Harrison* If dead, when

Mother's habits *Good* Occupation *Domestic*

Parents married? *Yes* ; Divorced? *No* ; Separated? *No*

Child to be admitted by reason of abandonment by parents, neglect, orphanage,

inability of parents to provide for *them*.

Witness hand this *16* day of *May* *1913*

Alice Johnson

B. H. Barman

With her signature, Alice surrendered her children on May 16,
1913, to the Clark County Children's Home, Springfield, Ohio.
Courtesy of The Andrew J. and Mary Jane Humphries Foundation.

Alice's children lived in the Clark County Children's Home, Springfield, Ohio, circa 1900. *Courtesy of The Andrew J. and Mary Jane Humphries Foundation.*

Alice (right side) is seated against the wall, fourth from front, at the 1961 Aultman Hospital Employee Appreciation Dinner, in Dayton, Ohio. She kept knowledge of her black family from her co-workers. *Courtesy of The Andrew J. and Mary Jane Humphries Foundation.*

Alice on a 1958 road trip to California with "Don," a man her black family never met. *Courtesy of The Andrew J. and Mary Jane Humphries Foundation.*

Elizabeth Johnson was twenty years old in 1930, and living in Detroit with her aunt, Pauline. *Courtesy of The Andrew J. and Mary Jane Humphries Foundation.*

Alice and Bud Johnson in Detroit 1953. *Courtesy of The Andrew J. and Mary Jane Humphries Foundation.*

Alice Johnson saw the fourth generation of her black family in 1956, Detroit. *(l-r) Alice,* great-granddaughter Alice Humphries, granddaughter Ellen Elizabeth DeBose, great-grandson Andrew D. Humphries and daughter Polly Johnson Leigh. *Courtesy of The Andrew J. and Mary Jane Humphries Foundation.*

CHAPTER 3

Pauline

A SNAPSHOT IN OUR FAMILY'S ALBUM captures one of my family's proudest moments: four generations of black women. It was taken in the winter of 1971. We, four women and a baby, were in my grandmother's living room. I was the youngest woman in the photo, and my infant son, Diallo represented the fifth generation. He was held by the oldest woman, brown-skinned Pauline, my grandmother's aunt. While the rest of us straddled the color line, she does not. Pauline is the matriarch and anchoring heart of the black side of my grandmother's family. She is John Henry Johnson's sister, and Alice's sister-in-law.

Pauline became the matriarch of the family after Alice's death in 1961 at the age of eighty six. She outlived Alice by some twenty-five years and died in Detroit at age one-hundred and three in June 1986. Pauline was the one Alice failed to convince in 1913 that education was more important than holding the family together in a traditional way. While Alice prevailed, Pauline lived to see two generations of women in the family take advantage of an opportunity Alice fought so hard to obtain: education. My mother attended Wayne State University in Detroit, and I earned two degrees there: a Bachelor and Master of Arts.

But Alice would definitely have something to say about her direct descendants putting Pauline Johnson in the seat of honor. Their relationship was contentious. Understanding the tension between them requires revisiting my family's black ancestry, and it begins with the Civil War.

Pauline and John Henry's father, Isaac Johnson, was a Union soldier. His Union Army enlistment papers said he was from Rockland, Maryland. When I searched for him in the 1850 U.S. Census for the Green Spring Valley section of Baltimore County where Rockland is located, I did not find him by name. But when I reviewed the 1850 U.S. Census of the first District of Baltimore County on Schedule C (commonly known as the "slave schedule"), which lists people by gender, color, and age, I was able to identify him.[1] He was enslaved by the son of William Fell Johnson, an elected Baltimore County official who also owned the Rockland Factory of blacksmith and wheelwright shops.[2] William's oldest son, Thomas Francis Johnson was listed as the owner of ten slaves; seven of them male. The youngest was a one-year-old boy. I think that was Isaac. His father, who Isaac grew up knowing, might have been one of the mulatto men listed on the schedule. There were no stories passed down to help identify if one of the women listed was Isaac's mother.

Abraham Lincoln was in the White House for barely six months when the first shots of the Civil War were fired on Fort Sumter in 1861. Maryland was a slave state that remained loyal to the Union, but since it was so close to the nation's capital, it was chaotic. Soon after the start of the Civil War, William Fell Johnson died. Disruption in Rockland followed. One man's death meant another man's freedom. Isaac and his father simply walked away from slavery. They might have left Rockland and walked miles to Baltimore. But it was more than likely the two were already in the city, let out by the Johnson family to work on contract. The black men were masons. It was a common practice among slave owners to rent out the enslaved. Sometimes they let the enslaved people keep all or a part of the money. Some enslaved people bought their freedom with this money.

Isaac and his father ran into the Union Army and marched behind them from Maryland to Ohio. Enslaved people who did this were known as "contraband." The term comes from a law that allowed the Union Army to confiscate any property of the Confederacy as "contraband." Enslaved people were considered as such.

Isaac and his father did not immediately join the Army. There was another law passed by Congress that promised to pay slave owners $300 for each enslaved man proved to have enlisted in the Union Army. Isaac could not read or write, but he could do simple math: $300 was a lot of money, more than he had ever had. He would not give his owner the satisfaction. It was not until October 1864, after Congress equalized black soldier's pay to white soldier's pay did father and son enlist in the Army. They joined Company H, 15th Regiment, United States Colored Infantry.

When Isaac enlisted, he was asked by Captain James Dereston, "You do solemnly swear that you owed no man unrequited labor on or before the nineteenth day of April 1861, so help you God?" Isaac raised his hand, and said, "I was not a slave."[3] He told the captain that he was eighteen and a farmer. Both were lies. He was born around 1849, which made him fifteen at the time of his enlistment, and our family knew him to be a brick and stone mason. He signed up for a one-year hitch. With Company H, he crossed the Ohio River and marched through Kentucky to Tennessee. The colored soldiers helped to contain Confederate General John Hunt Morgan, who became famous for his incursions into Kentucky. His troops drove through several towns in the Lexington area—Georgetown, Winchester, and Cynthiana—in an attempt to cross the Ohio River into Ohio. Although Kentucky was a part of the Confederacy, many Kentuckians disagreed with the war and fought against Morgan's troops. When Company H marched through Kentucky, they helped to thwart Morgan's attempt to invade the Union. The battles left Kentucky in tatters; the closer to the Ohio River, the worse the damage.[4]

In the fray, Isaac suffered two injuries: a grazing gunshot wound to the head, and a broken arm bone near his wrist. Company H marched through Kentucky to Tennessee and reached Nashville in October 1865. By that time the war was over. So was Issac and his father's one-year hitch. They left the army and set out to live as free men in a nation still writhing from the war.

Isaac's father did not want to return to Maryland or Ohio. He decided to go to Africa. This effort, now known as the "Back to

Africa" movement, was common before and after the Civil War. Some black people wanted to escape the long nightmare, and white people were happy to see them gone. Freed slaves settled in two free ports in Africa: Sierra Leone and present-day Liberia. Certainly that trip was Isaac's father's first time there, if he ever even landed. Many ships sank in the Atlantic ocean and Isaac did not want any part of it. He bade his father farewell and returned to Ohio to live with a woman he knew as "Auntie." She died soon after and he was alone in the world again. Isaac knew what it meant to have someone he loved leave him, to have no family. Slavery's greatest horror was the separation of families, but the loss of family is heartbreaking regardless of the circumstances. Giving up one's children voluntarily is almost unimaginable hence the hard feeling towards Alice when she surrendered her children to the orphanage.

From his auntie's house, Isaac went to Georgetown, the seat of Brown County. The town represented a proud military tradition that produced five Union generals, including Ulysses S. Grant. Set seven miles from the Ohio River bank on a well-cut road west to Cincinnati, Georgetown had been a stop on the Underground Railroad: the overland escape network for slaves. They would wade in the water and follow the gospel code. Conductors filled their boats with passengers, slipped their hands onto oars, and rowed silently in the dark across the Ohio River. The ferrymen shuttled between north and south; the enslaved people journeyed to Georgetown across the river toward freedom.

Historian Carl N. Thompson recorded an anecdote about Georgetown:

> "Before the war, when the 'Underground Railroad' was in active operation, we had a resident named Lindsey, who was quite active in catching runaway slaves, or at least in trying to catch them. One day a gang of boys concluded to have some fun at his expense. They dressed themselves up in old clothes that looked alike, blacked their hands and faces, and went into the woods and dispersed themselves over

wooded terrain. Then one, who was not disguised, wont to old man Lindsey and told him there was a runaway slave at a certain place. Lindsey went out after him and when he got there, one of the boys broke out and ran for life with Lindsey after him. The boy ran to where the next one was, stopped and hid in the underbrush while the second boy broke out and ran. This they kept up until the old man had nearly run himself to death, when the one he was chasing allowed himself to be caught and the joke came out. It was hardly safe to say run-away slave to the old man after that."[5]

Georgetown was friendly to black people, and it was there Isaac found his bride.

In about 1867, Isaac married a sweet fifteen-year-old gal named Celia Lydens. He and Celia stood up in front of a Presbyterian minister, then they headed for Kentucky where, thanks to John Hunt Morgan, work awaited stone masons like Isaac. The central Kentucky countryside was pretty much in shards just like Isaac remembered it. A lot of work was needed to be done to put horse country back together again. He secured work reconstructing brick walls, walkways, and houses in the Kentucky Bluegrass country.

Isaac and Celia had fourteen children. All of them were born in small towns near Lexington such as Winchester, Millersburg and Cynthiana. The family's location can be traced to the children's birth dates and places. His son John Henry, the seventh of fourteen children, was born in 1876 in Winchester, the seat of Clark County, known for its elevated walkways and stone fences that extended out into the country. Winchester's 3,000 residents were more than 50 percent black and lived in the section called Bucktown. Pauline was born in 1882 in Millersburg, Bourbon County, population 860. Millersburg Female College and Kentucky Wesleyan College were located there. The colored people of Millersburg impressed historian William Perrin as "very zealous in religious matters, and whose churches attest their devotion to the master's cause. They also had a school, which was attended by all the colored children who can afford to indulge in the luxury of education."[6] Millersburg was a good home for Isaac as he continued the work of rebuilding Lexington. His family stayed there for twelve years. The youngest Johnson daughter, Nellie, was born in 1889, in Cynthiana. This city of 2,500, in the southeast part of Harrison County, was a transportation hub with turnpikes to other key towns like Paris, Falmouth and Leesburg. That is the reason why Confederate General John Hunt Morgan targeted it during the war. His troops nearly burned Cynthiana to the ground in one of his futile attempts to get closer to the Ohio River. Cynthiana residents sued the Congress for war damages, and the town was still being rebuilt twenty-five years after the Civil War ended. Sometime before 1889, Isaac relocated there for work. Even though Isaac and Celia were married by a Presbyterian minister, in Kentucky they became Baptists, like everyone else.[7]

He and Celia had a big family. Here is the birth line-up of their fourteen children:

Sara, 1869
Charity, 1870
William, date unknown
Lena, 1873
Harvey, 1874
Billy, 1875
John Henry, 1876
Effie, 1877
Esther, 1879
Pauline, 1882
Lucy, 1884
Baby boy unnamed, 1886
Nellie, 1889
Baby boy unnamed, 1890.

Five sons were lost at birth or soon after, and John Henry was the sole surviving son. These deaths pained Celia and Isaac. Maybe they tried to avoid pregnancy, but birth control was limited, and they failed regularly. Celia suffered from neuralgia, a stabbing, burning pain due to irritated or damaged nerves, which can be caused by diseases such as diabetes or multiple sclerosis.[8] Since doctors at the time could not pinpoint the cause of neuralgia, there was no real treatment. Unfortunately, the health care services in late nineteenth century Kentucky was horrendous. Historians Lowell H. Harrison and James C. Klotter found late nineteenth century Kentucky to be "the worst quack-ridden state in the Union."[9] Celia was frequently bed-ridden, and unable to care for her home and family. Her illness was mentioned in the 1880 U.S. Census.

Celia's condition had worsened to the point that all she wanted was to return to her hometown to die. So Isaac took his wife and remaining children living at home to Georgetown. Toward the end of Celia's life, her and Isaac's older daughters were starting to leave the family to start their adult lives. They had cared for their inca-pacitated mother, and helped to raise most of their younger sisters and their one brother, John Henry. In 1894, their oldest sister, Sara Ann was twenty five years old, married, and pregnant with her third child. She lived in Millersburg with her husband, Willie Williams. On November 11, 1894, Sara Ann delivered a live, healthy girl, Laura Williams, and then soon after the birth, she died.

Since her mother Celia was unable to take care of her grand-children, Sara Ann's mother-in-law, Mrs. Williams, took the older children, but refused the infant; she just could not do it. As a result, Isaac took his granddaughter Laura home and placed the infant into the care of one of his younger daughters, twelve-year-old Pauline.

Little girls taking care of babies was so common during this era that Jacob Riis documented with photographs how young European immigrant girls were forced into being Little Mamas in New York City. That same thing was happening to black American girls. Riis' famous photograph, "Minding the Baby, A Little Mama," illustrated exactly what happened to Pauline.[10]

Being a Little Mama meant the baby was cared for, but it also meant the Little Mama could not go to school. Her education was sacrificed to help the family. Maybe the adults thought she could go back to school when the baby was old enough, but it was highly unlikely. Caring for children was what females were supposed to do. Even now in the twenty-first century, women with the best intentions find themselves in a similar situation—facing childcare issues. In the difficult choice between a crying, hungry, lonely, and needy child, and a book, the child wins every time. So it is not surprising that in 1894, most people believed that since a girl was only going to get married and have her own babies, there was no need for school. Some still think this way.

By around 1897, Pauline's mother Celia died in Georgetown at age forty-three. Laura's father, Willie Williams, was not dead but he may as well have been. Widowers did not and were not expected to care for their own children, it was women's work. Laura was separated from her siblings who found a home on their father's side of the family, so they never really connected. This was bound to create feelings of abandonment, dislocation, envy, and even anger. And Pauline, who was aunt-cum-guardian, mother and father to this baby, accepted her fate with the grace of Mary, mother of Jesus, and within the circle of her family, did her best to raise her. This was not unusual in nineteenth century America.

ဆ ∞ ဆ

Cincinnati, Ohio, 1899.

THE BEST VIEW OF THE QUEEN CITY was from the Kentucky side of the Ohio River. From there, one can see the splendorous display of north and south strapped together by pearls of light outlining wrought iron bridges over the fearsome, fierce and bountiful river. During the steamboat era of the 1850s, people flooded into Cincinnati, making it the biggest city in the state and the region. The population bloated to 300,000 with 37,000 people crammed in each square mile. People worked in trade, transportation, manufacturing and mechanics. Nearly 32,000 people were domestic and personal servants.[11]

Maybe Isaac had wanted to see Cincinnati when he enlisted in the Army at Hillsboro, which was some fifty miles northeast of Cincinnati. Maybe he did see it when he relocated to Georgetown, just a few miles from the river bank, but it was only after Celia's death, at the turn of the twentieth century, that he was ready to live there. The Queen City was the place everyone was talking about, it was like Paris and London. He took his family—we know it was at least comprised of John, Effie, Pauline, Lucy, Nellie and baby Laura—west to the city, joining some 14,000 black people already in Cincinnati. The Johnsons lived in the southeast corner of the city with other black folks who raised their families and supported their communities, and kept to their part of the city, separate but equal and in peace. In time, his younger daughters might find someone to marry and have children with, and a Baptist church where they could spend all day Sunday.

The Johnsons enjoyed this vibrant community. Pauline was almost sixteen and her younger sisters Lucy and Nellie were getting old enough to help with their niece Laura. But Cincinnati's southeast section was not what Pauline's older brother John Henry had in mind. Pauline was worried about her brother in Cincinnati, because she knew how he was. Like many younger sisters, she closely watched her older brother. Since John Henry was his father's only living son, he was spoiled rotten. He always did what he wanted to do, and his father let him. And John Henry did everything big and enthusiastic like the Kentuckian he was. He was free with his speech, independent in his actions and was always extravagant in his behavior.

John Henry's constant talk about horses marked him as a horse man, born and bred. He boasted he was on a horse before he could walk. John Henry quickly became a fixture on Vine Street, betting on and boasting about every little ounce of horse flesh he had ever seen or ridden or touched. He never tired of bragging about the "greatest"[12] jock to steer a horse around a turn in the run for the roses, the black jockey Isaac Murphy. And he shivered when he spun the tale of Jimmy Winkfield's "good judgment and cold nerve."[13] "Wink," as the jockey was called, won the Derby two times in a row, in 1901 and 1902, and would have won it a third time, but the Derby started requiring jockeys to take a written test. There was always another test for black people, especially for those who had beat the odds.

What Pauline saw in 1899, was her brother, John Henry romancing a white maid. They worked together at a Great House in the hills, and he the only black among the servants. Lots of colored men worked in those fine houses, colored women too. The smart ones were able to get those jobs, but they kept to themselves. They did not want to get into the type of trouble Pauline's brother John Henry was courting. Although it would be years later, it was the kind of thing that undermined heavyweight boxer Jack Johnson. Under the Mann Act, Johnson was accused, tried and found guilty of transporting a white woman across state lines for immoral purposes, and served time in Leavenworth prison. That white woman was his wife, his white wife. But Pauline's major concern was the Klan, the white men who lit flames to stop blacks and whites from being together. She was not happy about John Henry's relationship with Alice, because she did not want some liquored-up white men to lynch him over it. Yet what could she say? She was his *younger* sister.

John Henry always worked two jobs, at least. He worked for regular wages, either as a mason, porter, bartender, or a laborer, but he was also a sporting man. Being a Kentuckian, John Henry groomed, trained and bet on horses and dogs. It was legal. Later, he owned a Staffordshire Terrier, white with a black patch over his eye, called Spot. The big pit bull held up a great square head set with a mighty jaw. Did John Henry's sister wonder if this was why Alice liked him, because he had money? How could she know "nigger-rich" from real money? She was Irish.

With all this weighing on Pauline, leaving Cincinnati was a blessing sent from God. Isaac moved the family to Springfield, a smaller town about 135 miles north of Cincinnati. She could stop worrying about the men in her family because she would no longer have to hear about her brother's and father's shenanigans. Even Isaac, who was a widower, had become popular among the women seeking a husband. Springfield represented a fresh start that provided space between Pauline, and, John Henry and Alice.

ℰ ℭ ℭ

Springfield, Ohio.

SPRINGFIELD WAS "A CITY OF PROGRESS." In 1901, it had sixty trade unions, the Federation of Musicians being the most recent one.[14] There was work in the factories, but Isaac did not apply there. Not because he did not want to work inside, but because the only factory jobs that black men could get were dangerous, like pouring molten steel, bending smoldering iron, or breaking a strike. That was work for a young man, men who could jump out the way. No longer a young man, Isaac was more than fifty years old.

By the turn of the century, 4,253 blacks lived in Springfield. Most of them were unskilled laborers and servants, but some worked in government offices as well. Black men owned establishments in the drinking district. There were several merchants, doctors, and clergymen at the three Baptist and three African Methodist Episcopal churches, according to Darnell Carter, a Springfield attorney who studied the history of his hometown.[15] Springfield's black community had vibrant churches that did not look away from the plight of its people. The clergy were community leaders, the church spaces worshiping meccas, community centers and information hubs that organized efforts to improve everyday life.

As in Cincinnati, Springfield blacks kept up a busy, yet smaller, social scene. There were a dozen secret Masonic and Knights of Pythias societies and a Young Men's Christian Association (YMCA). They formed several baseball teams and numerous bands and vocal groups. Except for the 1904 and 1906 riots, Springfield was a good place to raise a family.

But life in Springfield challenged Isaac. He was in poor health. His decades of toiling as a brick mason caused constant pain. His war injuries—the bullet that grazed his head, and the broken bone in his arm — agonized him. The pain increased every year. He needed income because he would not be able to work any longer. He first filed for his Army pension in 1892, but it was not granted, so said a letter from the Department of the Interior, Bureau of Pensions, War Department on December 9, 1901. He was living at 312 Gallagher Street, two short city blocks from Irish Hill. Papers in his mailbox seemed a constant. They appeared at the most important points of his life—Army enlistment, marriage, his children's births, his sons' deaths. An illiterate, Isaac relied on his trusted readers and scribes. So on that Monday in December, he called for his youngest daughter, twelve-year-old Nellie. She opened the envelope to find a questionnaire inside. The preamble said that to prevent fraud, the Pension Bureau needed him to answer thirteen questions, in writing. The questions seemed like lie detector tests because they kept asking the one question he vehemently objected to: "Were you a slave? If so, state the names of all former owners, and particularly the name of your owner at the date of your enlistment." Isaac had answered this at his Union Army enlistment on October 6, 1864. He had said he was a farmer.

The matter at hand was money. A law at the onset of the Civil War had guaranteed slave owners $300 for each enslaved man who enlisted in the Union Army. Isaac knew that then, but it seemed to him that the federal government was determined to give former slave owners a payday thirty-five years after the war ended. I can almost hear him saying, "Naw, sir." He told Nellie to write, "I was not a slave." She did. Then, she wrote her father's name, and Isaac made his mark with an "X." With two witness signatures he returned the questionnaire one week before Christmas, December 18, 1901. No doubt, he hoped that the next communication would not be a lump of coal, but a check, but nothing would happen for a while.

On October 15, 1902, Commissioner of Pensions, B. S. Ware, asked the Department of the Interior to provide Isaac's personal description with "the name of former owner of the soldier." F. G. Arnsworth, Chief of the Record and Pension Office, received it the next day. He verified that "Name of owner not found." On October 27, 1902, two friends Daniel Baker, aged forty-one, and Noah Glenn, aged thirty-nine, both of Springfield, filed a General Affidavit on Isaac's behalf to the War Department:

> "We have known the claimant herein named for over 30 years and over 20 years respectively. We further declare that we know he has suffered and complained

of Lumbago and disease of the heart from July 25, 1898, to December 18, 1901. We met claimant very often from July 25, 1898 to December 18, 1901 and know that during said time he was greatly affected with said diseases. We have known claimant to be confined to his bed and room often on account of said diseases during the time. He often tried to work when he is not able to do so. His wife is dead, and he had a family of children depending on him and he makes every effort to work when he can. We do not think he was able to do a day's work between the dates above named, i.e., between July 25, 1898 and December 18, 1901. We have testified from intimate acquaintance and our own personal observation."[16]

The hope was that this affidavit would spur the Bureau of Pensions to award Isaac a pension. At age fifty-two, he could no longer work and earn money.

Everyone in the family had to pitch in to support Isaac. Pauline did her part. She was working as a maid in a private home. It was one of those easy-to-find jobs—cleaning up behind white folks—because few other opportunities were open to black women. African American women held their families together with "essential" jobs: "They care for our parents, our children, serve our food and clean....," wrote economist and educator Julianne Malveaux.[17] This was true when Malveaux mentioned it in her early twenty-first century writing; it was gospel in the early twentieth century.[14] It was not entirely clear if money was the reason, but in 1904, Laura went to work as well. She was ten years old when she left school in the fourth grade. Laura was tall and skinny, talkative as a magpie, and nervous, as individuals with tenuous family ties can be. Maybe Pauline did not like Laura leaving school, but what could she do? The family needed its people to work to support themselves and their old man, so even Laura got a job. Pauline's life was of obedience and duty, with her only respite attending church, where she met her husband.

Early on in my efforts to understand this story I never stopped to consider Pauline's place in the world. Initially, I considered her and Laura the villains. But I soon ed they were women of their times. Their behavior was proscribed, and when they went outside of their roles, they were rarely rewarded and often punished.

Marriage became an institution that was as cultural and social as it was legal and a state of being, with men pulling the strings. Its primary purpose was to bind women to men, and thus guarantee that a man's children were truly his biological heirs. Religion played a major role. As the Roman Catholic Church became a powerful institution in Europe, the blessings of a priest became a necessary step for a marriage to be legally recognized. By the fourteenth century, at the Council of Trent in 1563, the sacramental nature of marriage was written into canon law. While church blessings did improve the lot of wives, the church still held that men were the head of families, with their wives deferring to their wishes. This was transferred to the new world.

By Pauline and Alice's generation, getting a man was a woman's top priority because it was expected of her, and society enforced that standard by limiting a woman's opportunities. Until the laws changed, a woman's success was about getting a productive, profitable, hard-working man and making sure he was happy enough to come home every night, with the fruits of his labor. Women became the keepers of "the muses and the graces," which is what my sorority, Delta Sigma Theta founded in 1913, ritualistically called behavior of moral good.

As daughters, the social and financial pressures Pauline and Alice faced were complex. They tried to figure out how to live in the belly of the beast, each in their own way. Alice was a fallen woman, in the sense of race betrayal. As a result, she was abandoned by her family. When her husband John Henry died, Alice, as a widow with children, became more vulnerable because she was unable to work and take care of her baby unless she pulled her daughter out of school. That was something Pauline could not understand. As a daughter, Pauline did what was expected of her by quitting school and taking care of her orphaned niece. When her father was in need and her income as a domestic was insufficient to sustain them both, Pauline did what most women did to secure more income: become a wife.

James Ferguson was born in Gallipolis, Ohio. Their marriage license said he was a farmer. Ferguson owned the house located at 320 Buxton Avenue, on the corner of Kenilworth Avenue, near the hospital at the edge of town. He lived there with his brother.

On June 23, 1904 at St. John's Baptist Church, Pauline and Jim married in a ceremony officiated by the Reverend Timberlaker. Jim's brother moved out of the house and Pauline gussied it up. She continued to work as a domestic, and helped people at church, where people who needed help could always be found. Ten-year-old Laura lived with the Fergusons, which gave Isaac peace of mind to know that his daughter and granddaughter were well-situated. Nellie, John Henry and Pauline's youngest sister, sometimes lived with Pauline and sometimes was fortunate to find a live-in work situation. Pauline's marriage meant that she could help her father. Family had to take care of each other.

John Henry and Alice arrived in Springfield in time for Pauline's wedding. They came with their pretty two-year-old daughter who was named for John Henry's sisters, Pauline and Lucy. But that show of affection from John Henry to his sisters was the beginning of a whole lot of mess. Alice called her daughter Polly, an Irish nickname, but John Henry's sisters called her Little Pauline because John Henry's sister was Big Pauline. It was like they did not know a nickname must be significantly different to serve the purpose, but as neither of John Henry's sisters had children, the aunties called Alice's child in a way that bound her more closely to them. John Henry and Alice had a second child born in Springfield on June 2, 1904; a boy, named Elmer, called Bud. On his nickname they all agreed.

John Henry and Alice lived with Isaac because of Isaac's financial situation, but probably told the old man that they needed his help. John Henry did need time to situate himself in the heavily unionized city of Springfield so he could continue to help his father while supporting his family. He cobbled together work by doing a bit of masonry, and some buckboard wagon driving. Among other jobs, he was a bartender in Springfield's red-light district often referred to as The Jungles. It was on Columbia Street, near downtown. A first thought was that The Jungles was where black people lived, but maybe it was also called that because eight saloons were owned by black men. George Hurley at the Honky Tonk was one of them. Plenty of white men came to The Jungles for drinking, carousing, gambling, and prostitution.

John Henry was a great bartender. Every whiskey or rye he poured came with a paid-for tip on the horses. The job would have lasted forever if he had not been a married man with a wife and two young children at home, plus a sick father, two younger sisters, and an orphaned niece. Bartending was a night gig, but he had to get up most mornings to help his family. He did not need to be a bartender to make money on race tips; he could do this at the pit. He owned his own dog, Spot. John Henry was just waiting for his big break, and he got it when he came to the attention of the governor's son.

The former governor, Asa Bushnell, who had lived in Springfield, died in 1904 from a heart attack. John Henry arrived in Springfield and met the governor's son, John L. Bushnell, who had become his own man. He owned and oversaw all the businesses his father started, but Bushnell's heart was into prize show horses such as Hackney Morgans, a fancy English breed of high-stepping trotters. They stand about fourteen-fifteen hands in height and come in bay, brown, black or chestnut color, and their legs carry some white markings. A Hackney is a well-defined horse from its antenna ears to its skinny legs, and has a gait that is brisk and elastic. In other words, in the world of horses, Hackney Morgans were precise. It is not known how John Henry and John Bushnell met, but no doubt the pleasure was mutual. John Henry needed a well-heeled patron and Bushnell needed a man who knew horses. John Henry took owner-ship of Bushnell's stable. He got to work at 4:30 every morning to exercise and brush down the horses, and coo in their faces. They all had Irvington or Gipsy in their names. One mare was called Irvington

Nelly after John Henry's youngest sister. Working for Bushnell, John Henry learned to drive a fancy horse carriage called a phacton and would later have his photo taken in a driving coat and hat. Also, Bushnell and John Henry did a little construction business together. Doors opened in this new town, Springfield, for John Henry Johnson, a hail fellow well met.

In Springfield, the Johnsons had a chance to enjoy John Henry's children. Alice allowed them to take the children on trips. Polly remembered her grandfather taking her to the Ohio State Fair:

> "Once a year Grandpa took us to Columbus, Ohio, where he collected his pension in person, and to the Fair. That day was a day to remember. The interurban car ride to Columbus, lunch in the big building where he picked up his check, the Fair attraction and rides, all the snack foods we could want or eat, then the ride on the interurban back to Springfield. We arrived home tired, grubby, sleepy and very happy."

Isaac loved his grandchildren and his daughter-in-law, and called her "Irish," with affection. Alice was good about sharing the children, letting them know their family, but, the Johnsons noticed many things amiss.

The food Alice served? Plainest fare ever. White potatoes, always white potatoes, barely seasoned with a dash of salt and pinch of pepper, and tea biscuits, a kind of bland cookie. Irish stew made with a variety of root vegetables cooked into a mush too awful to describe. Isaac used to conjure up game stew on the cook fire in the cellar of their house and feed it to John Henry and the children. Alice would not touch it and did not want her children to eat it either. Polly remembered that. And Alice, who did not attend church, did not get the children baptized. Who ever heard of an Irish woman who did not go to church? John Henry was raised Baptist, Kentucky's pioneering religion.[18] As far as his family knew, he never pressed his wife on the issue of church, although maybe it was he who wrote their children's names in the Donlan family Catholic prayer book. Their names were written across from a scripture Baptists loved: "In the beginning." The spelling echoed a Kentuckian accent—he spelled "born" the way it rang on the ear in Kentucky—bor-n. "Borned."

Isaac took Polly and Bud and another little boy, George Walker, the son of a friend, to a tent revival. And Isaac was proud that his grandchildren saw him work as an usher at the revival. Polly recalled watching the spectacle from a bench in the back of the tent. Billy Sunday, a former baseball player turned rough-talking evangelist to the masses, was the revivalist.

> "The tent was huge and hot, the crowd excited; they were crying, shouting, moaning, singing and clapping. When Billy Sunday gave the invitation, folks were told to go to the back of the tent and come down the center aisle. This aisle was covered with sawdust and going down to the front was called 'hitting the saw-dust trail.' As an usher, Grandpa sang and clapped and assisted people up and down the sawdust trail many times during the revival."

A year went by. Life was good. And then it got better, Alice was pregnant with their third child. It was also time for her and John Henry to move into their own house. Their second son, Levy was born July 23, 1906, and they named him after a man in the Bible. John Henry started designing Alice's house the way she wanted: white clapboard with fancy wooden trim around the porch edges to match her lace curtains. Isaac helped with construction. He dug the cistern in the backyard. The first time he pitched in his shovel, a spring popped up. People were talking about that nearly a century later when I visited the homestead. John Henry put a white picket fence out front and a dog house in the backyard for his fighting dog, Spot. He loved his pit bull, loved the feel of his thick muscles twitching under his smooth coat. In spring 1907, they walked through the door of their new house on Harrison Street, with almost one-year-old Levy in Alice's arms, three-year-old Bud and five-year-old Polly. Life was good.

One year later, in 1908, Polly started school. John and Alice discovered their Irish Hill house was in the wrong neighborhood for the Springfield school she wanted their daughter to attend. It was not the black school, but no matter. In the Johnson family, girls' duty to family came first; most schools would do. Still, as long as John Henry lived, his family tolerated Alice and her hoity-toity ideas.

First of all, no black school for Polly; not the Garfield school, where Laura had attended, briefly. The Johnsons always attended black schools. In Kentucky, they were run by the church, taught by a school marm who had a bit more education than the pupils in front of her. In Springfield, Ohio, the black school was a part of the district, in a rented building. Seven years after the Civil War ended, in 1872, the black community thought its children deserved the same schooling as any other (white) child in Springfield. The talented tenth of black Springfield led the way, filing a lawsuit for an integrated school district. They relied on the Fourteenth Amendment, ratified four years earlier in 1868, which guaranteed equal protection under the law for all citizens, including former slaves. But the Board of Education settled the suit. They offered the black citizenry a school of its own, newly built in their community, and it was accepted. Thus, the Pleasant Street School, the first building owned by the Springfield, Ohio, Board of Education was built for the purpose of educating black folks. That deal lasted a little over a decade until 1882, when a second lawsuit, was filed. It took five years for it to twist through the entire judicial process and this time there was no settlement for segregated classes or second-class education for second class citizens.

It was a cause rooted in morality so the clergy took a point position in the case. Leadership for the desegregation lawsuit came from the African Methodist Episcopal (A.M.E.) Church and its minister, the Reverend John Gazaway. His daughter, Eva, was the plaintiff. In 1887, the Court ordered the public schools to desegregate. Even after desegregation in Springfield public schools became law, the Pleasant Street School remained a black school. Integration was selective. Some schools only allowed a few blacks to enroll, like the

Bushnell School, for instance. Whether the community resented or contested the continuing segregation hardly mattered. In 1896, the U.S. Supreme Court's decision in *Plessy v. Ferguson* rendered the issue moot; "separate but equal" was the law of the land. About the same time, the Board of Education removed children from the Clark County Children's Home from the Springfield schools as well. The Home Board of Trustees hired a teacher to teach inmates at the Home, and she was a member of the public schools' faculty. Poor children and black children would not have full access to Springfield public schools again for a long time.

In 1908 when Polly was six years old and starting first grade, Pleasant Street school was no longer open. There was a new school on Pleasant Street, The Garfield School, named for the assassinated twentieth president of the United States, James A. Garfield, a Republican from Ohio. Garfield School sat on Pleasant Street just west of Fountain Avenue. It was among the smallest of Springfield's schools with 350 students, including 96 black children. *Plessy* was still in place, but the Board of Education did not heed it. There were some black kids at every school, even Bushnell. But it did not matter what was going on with the other schools. Clifton was the school Springfield bragged about in its Centennial Program:

> "The Board of Education has the largest expenditure of any municipal department and nearly as much as all other departments combined....and while there may be room for criticism, yet the educational advantages of Springfield are admittedly first class."[19]

Alice enrolled Polly in the Clifton school. One of Polly's first textbooks was *The McGuffey Reader.* It contained religious messages, and the school day schedule included prayer every day. Pauline, the good Baptist, did not lord it over Alice when Polly let that be known.

℘ ℭ ℭ

THE FAMILY CELEBRATED a big Christmas at Pauline and Jim's house in 1908. It was Polly's first Christmas vacation from school. John Henry put his daughter on the streetcar and asked the conductor to let her off at Buxton Street where Pauline's husband Jim met the little girl. By this time Jim was a cupola tender in one of the factories, one of those dangerous factory jobs reserved for black men and others like him. But the job meant the Fergusons had money, even if after four years of marriage they still had no children.

That Christmas, every one of Pauline's living sisters came to Springfield and they had such a good time. The tree was decorated with popcorn strung with cranberries. Two tables were set up in the dining room to seat the sixteen family members there for Christmas. The buffet held the punch bowl, mince meat pies, and the floating island dessert. John Henry made fun of it; so much meringue! That and the homemade ice cream Isaac cranked his arm off making. So many good things to eat: the turkey and ham, the sweet potatoes and rolls, collard greens, and a whole bunch of good southern food. It was a day for laughter, fun and family. Just as the Johnson sisters had spoiled their brother, they also spoiled his children. The new baby was Levy, a sweetie-pie at two years old. They had a great time that day, but good times do not last forever.

In the fall of , Levy got sick with whooping cough. His illness took the whole family down. Those few days he was sick, Pauline stepped right in and took the other two children to her home and cooked for them, all their favorites, and put them to bed. She got the children up for school in the morning, kept a smile on her face though she worried about little Levy like everyone else. Still, this had always been her job, to watch the children when their parents could not.

The disease's progression was cruel. The cough reminded one of a crane, and developed into croup that became a sticky phlegm in his throat. The symptoms abated in the daytime, but at night Levy was unable to breathe because his throat was so full of phlegm that could not be broken up. Alice could barely talk about it, or keep a dry eye. Pauline came to understand in bits and pieces that Alice had a brother who died from the same disease. But to her credit, Pauline did not burden Alice with talk about the heartbreak in her family when every baby boy died except John Henry. They hoped and prayed over Levy for five days, but the Johnson family's curse on sons struck again. He passed away on November 5, and there was more tragedy to follow.

The first time Pauline was glad her brother John Henry was in good with the white folks was when the doctor came to John Henry and Alice's house. It showed that John Henry had prospered and was well-respected. The doctor nodded cordially to the assembly of the Johnson family gathered on the first floor of the house, but he saved his words for Alice. She told them the problem was John Henry's heart, but this was long after Pauline noticed the change in her brother.

Pauline had to be strong. She idolized her brother. He was just six years older than her. She wanted to speak kindly to him and offer some comfort, show her concern, but John Henry was a proud man who would have never admitted that he was failing. And so, those around him played along, even though it was clear he was not getting better. The doctor had already ordered his patient to limit his excitement. John Henry stopped working on construction sites, gave up gambling and dog matches.

However, Pauline's brother continued to tend to Bushnell's horses because it offered a slower, calmer pace for a man with a weak heart, but it was not enough to save him. Knowing this, Pauline did all she could to help. The house smelled of the frosty green scent of eucalyptus. She carried her share of kettles filled with steaming water to pans filled with oval green leaves, the treatment for a bad heart. First she carried water to the dining table where John Henry sat and read the sporting pages. And then she carried water upstairs as he lay in bed. Alice thanked her for the help because Pauline also helped with their fourth child, their baby girl Elizabeth Loretta.

It was a sad time as Pauline watched her beloved brother decline. She had never known life without him, except those few years he stayed in Cincinnati with his new wife and baby after the family moved to Springfield. The times she found herself alone with him—when the children were in school and Alice and the new baby were sleeping—he would not allow any talk of what was staring them both in the face. She found herself choked-up and on the verge of sobbing, and apologized for not being a good conversationalist. He joked, "I am good enough for both of us," and he was until he could speak no more.

Saturday, June 2, 1912, was Bud's birthday and also the day of John Henry's funeral. The coffin had sat in the parlor for two days. Pauline wore a blue tinged smile as she directed the household, got the food and made sure Alice and the children got their rest. She stood over her brother's body, gazing at his face. She said what all grief-stricken mourners say, he looks so good, like he was not even sick. And she cried in the kitchen when she was alone.

Undertaker Ewing's horse-drawn hearse carried John Henry to Ferncliff cemetery. They returned to find the photographer waiting. He had set up his Kodak Brownie camera in the street in front of John Henry and Alice's house, allowing enough space for the lens to gaze upon the entire group. Photographs of mourners were customary at funerals; sometimes a photograph was taken of the deceased in their coffin, but not of John Henry, at least not one that came down in our family. The photographer screwed the box camera onto the tripod and attached the curtain to block out the sun so he could see the image through the lens. He would be shooting into the dark recessed space leading to the front door, there was no help for it. What mattered was the sun was over his shoulder. White clapboards of the house provided enough contrast to show the house numbers, 606, on the front façade. In these early days of summer, the vine growing on the house next door was just starting to flower.

As the patriarch of the family, it was Isaac's duty to tip the man, and he was able to because his billfold held his precious pension dollars. His Army pension had come through. At first, he was receiving ten dollars a month, then he received a two-dollar raise. In 1912, Isaac was about age sixty-three. Closing his fingertips to pinch apart the bills sparked rheumatic pain into his war-injured wrist. Still, a tip for the photographer was little enough to offer, though the undertaker included a photograph as part of his services.

The Johnson family was a big group—eleven people in the family—and getting them to come together took time. The first grouping was Isaac and his daughters. Four sisters had traveled from out of town, gone from their father's care to that of husbands in Florida, Milwaukee, two in Detroit. Two others lived in Springfield: Pauline had been married eight years to a husband now sick, and Nellie and her beau, William Browning, who had been hanging around for more years than any of them like to think about. Neither Alice nor her two older children appeared in this photo. She declined it, saying she had business with the undertaker. She held the baby out to her father-in-law. The old man was aching with war and work wounds, and now his heart was sorrowful. The old man accepted Alice's first refusal, knowing the Johnson sisters wanted a photo with just themselves. He took the baby.

Pauline and her five sisters stood in a line behind the picket fence. They all wore black mourning dresses with high collars, and long sleeves. Ornamental brooches pinned the high-necked frocks of three of the sisters. Two sisters marked their cinched middles with broach pins. Only the petite Lucy had not pinned her dress, the voile fabric as fragile as her face. Nellie pinned a broach to her bodice. It looked, for all-the-world, like a medal—perhaps for courage. Pauline stood straight as a soldier. Most families stack their people in photographs by birth order. John Henry was born in the middle of the pack of sisters, and he divided them into the older and the younger set. Today the sisters mixed themselves up; younger sisters holding tight to the older ones. Flat-line, joyless mouths, wet eyes staring directly into the camera. In the previous days they had laughed and joked over their brother, but the day of the funeral brought sadness in such ample supply it could be scraped off into a bucket. Effie cocked her head right, an inquisition of the occasion.

In the opening of the white picket fence, Isaac sat on a chair. He wore a black jacket and a black tie around a white collar. His shoes wore a coat of grey from the dust on Harrison Street.

He held his two-year-old granddaughter on his knee; her white dress mussed and curly hair tousled. His strong arms wrapped around her, with his fingers in an intertwining lock on the girl. Elizabeth sucked her thumb, while fingers on her other hand worried her grandfather's sleeve. If she started to cry, no doubt the old man would jiggle his knee to distract her, but despite cajoling, charming and chatting children down, they always squirmed in front of the camera. Everyone in the photo needed to be still while the film was exposed, however long it took, or else it would blur.

Inside the house, Alice sat at the dining table with the undertaker certifying her husband's transition. She had to ask her father-in-law for information unknown to her: the spelling of John's mother's maiden name, and her birthplace. In every existing record, Celia's last name was spelled differently, but the pronunciation very similar: Cydens, Sidens, or Lydens. Pauline's marriage license spelled it Lytes. Isaac's information was well-known because he often told her stories about Maryland, the Civil War and Kentucky.

Isaac put Elizabeth in her mother's arms and pointed his son's family to the door. He refused to let his daughter-in-law beg off the second photo. "They waiting on you," he said. After he pushed her out the door, he heavily lowered himself into the empty chair.

John's sisters rearranged themselves in the next photograph. They lined up, but in a different order. This time the three youngest sisters, Pauline, Lucy, and Nellie stood shoulder to shoulder on the far left end, putting distance between them and Alice at the far right. Three older sisters formed a buffer in-between. Their young faces frozen by the strained relations, Polly and Bud stood in front of the aunties who were not part of their everyday life. These women felt safe. The sister with the big bosom—Esther—looked away from her younger sisters and gazed toward heaven in stern disbelief of the chilliness Pauline, Lucy and Nellie sent Alice's way. Lena's shoulder offered Alice comfort. This sister was closest to Alice's age, though they rarely met. With her shoulders going in one direction and her head tipping in the other, Alice looked lopsided. In her arms, her baby acted as a counterweight, giving her mother some semblance of balance, steadying her on her feet. Alice looked distressed and exhausted.

This photo tested the photographer. Death spiked high feelings, requiring utmost patience and courtesy of the photographer, but the family's variety of skin tones challenged his technical skill.

He could either adjust the aperture to capture a true image of the white woman and her near-white children, or set the exposure for the formidable women of his own race. He worked for Ewing, the black undertaker, and if the photos showed the black people's faces as ink spots, without eyes to see, noses to smell or mouths to talk, the photographer might as well look for another job. Finally, he adjusted the aperture for the black women. In the printed photograph, the white widow appeared darker. Was this not what this family was about? One could see it clearly in the children.

The Johnson family photographs were less than satisfactory. The photo with the white widow was blurred, and dark. She looked like she was colored. One photo after a funeral was customary, but two went a step too far for everyone. They were all tired, and their hearts wrung out.

ℰᴏ ℭʒ ℭℛ

The sisters talk about Alice's situation.

THE SISTERS CAME to 606 Harrison Street, the house the Johnson men built, with food in hand, warming it in Alice's kitchen. It was more for the children than Alice, who would not eat. Maybe they tried to call her daughter "Polly," but "Little Pauline" came across their lips naturally. They hugged Polly and Bud, and nearly two-year-old baby Elizabeth straddled on one or the other of her aunts' hips. They talked about how glad they were when everyone came together for Christmas four years earlier; they had a chance to see Levy and John Henry before the curse of the Johnson family struck again. How many times did they quote the Bible: "Watch therefore, for ye know neither the day nor the hour" (Matthew 25:13). They were Baptists, after all. When John Henry died, Polly was ten years old in the fourth grade, and Elizabeth was age two. It was like history was repeating itself. What the sisters said was true: in 1908 just four years earlier, they had been whole and healthy, Levy, three years old and John Henry, a happy man. And in 1912, both were gone. Finally, the aunties put the baby down and said to their sister-in-law, "Ally, let us know how we can help."

They gathered by themselves at Pauline's house. Huddled in the kitchen, they wondered, what was Alice going to do with three young children? She needed help. They were late in ing that Alice's family had abandoned her a long time ago, as soon as they realized she was with John Henry. The truth came out when Levy died, no white people came to comfort her. That put all the responsibility for the new widow and her children on John Henry's sisters, but what could they do, especially the ones who lived at a distance? Besides, they all worked as domestics, and none of them had a lot of money.

Alice no doubt would be returning to work. The house was free and clear, and John Henry left some savings, possibly insurance, the kind people paid a premium of a dime each month. After paying the undertaker, there was some money to tide her over. John Henry's sisters had chipped in with what they could. The big concern was care for the baby until she was old enough for school. That was a long three years away four years, if Alice refused kindergarten.

Each sister promised to help as much as she could—even Lena the Army wife stationed in Florida, and Effie in Milwaukee. But due to geography, the job fell to Pauline, Lucy and Nellie. They were childless. Lucy and her husband Ray were riding the crazy crest of the Detroit boom. He worked as a hotel porter, and with housing in such demand, Lucy ran a boarding house, renting out sleeping beds, eight hours at a time. She said any one of the children could come live with her and her husband in Detroit for as long as necessary, even the baby. Esther lived in Detroit as well. The two might have partnered to care for the child, but Lucy was forever doing linen and making up beds, so she was never a serious option. Most importantly, the children should stay together so they could know each other. John Henry's niece, Laura Williams, was a stranger to her older siblings who were raised by their father's family after their mother died. Her grandfather Isaac, her aunts, uncle and cousins were Laura's closest family, but that never seemed enough, even Pauline saw that. Laura was nervous as a bird, always chattering. Pauline and Nellie lived in the same town with Alice, but Nellie worked and was waiting, four years now, to marry Will Browning.

Of all the sisters, Pauline, the "guardian of the family's orphans" was the one they looked up to for a solution. Appointed at the age of twelve as the guardian of the first family orphan, she was expected to step in and help. Pauline told her sisters she would help as much as possible, but like all her sisters, she worked as a maid. Still, when she could, Pauline brought the children into her home. She lived way out on the East Side on Buxton Street, just a block or so from the city limits. It was a long haul from Irish Hill, near the center of the city, but worth the trip. It would be just like Pauline to have supper waiting, and how great it was for Alice to be able to sit after supper with another adult to discuss her children, and hear about their day. Against all good judgment, Pauline allowed them to play in the parlor, fighting to be first to stare into the pictures on the stereo optician. She fed them the southern food their mother detested, but in that summer of tender grief, Alice said nothing critical of her sister-in-law's care.

Pauline felt appreciated for every minute she spared. With no child of her own, she enjoyed them, their laughter and bright voices, and their politeness, "Yes, Aunt Pauline." Their willingness to be distracted from grief helped their aunt as well. In 1912, she had a husband, but after nearly eight years of marriage her hope for her own family was quickly fading away.

Pauline may have suggested doing with Polly as it had been done with her: keep her home to care for her baby sister while their mother worked. It was a workable idea, as shown by any number of families, including the Johnsons, who pressed a daughter into similar service. There was little other help, especially for black people. Family had to take care of their own.

Death in the family pushes relatives to make certain vows, and before the sisters boarded trains to Detroit, Florida and Wisconsin, their last tears came with a vow to reunite before another funeral. Death caught the sisters short of their well-meaning intentions. Effie died in November 1912, "when I was in fifth grade," Polly recalled. Effie was John Henry's next younger sister. Grieving in Springfield became too much for the old man. Isaac moved to the National

Military Home in Sandusky, Ohio, the closest one near to where his third daughter lived. Lena Harris lived in Detroit's Black Bottom on Lafayette Street. She was one of only two children from his first eight still alive. She took charge of their father. He never felt more discouraged, more in need of prayer. She could talk to Isaac about the old days when Celia, Sara Ann, John Henry and Effie were alive, and knew not to ask about the others.

Back-to-back deaths often spur a family to quit talking and do what they said they were going to do. Early in spring 1913, the sisters took a trip together—Pauline and Lucy, their husbands, Jim and Ray; their sister Esther, one niece, Nanny, her husband, Tracy; and Nellie and Will, still not married. If invited, Alice begged off, the children were in school. The sisters met in Dayton to have fun at Lakeside Park. It was an amusement park with a wooden roller coaster, a carousel, shooting gallery and all the fun of a state fair. They went to the photographer's studio, which had for a prop the newest thing: an automobile. The nine of them piled into a black Ford Model T for a photograph. Solemn faces, all around, but that was the style, and no one had more of that than the Johnson sisters, especially Lucy. She wore her best suit, and Pauline donned her new waist with ruffles of lace at neck and sleeves. They wore their new $1.98 hats decked with pom-poms.

In the early twentieth century, photographs of this sort were printed as picture postcards. One portrait shows a slender thirty-one-year-old Pauline seated, her brimmed pom-pom hat a frame above her plain face. Both sisters sent their photos back to Alice, inside envelopes. Pauline was worried and concerned about being away. She was helping Alice take care of the children: her namesake niece, the rambunctious eight-year-old nephew, and darling little girl. She cared for her brother's children like she would for her own and she missed them. "This was taken on Sunday," she wrote on the back of the photo. "I was wondering what you all was doing?"

They were trying to manage an unsettling situation that was spiraling out of control. Pauline knew that, but she had nothing more to say. After John Henry died, his sisters did what they could do to help. When Alice got a job, Pauline, who was a doer, stepped in like a relief pitcher in the World Series. But they were juggling the care of a toddler too young to attend school. Alice, Pauline, and Nellie were putting their jobs in jeopardy when one or the other stayed home with the baby. Agonizing scenes took place when Polly demanded to know why she had to stay home from school with the baby. Her mother never shared how her going to school was in peril. Pauline kept mum, but tried to get Alice to be more succinct about what she wanted and needed from them. They were frustrated when Elizabeth wailed for her mother when she went to work. Something had to give.

I am sure when Alice told Pauline of her plan to put Polly, Bud and Elizabeth in the Clark County Children's Home, the fireworks ignited. At first it sounded like an idle threat. Most orphanages did not accept colored children, not the Lutheran Home, or the Knights of Pythias or the Odd Fellows. It was as Booker T. Washington, president of the Tuskegee Institute, and Richard Carroll, manager of a South Carolina home for destitute colored children, said at the White House Conference on Dependent Children that black people had to take care of their own.[20] But then it dawned on Pauline that Alice was serious. Pauline feared that once the Home admitted the children, they would be given to foster homes, especially Elizabeth, who might even be adopted because she could easily pass for white. All this swirled around Pauline who cried that the children were all that was left of John Henry. She pleaded with Alice that family takes care of its own.

When Alice explained how important it was for her children to complete at least ninth grade, they did not believe this warranted surrendering her children to an orphanage. Pauline, her sisters and niece had even less schooling than Polly had in 1913 at age eleven as a fifth grader, and they turned out fine. Laura told Alice that she was "putting on airs," thinking she was better than everyone else. Alice responded curtly to Laura, "Who puts on airs for you?" as Polly remembered. Pauline stood by in silence feeling a guilty pleasure that Laura had repeated what Pauline had said to her. But Alice also implied that Laura's lack of schooling made her a rude and disrespectful young woman who never showed Alice any respect as her elder. This battle over the future of John Henry's children got so heated because they were nearly the last of the family line. Pauline and Lucy never had children. Nellie was still waiting to marry William Browning. Who thought that would ever happen?

There had to be a day when Pauline and Alice's conversation about the children ended in disaster. Exasperated, Alice may have pointed out these were her children to do with as she saw fit, and if God had wanted Pauline to have children, he would have sent them to her. And Pauline could say nothing because she was married for eight years with no children. The heart of the matter was that Pauline could not understand why education mattered so much to Alice, and why Alice was willing to sacrifice her family so that her daughter could have an education. How could she not see the importance of holding family together? Alice's family had cast her out, did she not want to have some kind of family around her? If the Johnsons had not taken care of each other, Alice would never have had a husband. Life was hard, family had to stick together in order for them to survive. But maybe only black people thought this way. Pauline did not know about all that, she just knew what had worked for them. What was wrong with Alice?

After Alice surrendered her children to the Clark County Children's Home, Pauline perhaps threatened Alice about getting them out herself because she was a married woman. The one thing a woman needed in order to take home a public ward was a husband. But if she was considering it, she was running out of time. Her husband Jim was diagnosed with Hodgkin's Disease, a cancer of the lymph nodes. He was thirty-eight years old, and he had been sick for six months. Five days after their tenth wedding anniversary, on June 28, 1914, Jim died at home at two in the morning. Pauline and Jim never had any children. Pauline was alone.

In 1915, at age thirty-three, Pauline did something Alice never considered; she remarried. Her new husband was Cleo Hardy, a jovial man. While Jim was sharp and his face was angled, Cleo was round, smiling and happy. Isaac moved from the Old Soldiers'

Home at the north end of Ohio, and took up residence at the Soldiers' Home in Dayton, twenty-six miles south of Springfield. He still needed looking after, and Pauline was the one to do it.

One of the black people who worked at the Children's Home was related to William Browning, Nellie's husband, finally as of 1914. The Johnsons were able to keep up with John Henry's children without going there in the first tender years when nobody knew what was going to happen. Whether Pauline visited John Henry's children at the Children's Home was not known. Alice saw her children regularly and she brought them several times on the interurban car to visit their grandfather at the Old Soldiers' Home in Dayton. When he died from a stroke in 1917, Polly recalled everyone—her brother, sister, and mother, her aunts and cousin—were all at the funeral. "He was given a military funeral which impressed me so much I could recall all of it for years," she wrote in her journal. "My grandfather's flag-draped casket was placed on a flatbed wagon frame attached to a caisson drawn by horses. Soldiers followed the caisson in a slow, dignified march from the chapel to the grave site. A soldier's farewell that included a volley of shots and taps closed the service, a service that left a lasting impression of honor, dignity and pride with Private Isaac Johnson's grandchildren."

Springfield had been a place of great joy and deep sorrow, and after Isaac died, Pauline had no reason to stay. She sold her house to Nellie and Will Browning. They raised their son, Bill, on Buxton Street. Pauline and Cleo moved to Detroit. He earned a good living as a distributor of musical juke boxes, but they never had any children. In 1920, when Polly graduated from Springfield High School, Pauline knew how her namesake niece wanted to get her sister out of the Home. But she decided not to interfere, possibly in fear of angering Alice. Lucy had no such qualms. She and her husband, Ray Culberson were the first to sign Elizabeth out of the Clark County Children's Home when Elizabeth was ten years old. After one year, they returned Elizabeth to the Home. The reason is unknown. Two years later, when Polly married, she and her husband, James Leigh Jr., removed Elizabeth from the Home for good, but once in Detroit, the newlyweds let Elizabeth live with Pauline. It was Pauline who sucked up Elizabeth's feelings of outrage over being rejected by her mother, and dealt with Elizabeth's delinquency and poor performance in school, before she eventually dropped out.

There is a photograph in the family album taken years later in Detroit when all these women were old ladies. The one where Alice and Pauline are together has a brittleness about it. They all look so out of place and out of time. There is another showing Alice, Polly, and Pauline in a garden. The two older women stayed at opposite ends of a flower bed, with Polly in the middle. They tried to make up but people, especially women, take it hard when their family traditions are rejected or condemned. When the welfare of children is at stake, the pain cuts deep, so deep it stabs the core which never heals.

Pauline Johnson Ferguson Hardy died in Detroit on June 7, 1986, at age one-hundred and four. She was a member of St. Stephens' A.M.E. Church on Detroit's West Side for more than fifty years, having split her religious life almost evenly between St. Stephens and the Baptist church. Her other affiliations were K.P. Lodge, Courts of Calanthe, Detroit Progressive Court No. 458, and the Semper Ami Club. She left to mourn her passing and to cherish family memories four generations of nieces and nephews. The Bible verse printed on her funeral program came from the gospel according to John, "I am resurrection, and the life, he that believeth in me though he were dead, yet shall he live: And whosoever liveth and believeth in me shall never die" (John 11:25-26). ⌘

NOTES

1. *Seventh United States Census, Schedule 2,* for the 1st District in Baltimore County, July 23, 1850, slave owner Francis Johnson

2. *The Green Spring Valley: Its History and Heritage,* (Baltimore: Maryland Historical society, 1978), 52

3. Company Descriptive Book, Co H, 15 Reg't U.S. Col'd Inf., Isaac Johnson (Hillsboro, Oh., Oct. 6, 1864); United States Department of the Interior, Bureau of Pensions. Form 3-474 (old No. 3-493) Isaac Johnson, No. 1092802 (Washington, D.C., Dec. 7, 1901).

4. E. Merton Coulter, *The Civil War and Readjustment in Kentucky* (1926, repr., Gloucester, Mass: P. Smith, 1966), 386. William Perrin, *History of Bourbon, Scott, Harrison and Nicholas Counties, Kentucky* (1882, repr.; Cincinnati: Art Guild Reprints, 1968), 257; Lewis Collins, *Collins' Historical Sketches of Kentucky* (Covington, KY: Collins & Co, 1874), 135.

5. Carl N. Thompson, *Historical collections of Brown County* (Piqua, Ohio: Printed by Hammer Graphics, 1969) 134.

6. Perrin, 126.

7. Collins, 422.

8. William Pepper, M.D., L.L.D., assisted by Louis Starr, M.D,, *A System of Practical Medicine by American Authors.* (Philadelphia: Lea Brothers & Co, 1886), (5) 1215.

9. Lowell H. Harrison and James C. Klotter, *A New History of Kentucky* (Lexington, KY: University Press of Kentucky, 1997), 259.

10. Jacob Riis, *How the Other Half Lives: Studies among the tenements of New York,* 1901 repr.; the Museum of the City of New York (new York: Dover, 1971) cover.FN

11. Charles T. Greve, *Centennial history of Cincinnati and representative citizens,* (Chicago: Biographical Pub. Co., 1904), 1016.

12. James Robert Saunders and Monica Renae Saunders. *Black Winning Jockeys in the Kentucky Derby* (Jefferson, North Carolina: McFarland & Company, Inc, 2003), 90.

13. Saunders, 54.

14. Benjamin G. Prince, ed., *The centennial celebration of Springfield, Ohio, held August 4th to 10th, 1901.* (OH: Springfield Publishing Co., 1901), Section VIII.

15. Darnell E. Carter, *1904, 1906 and 1921 Race Riots in Springfield, Ohio, and the Hoodlum Theory.* Master's Thesis, The Ohio State University, 10.

16, Daniel Baker and Noah Glenn, *General Affidavit, State of Ohio, County of Clark,* October 29, 1902, np.

17. Julianne Malveaux, "Still at the Periphery: The Economic Status of African Americans." *Race, Class and Gender in the United States: An Integrated Study.* Paula Rothenberg, ed., 8th edition (New York: Worth, 2003), 293.

18. Collins, 416.

19. Prince, 112.

20. Proceedings of the Conference, 115 and 136.

Celia Lydens Johnson birthed baby after baby, fourteen children in total, including John Henry Johnson. *Courtesy of The Andrew J. and Mary Jane Humphries Foundation.*

Isaac Johnson was a mason, a son, a father and grandfather. He loved to tell his tales of being a Union soldier during the Civil War. *Courtesy of The Andrew J. and Mary Jane Humphries Foundation.*

Pauline Johnson, John Henry's younger sister, at Lakeland Amusement Park, Ohio, 1913. *Courtesy of The Andrew J. and Mary Jane Humphries Foundation.*

Lucy Johnson, John Henry's younger sister at Lakeland Amusement Park, Ohio, 1913. *Courtesy of The Andrew J. and Mary Jane Humphries Foundation.*

John Henry Johnson's sister, Lucy Johnson Thompson (l), and niece, Laura Williams Harden (r), circa 1940, in Detroit. *Courtesy of The Andrew J. and Mary Jane Humphries Foundation.*

John Henry Johnson's two sisters, Nellie(l) and Pauline (r) with Nellie's husband, Will Browning (c), in Detroit in front of Polly's house in Detroit, circa 1960. *Courtesy of The Andrew J. and Mary Jane Humphries Foundation.*

In 1961, Polly (c) failed to reconcile the two women she loved most, her mother, Alice (l), and aunt, Pauline (l), in a visit to Belle Isle Park in Detroit, 1961. *Courtesy of The Andrew J. and Mary Jane Humphries Foundation.*

John Henry Johnson's sister, Pauline Hardy (l), and niece, Laura Williams Harden (r), circa 1970, Detroit. *Courtesy of The Andrew J. and Mary Jane Humphries Foundation.*

In Detroit, John Henry's sister, Pauline, seated, holds the fifth generation of her brother John Henry and Alice's family, a baby boy born in 1971, Diallo K.B. Humphries. L-r: Dedria A. Humphries, Polly Johnson Leigh, Mary Jane Leigh Humphries. *Courtesy of The Andrew J. and Mary Jane Humphries Foundation.*

CHAPTER 4

Polly

I LOVED GOING TO my grandmother Polly's house. It sat on a corner of Underwood and Northfield streets on Detroit's West Side, a traditional white house, with a wide shaded porch across the front. Inside, the living room spanned across the full beam of the place. Entering through the front door, one can see the red brick fireplace on the far end. Brass fireplace tools: a little broom, and pan, a poker, a small shovel, were hung from a stand sitting on the ceramic tile hearth. Cabinets with doors of clear glass flanked both sides of the fireplace. In front of the fireplace, a low river barge of a coffee table floated over a nubby, blue carpet. The only other furniture in this area was my grandmother's rocking chair next to the east cabinet, and on the other side wedged into the corner by the front windows, a small, upholstered stool.

I felt comfortable at Polly's because I spent a lot of time there. In addition to Sundays after church and holidays, I helped her at her house every Saturday when I was a teenager. From 1968 to 1971, I earned my spending money running errands up and down the stairs, basement to the second floor, to save her arthritic knees. Except for me earning spending money, the housework seemed unnecessary. My grandmother's house looked the same before and after a cleaning, though she knew when I overlooked a spot. Every week I cleaned the bathroom, vacuumed the living and dining rooms, and dusted. I dusted around and under the many books, including the yellow-bordered *National Geographic* magazines my grandfather read. Eva Rutland's *The Trouble with Being a Mama* was always on the table next to Polly's rocking chair. It was Rutland's memoir of mothering children in the racial conflict of the South and the social upheaval of California.

One spot I never overlooked was the corner by the front windows. I sat on the upholstered stool, back against the wall, feet snuggled in the thick blue carpet. Under the ruse of cleaning the glass door of the cabinet, I took out her leather-bound photo albums, and flipped the pages. She filled them with images: flowers from gardens, postcards from the Caribbean and so on. The ones I loved were filled with people. Our people. My favorites were those of me and my sisters, brothers, and parents at Christmas and Easter as babies and toddlers and graduates. I studied every image of my grandmother's past. I never had to ask who the white lady was because Alice had always been there in the album and in person, but some of Polly's relatives never showed up much. Some were cut out. People used to cut out a relative they did not like in a group photo since snubbing a relative was something most people of her generation did not dare do in real life. People were too hard to come by and keep.

This is what absorbed my attention and sparked my imagination. I could sit for hours with a photograph album on my lap. On a Sunday afternoon when I was visiting, she would let me, but Saturday was a work day. Once detected, she would break into my cocoon of silence and rouse me from the corner. I rarely heard her heavy tread over the floor until she stood over me.

Pauline Lucy Johnson was born February 7, 1902 in Cincinnati, Ohio, the adored first child and daughter of Alice Donlan and John H. Johnson, two American renegades in an America still struggling to become "one nation indivisible with liberty and justice for all." It was having great difficulty respecting the different peoples within. There were other places Polly could have been born in the U.S. There were many people like her in the American South, white and black. Yet she was distinct. She came into this world from the hope of two giddy young people in love: two halves, opposite in form (man and woman), color (black and white) and nature. John Henry was born free, and Alice sort of free, as free as any woman in the late nineteenth century. Certainly she took advantage of all of the liberties available to her at the time.

Growing up, Polly did not know about the error on her birth certificate. She did not know that it was racism that purposefully misidentified her mother as black. She did not fully understand that her white mother and black father crossed the color line. For her, John and Alice were Mama and Papa. She was their child. She had extended family, her father's father, and his sisters. They did not always get along with Alice. Polly did know that, unfortunately.

I like the idea that Polly spent her early childhood in one of Cincinnati's romantic alleys, a crevice of a street where people lived in a cozy way, taking only the space they needed. They were small people. The Irish were made small by the cruelty of the English, a people who settled on an island that had too little land and few resources. The Irish struggled to survive and personified the adage, "necessity is the mother of invention." But Polly did not know that. What she knew was her mother called her Polly, her father made her laugh, and she loved them both. It may have seemed a good thing when they moved from that alley to a house that held other people who loved her as well. Her grandfather and her aunts loved her as her mother did, unconditionally. Their dark skin had no significance to her. There was nothing to question; they were one big happy family.

When Polly came with her parents to live in Springfield, Ohio, closer to the Johnson family, she was two years old. Springfield was uneasy when they arrived. Darnell Carter, a Springfield native, studied the Springfield's race riots for his Master of Arts degree in history at The Ohio State University. The title of his 1993 thesis was *The 1904, 1906 and 1921 Race Riots in Springfield, Ohio and the Hoodlum Theory*. Carter examined the cause of those riots using books, magazines, newspaper articles and interviews. To understand the riots, Carter also examined labor strike controversies of the 1880s, school desegregation of 1882, and the *Plessy v. Ferguson* ruling from the U.S. Supreme Court, which removed any obligation to desegregate. To its credit, the Springfield Board of Education did not roll back the progress that had been made before *Plessy,* and black students remained enrolled in varying percentages in most of its schools. Still, in March 1904, "Springfield had become a powder keg of racial and political tension awaiting a match," Carter wrote. [1] As in Tulsa, Oklahoma, Springfield was a city where blacks had established a vibrant community. A section of Springfield know as the Levee provided housing for black industrial and day laborers, as well as being a black business district conducting more informal industries such as prostitution, drinking and gambling. The 1904 race riot was instigated by police involvement in a domestic dispute in the Levee that turned deadly.

When Richard Dixon went to the Jones Hotel in the Levee to retrieve his clothes from a woman, Mamie Corbin, who was pur-ported to be his common-law spouse, Dixon requested that a police officer accompany him. Various newspaper sources reported that Dixon and Corbin quarreled until Dixon took out a gun and shot the woman. When the police officer attempted to subdue Dixon, he was shot too. Dixon escaped and immediately turned himself in at police headquarters. When news of the shooting and the death of a white police officer by a black man reached the Springfield community, white men gathered at the jail demanding the release of Dixon. After they succeeded in overpowering the police, they took Dixon away and lynched him. This is what provoked the 1904 race riots and welcomed Polly and her parents to Springfield.[2]

In March 1904, two-year-old Polly was living with her parents at her grandfather Isaac's home in a black neighborhood called The Jungles. She was not too young to pick up the emotional tremors of her parents. She must have been nervous and clinging to them. Then her little brother Elmer (called Bud) was born on June 2, 1904. In Springfield, Polly also had to deal with gaining another identity. That was tied up in the new nickname, "Little Pauline." She was only called that by her aunts, those ladies who smelled so good. The Johnson family already had a Big Pauline, who gave her delicious things to eat. Soon she figured out she was Polly at home with her parents and brother, but Little Pauline with her grandfather and aunts. Still too young to know who she was—Polly? Little Pauline? Black or white?—in time she would figure it out.

In February 1906, when Polly was five, Bud was two, and Alice four months pregnant, John Henry was working as a bartender in the drinking district known as The Jungles. He spent most of the night pouring drinks, and running the cloth over the already gleaming dark, shiny wood bar waiting for the signal that a man at the rail wanted another pour. John Henry always kept a keen eye and ear. Sooner or later, he caught a warning. There was another race riot brewing. This one was a little different: the trouble started with a barroom brawl between black and white men that spiraled out of control. This time around, the attack was on The Jungles, where the Johnsons lived.[4] Polly remembered her father telling her mother the next morning, a black woman had already been burned out of her home.

"There might be trouble, Irish," he said.

"I suspect," she replied, "downtown."

"No," he said, "here."

They were still living with Isaac. Alice's solution was to run to her aunt's house, Polly recalled, but her mother did not have an aunt in Springfield. Alice had no blood relatives in Springfield—she had none anywhere in the world that would claim her. She did have a friend—an older woman in the Irish neighborhood whose name was Mrs. Cathill. Alice said, "We can all go to my aunt's until the trouble passes."

"No," John Henry said. "I'm not running. I'm staying here. I know these fellows."

Alice spoke low. "You know these men, and you don't know them. When they get in that mob, they won't know you."

John Henry replied, "I'll open the gate and let those dogs out if they try to get in my yard, and I've got these rifles."

John Henry sat on his front porch all day, rifle across his knees, and Spot laid on the wooden floorboards. "Steady boy," he murmured, as he rubbed Spot's block head. He had other dogs in the back yard and if trouble rose its head, he could sic Spot on the first man, leap over the rail, quickly run down the short path alongside the house, and open the gate for the other dogs. The path to the yard was narrow enough that Spot could hold the men off. Behind John Henry, the door opened. Light footsteps. Polly and Bud came to stand at their father's side, Alice behind them. John Henry said to reassure his wife, "I'll open the gate and let the dogs out," he said, "I've got this rifle and I'll open the gate."

Alice gave the children a little push off the porch down the steps. She was taking Polly and Bud to Mrs. Cathill's to hide them under the feather bed, Polly remembered.

John Henry waited for a long time the second night of the riot of 1906. He waited until it was pitch dark. So when the bouncing balls of torch light came, it lit a bright line headed towards him, and John, being dark skinned and perhaps not visible at first, surprised the men when he said, "Well, boys, if you don't pass on I'll turn my dogs loose," and he called out a few of their names, "William. Bob." Now the men could see him sitting there at the edge of the shadows with his rifle and his dog Spot, who tensed his muscles, waiting for the command to attack. The men then called out John Henry's name and then marched on, their voices, faces and torches fading into the darkness.

Polly recalled this story from her childhood, and it was similar to the one Carter reported in his thesis. He wrote that Charles Fillmore and Rueben Campbell, who lived on Summer Street, appeared on their porches with shotguns to defend their families and homes, and John Henry did the same.[3] Springfield had some audacious and committed black men who stood their ground, including Polly's father. Polly understood the necessity of guns in early twentieth century America. Toward the end of her life, she told me, in a matter-of-fact tone, everyone had a gun because you never knew what was going to happen. Polly loved her papa for his courage.

In summer 1906, the family grew bigger following the birth of Polly's second brother Levy on July 23. Now Polly had two brothers just like her mother had. During the year of Levy's birth, the family moved into a new house. Her father had a new job. He worked with the governor's son, John L. Bushnell, whose show horses John Henry took care of. This turn of fortune meant Polly's father could build a house on Irish Hill. Alice was happy to be living among her people; this was clear when she baked dozens of cupcakes to give away to neighbors up and down the block. Polly had her own bedroom upstairs across the hall from her parents' room.

In the fall of 1908, Polly went to school. Polly did not know why some people in Springfield hated integrated schools, and did not want their children sitting next to black children, but school mattered to Alice. She enrolled her daughter at the new school built just seven years earlier. Clifton was the biggest elementary school in Springfield, with more than one hundred students in each of its eight grades.

Years later, Polly wrote about this day in her journal. It was "awful." Being "spoilt and shy," she cried the entire first day. Two sisters, Gertrude and Christine Leach befriended Polly and took her out on her first recess. Her teacher was a strict German woman, Miss Frattwin. First grade students reported at 8:30 a.m. for devotions. Prayers were said in the morning and afternoon. The day progressed in 15 and 30 minute periods. Afternoon sessions were longer than the morning's. There were five sessions in the morning before ten o'clock. Music, reading, two arithmetic sessions met every day. Geography, history, physical education, civics and morals met one day each week. "Intermission," known as recess in Polly's journal, started at ten. After morning intermission, the schedule continued with gymnastics, art and drawing, language, writing, and spelling. Second intermission began at 11:15 a.m. for children to go home for lunch. School re-opened at 1:00 p.m., and the subjects repeated. First and second graders were dismissed after their 2:45 p.m. reading class.

This was the kind of schooling Alice wanted for her daughter. Reading and writing, the foundation of good Irish storytelling. Her first day of school was perhaps the first time Polly realized the burden of being her mother's daughter. In addition to body sustenance, going home for lunch provided a bolstering from her papa and a hug of encouragement from her Mama. Eventually, Polly started to enjoy school.

After four months, Polly learned that school led to Christmas break. Polly was a big girl, a first grader in school. Alice let her ride the street car to her Aunt Pauline's house. The streetcar trundled along the length of High Street, from York Street to Buxton Lane. She admired the mansions and recognized the Bushnell house where her father worked, and the Great House where her aunt Nellie was a live-in maid. After jumping through the snow in the big boot prints of her uncle, Jim, Polly arrived at the house. For the first time in years, all the Johnson women were in town for the Christmas holiday. Her aunt, Esther from Detroit, hugged Polly to her "ample breast and tells me I am the prettiest little girl she knows." Another aunt, Lena, an Army wife who lived in Florida, brought Polly a gift: a beautiful large doll. This day she recalled her mother looked "small and pretty, and her beautiful chestnut brown hair hangs nearly to her waist." Except for her grandfather Isaac, no one asked about school. After he rewarded her with one copper for showing him how to read a word, she could forget about the mind torture inflicted by her teacher, Miss Frattwin.

In her remembrance of this day, Polly betrayed her love of desert. The list of Christmas deserts included mincemeat pie, sweet potato pies, a coconut cake, a pound cake and floating island, a traditional Christmas custard her father called "air pudding." She recalled the exquisite cut glass serving dishes that were piled high with curled celery and relishes, and how the facets of the smaller dishes shimmered with jellies and jams. Polly was needed to set the table, but in the meantime, her aunt, Pauline told her to go upstairs to Laura's room. Immediately, Polly's fourteen-year-old cousin, Laura, started to boss her around. Tired of that, Polly retreated to the living room where she smiled at a "wall picture of a little girl in a blue dress playing a clavichord in a garden where several other little girls are dancing."

When Polly's parents arrived, her father was the center of his sisters' attention, as always, but this time they also crowded around her mother "to get a look at the newest member of the family," two-year-old Levy. During dinner, he stayed in his mother's lap while the rest of the children slid onto an ironing board serving as a bench at Grandpa Isaac's table. He was full of "folktales from the days of slavery, stories from his travels as a bricklayer, and his adventures as a Union Army soldier," which his children had heard at least a thousand times. At last, the lady of the house bumped open the swinging kitchen door with her hip, turned and revealed the huge and beautifully browned turkey in her hands. Pauline set it in front of her husband, who offered "thanks to God for this family here gathered and for the food that nourishes." All sixteen relatives responded, "Amen." It was a great Christmas.

In , seven-year-old Polly started second grade in Miss Hunt's class without crying. However by November, misfortune struck. Her parents took Levy to the hospital and he never came back. It made her Mama cry and Papa sniffle all the time. They buried Levy in Ferncliff Cemetery. He died from whooping cough that turned into the croup. Polly did not know the reason why she has so many aunts and no uncles, nor did she understand why her father was inconsolable. After the visit to Ferncliff in the cold of November, Polly returned to school and found that she liked it more than the grief in her house. Her father tried to act hard when he said, "People die. I have a family to raise," but he sniffled and wiped his eyes and nose a lot.

In September 1910, Alice was getting eight-year-old Polly settled in the third grade. One of the teachers brought a huge Chinese lantern from San Francisco. On September 10, Alice went to the hospital, and a few days later came home with a new baby. "This is your sister, Elizabeth," her Mama said. And Papa was smiling, again. Now Polly was not the only daughter, but the oldest daughter.

That same year, about six blocks from Irish Hill, the city's new high school opened at Limestone Avenue and Miller Street. Like the Clifton school, Springfield High School was a testimony to the city's 1901 boast about first-rate educational opportunities. The Board of Education's budget was the largest of all the municipal departments; sometimes its budget exceeded that of two and three city departments put together. The Board had spent seven hundred thousand dollars on the new high school to become a replica of the U.S. Library of Congress. Both buildings have high balustrades and soaring domes, which symbolized the universality of knowledge. However, Springfield High School did not have the ornate bubbling fountain or the twenty-three-carat gold gilded dome. Polly would attend the school later, fulfilling her mother's dream from the time the building was finished in 1910.

In 1912, Polly was ten years old and in Miss Smith's fourth grade class. The Clifton School was renamed the Emerson School that same year. Her father also changed. Something was wrong with him. John Henry was home more often, resting on the davenport, or in his bed. Her mother was worried and fretful; she became less patient and she raised her voice more. *Everyone was anxious.*

Aunt Pauline came by often to get Polly and her siblings; someone had to watch baby Elizabeth. When Alice toted boiling water up the stairs to their bedroom, and poured it into the pans lifting the smoky green ice smell from the eucalyptus leaves, Polly did her part by keeping Elizabeth out from under foot. Throughout her father's illness, Polly went to school every day. She was in fourth grade, and did not miss a day. She was slated to receive an award for perfect attendance on Decoration Day, May 30, 1912, but the day before her father died. So Polly did not go to school to receive the award. As customary, John Henry's funeral was held three days later, on Sunday, June 2, 1912. It was Bud's eighth birthday.

Polly was ten when John Henry succumbed. Later as an adult, she wrote, her childhood years to ten years old were "years of wonder, enchantment, adventure and sweet innocence. A beautiful and impressionable period of life. These should be years of make believe of oneness with man, nature and animals, without question without grief." *And then all that ended.*

Mr. Ewing laid her father out in the front room. Polly knew the deep sorrow her father's death brought to herself and everyone she loved. She did not know how bewildering the next year would be or that she would eventually recover. She documented all of the deaths in her journal: "In my fifth year my aunt, Effie, died. The day before Decoration in my fourth year my father died. In my second year my brother died." She also wrote about her grandfather moving from Springfield after his daughter died. She reminisced about the time they spent on the streetcar going to and from Irish Hill to Buxton Street. When she returned to school in the fall of 1912, the Clifton school was renamed Emerson. Miss Smith promoted her to fifth grade, to Miss Glenn's class. She did not mention how her mother went back to work as a maid, but Polly noted, "I left Emerson in May of my fifth year. Did not enter school again until the next fall." She did not mention the reason. She did not mention her mother's new job as a maid at the big hotel downtown. She did not mention going to the Clark County Children's Home. In her journal, she just appeared there.

It was summer 1913 when Polly arrived at the Clark County Children's Home. She was in shock, to say the least. During her first few days, she heard someone whisper, "Oh. When did she come? Well, there were two others a while ago." The words made her angry. She bristled at being singled out. In an upstairs hall, the boys were throwing rocks when Polly walked by. Caught in the crossfire, she got beaned in the head and it startled her. Rubbing her head, she walked to a chair and sat down. The governess came by and asked Polly to walk with her to join some other girls, but Polly told her, "I'm going to sit here the rest of the day and I may sit here until my mother comes back." And she would have, but the governess would not let her. Polly did not know when her mother came back for Elizabeth. But soon after, she knew her mother chose the baby. The governesses tried to make it better for Polly. Some of them were former Home "inmates," which is what the children in the home were called.

The start of school in the fall of 1913, was more than distracting. The Home school was one big room with all the grades together. Polly was in sixth grade. Her brother Bud was two grades behind her. Miss Stickford would be her teacher one year; in fall 1914 Harriet Graham directed Polly through seventh grade studies, which included reading, writing, arithmetic, humanities courses, science, and English and German government. The U.S. educational system's continued interest in Germany made World War I of great interest and a current event for seventh grader Polly.

The assassination of Austria-Hungary's Archduke Franz Ferdinand, and his wife Sophie, Duchess of Hohenberg on June 28, 1914 by Serbian nationalists, may have had no reason to alarm people in the U.S., but it was the match that ignited the complicated relationships in Europe and the start of World War I. For three years, the U.S. refused to be drawn in, though it was helping Britain with its war efforts. By the time the U.S. declared war in April 1917, the war was ending. Less than two years later in November 1918, the war of Polly's youth was over.

She spent eighth grade at the Country School in a room at her teacher, Miss Davis' house. The class had but three pupils, Charles, Robert and Polly. Miss Davis combined the county and town curriculum as preparation for the state's required Boxwell-Patterson High School admission examination. Mornings were spent reciting at Miss Davis's home and after that Polly and the two boys took exams. The three studied in the afternoon. It was tough and Robert did not finish the year. The governesses at the Home felt great sympathy for Polly's academic plight. They helped lighten her load by letting the girls raid their closets for extra clothes to play dress-up. A photograph taken in the yard of one such playful moment showed Polly, laughing, her mouth open, with four friends, Grace, Lynda, Mary, and Katherine. They dressed in layer upon layer of scarves and blouses, though it appeared to be summer. In the background, the sun shone through the trees. Polly was an eighth grader. She wrote on the photo, "All dressed up with no place to go." Though jovial, and good-spirited, Polly was not prescient. She was going somewhere. Her excellent grades exempted her from taking the Boxwell-Patterson high school entrance exam. She was on her way to high school in fall 1916.

At the same time Polly was receiving this good news, a jolly moment in the Johnson family came up with the return of her grandfather to the Springfield area. Isaac moved from the Old Soldiers' Home in Sandusky, Ohio, to the Old Soldiers' Home in Dayton, Ohio, just 30 miles west of Springfield. The family was slowly knitting itself back together again. Now Isaac was close enough for Alice to take the children on the traction line, a sort of long distance street car, to see him. Polly recalled that they walked the Home grounds peering for squirrels, chipmunks, ducks and other little animals and eventually wound up around the supper table in the public dining room with a plate of oysters set in front of each of them.

On the first day of the new fall semester, a governess took Polly on the Limestone street car south into the city. Long before the high school entrance could be seen, the high school dome grew larger and larger on the horizon. They descended from the street car at the school entrance and climbed the stairs to one of the most important buildings in town. Polly was nervous; she showed it in the constant smoothing of her hair. It was a madhouse that first day, with crowds of returning students greeting each other and finding their way to their classrooms.

It had been three years since Polly left the Springfield public schools district due to changes in her life: once a daughter, now half-orphaned; once a neighbor, now an inmate. Inside the school, a teacher directed new students to Principal Tiffany's office. He asked the governess accompanying Polly what Polly wanted to be. The response was "a nurse," a decision she arrived at in consultation with her mother and Miss Davis, in light of the nursing care her brother and father had required, plus Polly's excellent test scores in science. Polly heard the principal say Room 50, in the hall a teacher pointed her in the right direction. But she was misdirected—it was room 53—small first day of school mistake. She could not see a real difference in the classes on the schedule given to her—English, algebra, botany and physiology, gymnasium and commercial geography—and what she supposed the nursing program might look like, so she stayed in room 53. Thus her first year in high school began. She recalled looking for classmates from her old school, and thought she saw two, who ignored her. She did not see the Leach sisters. After Christmas, she was sick for nearly the entire winter but passed her classes nonetheless. She started summer of 1917 thinking high school was no fun and was not looking forward to a second year.

Alice had won the directive from the acting superintendent Brubaker that Polly, Bud and Elizabeth were "Not to be Put Out" of the

Home, but in the summer 1917, Robert S. and Edith W. Rodgers appeared at the Home. It is not entirely clear if Mr. and Mrs. Rodgers' priority was for a wage maid, or if they wanted academic help for their daughter. They had two servants employed at their new home, a housekeeper/cook, and a chauffeur. Once a farmhouse, it was now a mansion with six bedrooms and three baths, a huge front room with French doors and walls of windows. Servant quarters on the north side of the house had four rooms. The chauffeur lived in the apartment over the carriage house. Mr. Rodgers was part of Springfield's old monied families, and the superintendent of the vast American Seeding Machine plant. He was also the president of the board of the City Hospital, director at two banks, and a member of two country clubs, and the Rotary.

The Rodgers had two daughters, Alice and Lucinda. The oldest daughter, Alice, was a moon-faced thirteen-year-old girl who tried their patience. She was a class clown and a poor student, especially in math. The Boxwell-Patterson High School admission exam loomed before her. The Rodgers immediately liked the academic achievements of fifteen-year old Polly. Pleased that she received excellent placement, Alice agreed, but only after the Rodgers promised that Polly would continue high school in the fall if it all worked out. Summer was to be the trial.

On June 21, 1917, the first day of summer, the Rodgers sent the chauffeur, Mr. Jackson, to pick up Polly. Riding in the automobile up the long drive, Polly took note of the two-story playhouse in the side yard. She felt small indeed in the marble foyer where the ceiling was 25-feet high. Polly's room was at the rear of the second floor, on the northeast corner of the house. Her window looked over a stand of maple trees. The family rooms on the south side enjoyed warm light air. Polly's summer duties were to assist the housekeeper/cook, Mae Johnson, including setting and clearing the table, and dusting. Polly was a companion for the two daughters, spending the days in their huge bedroom that had a fireplace, and a dressing room with built-in drawers and closets. Sometimes they went into the playhouse where, if they pleased, each one could have a room to themselves. Polly would read aloud. Thus Polly's summer away from the Home passed in a patchwork of having fun with new friends, earning money, and feeling guilty about leaving her brother and sister in the Home, which grew more crowded every day.

Then in August she received very sad news. Her grandfather died on the fourteenth of that month. He had a cerebral hemorrhage, otherwise known as a stroke. The funeral was three days later on Friday, August 17, in the chapel at the Old Soldiers' Home. The casket at the front of the Chapel wore the stars and stripes, and was attended at the front corners by a military honor guard. Polly remembered the family sang the old hymn "Blessed Assurance:

"Perfect submission, perfect delight!
Visions of rapture now burst on my sight;
Angels descending, bring from above
Echoes of mercy, whispers of love.
This is my story, this is my song,
praising my Savior all the day long;
this is my story, this is my song,
praising my Savior all the day long."

After that, Polly returned to the Home for ten days to say her good-byes. Another girl was already folding her things into Polly's empty bureau drawer. On September 3, she left the Clark County Children's Home for good. The day was a chilly 40 degrees and emotionally overwhelming. Polly was leaving her brother and sister to return to the Rodgers' home.

Later that week, she was back in school for the 1917-1918 school year, facing a tenth grade schedule of six classes. Of all her classes, she was most grateful for Mr. Shively's ancient history class, and Miss Hullinger's cooking class where she met a friend, Ernestine Roberts. Ernestine was in both these classes. She was taller than Polly, with brown eyes that swallowed up the whole rest of her face. The way she pulled her straight hair back into a bun was sweet, and it made her look as schoolmarmish as the teachers. Polly soon abandoned her softer, curly hair style for the schoolmarm look.

Except for the rest of their classes—Ernestine was in college prep and Polly was in business — they did everything together. A friend in school was what Polly needed. She wrote about Ernestine, "Who should be more likely to head the rest, then the one who loves me best?" In June, the two sixteen-year-old co-eds decided it had been a great school year. They passed all their courses and knew all the boys by sight; a few by name. And it came to no surprise to those who watched, particularly Polly and Ernestine that Polly's business arithmetic teacher Mr. Conover married Miss Short.

But just two friends would not do. In junior year, 1918-1919, they became a threesome. Irene Browne was another girl with her hair coiled at the back of her neck, but Irene let a few tendrils fly loose. She may have had some Native American in her that accounted for her wavy and thick, dark, jet hair. She had a beau, Gail Whetzil, who concentrated on school because he wanted to marry Irene as soon as they graduated. The two boys in their clique were George Walker and Goff Roberts. George accompanied the young women everywhere but especially to the Center Street YMCA where almost all the social life for the black youth of Springfield took place.

Many years before, George had been the other little boy who her grandfather had taken to the Billy Sunday tent revival with Polly and Bud. George had grown into a handsome young man. He had gentle brown eyes with a stallion's wild glint. He smiled a sneaky smile under his thin mustache, and parted and slicked his wavy hair to one side. George dressed exquisitely, everyday draping his broad shoulders in a proper jacket, inverted pleats sewn into the blouse back. The other boy, Goff C. Roberts, was a jock who loved basketball. Barred from playing for Springfield High School basketball team because he was colored, Goff joined the team at the Center Street YMCA. It was built around 1895 as a continued show of the strength of the black community. They had won integration of the schools and now they had a branch of the Young Men's Christian Association (YMCA). It did not have the same operational budget that the white Springfield YMCA had, which brought abolitionist Frederick Douglass to town to speak, but the black YMCA started a Dunbar and

Washington Debating Society, named for the poet Paul Laurence Dunbar and southern educator Booker T. Washington. The team at the Center Street YMCA, called the Olympics, made up of World War I veterans, and Goff, was widely followed by the black community. At school, the most Polly saw of Goff was waving bye-bye to his back as he sprinted after class to the YMCA for practice.

In her junior year, Polly owned a new Kodak Eastman Brownie camera—a perk of getting paid and being able to buy what she desired. A photograph was taken in front of their school of the three girlfriends: Ernestine wore a pointy top Canadian Mounties style hat, while Irene covered her dark hair with a wide-brimmed felt. Polly went hatless. Junior year was when she wished she had paid better attention to which room to go to on the first day of high school. Stenography, bookkeeping and typewriters forced her to the counselor's office looking for a curriculum change. The counselor said it was too late; she was stuck. That year, she ended up dropping bookkeeping and flunking stenography. Summer 1919 was the season for good hard study.

In her senior year, 1919-1920, Polly kept busy with her studies. Her social life was increasingly active. She was elected secretary of the Friendship club, while Hetty Fehr, a German, was elected president. They masterminded a Halloween dance with the Freshman Club. Polly helped with decorations, and then rushed home to dress as a Grecian goddess, a drape of green chiffon over one of her shoulders. Afterward, she went with Ernestine, Irene, George and Goff to Herb's party in the colored part of town, and there she won a prize for her Flower Dance. She wrote that it was "for being more capable of disgracing myself than anyone else." But she could get away with that. Color, especially light-skinned color had its privileges. In December, the junior class hosted a party for the seniors. At the end of it, seniors received their class colors in the form of two ribbons: one purple and one gray. After that ceremony, the colored students walked in the frosty night air to the Center Street YMCA where the Olympics were playing another Negro team from a nearby town. Goff was there on the court with his basketball teammates; he had skipped the school party. Even though Polly was neither baptized nor went to church, she went to the YMCA for meetings of the Philathea Club's Bible study for women.

Polly, the light-skinned girl, preferred the company of black people, and fit in like a star. She chose to be black. And at school, she was not always a mismatch, not always an "either/or," as in the rest of the society, she was just Polly, the light-skinned girl.

In her other world, the Rodgers kept Polly's eye on her studies; it was in their self-interest. Their daughter's progress in school could be tied to Polly's presence in their house, and the parents were grateful. Under their Christmas tree Polly found a gift: a beautiful ink pen and a jar of Indian ink. In February 1920 she turned eighteen years old.

That spring, the *Springfield News* published two events readers would long remember. First there was an ad for the Ku Klux Klan's Dancing Carnival at the Palace Gardens. The other event was the publication of the senior class photos. Polly sat on the end of the first row in her home room photo. The whole town talked about the 160 high school seniors and residents dreamed of the time when they could send their children to the high school. It was the path to a better life. Springfield's investment in its public schools outstripped their investment in any other public function.

In spring, Mr. Rodgers gave Polly a gift of a scrapbook embossed in gold on the leather front cover, "The Girl Graduate: Her Own Book." It was designed with the outline of a gold locket hanging from a ribbon. The heavy pages inside were oyster gray and printed with the names of their contents: Prophecies, autographs, and gifts. The book became her diary, her chum, her album, her confidant. Her secrets went into this book, some written in shorthand learned in school. Some pages were torn off and discarded. Every gift, every photo, every event, every person who crossed into her seniordom was noted in "The Girl Graduate." In there, Polly time traveled, recorded events from the Home, pasted photos of her family. When the book asked for the names of her teachers, she included Miss Graham from the Home, and Miss Davis from the country school. Beginning with the *Springfield News* article announcing the Class of 1920, every newspaper article about the senior class found a space in her book, including the photo of her friends, and one of Springfield basketball team player Ed Dye. She cut out his newspaper photo, edging the scissors around his broad shoulders and swept-back hair, his tank top, shorts, and knees wrapped in bandage. She pasted him in on page 115.

Then came the Senior Dinner, a five-course meal served to the VIPs of the school district, the high school principal, the school district superintendent and Board of Education members. Polly and Rosa Shulze, the class valedictorian, greeted their guests at the door. Polly also monitored the entrée — roast beef — as it reached perfection. Ernestine set out baskets of lilies of the valley and violets on snowy white linens. As for every senior event, the newspaper carried the news. It quoted Principal Tiffany telling the senior class women, "There is every indication that you will make very efficient women, the kind that make home keeping an art."

Baccalaureate was one of the few church services Polly had been to in her life. The ceremony was held at North Street A.M.E. Church. Reverend Scott preached on the beleaguered but faithful Job, Chapter 28, "Where Wisdom is Found." Polly said the preacher gave "some very good thoughts. A lot that went home." Class Night presented Polly with two choices of attire. One was a custom-made pea green silk taffeta and Georgette dress with matching hat and stockings that her mother gave her. Mrs. Rodgers gave her a hand-made blue silk taffeta dress, white stockings and hat. Claiming the pea green as "almost pretty," Polly, hummed the song, "In My Sweet Little Alice Blue Gown" from the hit musical *Irene*, as she slipped on the blue number. It was the first time that the Rodgers overpowered Alice's influence on Polly, but not the last. Before the graduation season ended, Alice saw every one of her gifts to her oldest daughter matched by the wealthy woman in whose home Polly had lived for three of her four high school years. Though the White House Conference on Dependent Children passed a resolution in favor of private family care for children whose parents could no longer support them, it was this type of alienation of affection that parents feared.[4] Rodgers genuinely liked and appreciated Polly's help with her daughter, who was enrolled in high school when Polly graduated. On June 17, 1920, at the eleven-hundred-seat county Memorial Hall auditorium, 150 young men and women graduated; seven were colored: Polly, Ernestine, Irene, Charlotte Lytle, Margaret Speaks, Catherine Singleton, who had been in Polly's first grade class, and George, the only black man. The other black young man who should have been at the graduation ceremony was Polly's friend Goff. He was among the ten seniors who did not complete their studies and receive a diploma. The superintendent of the Home, Mr. Thomas and his wife, the Home matron, and their daughter, the Home teacher, sent Polly a note of congratulations on her "untiring energy" in "finishing your chosen course of study." Polly received $24.50 in graduation gifts.

Parties and picnics were part of the ritual. Polly's party was held at the Johnson family home at 320 Buxton Street. After Pauline remarried, she moved and sold the house to her sister, Nellie, and her husband, Will Browning. They lived in the house with their three-year-old son, William Browning Jr., called Bill. Alice helped serve dainty refreshments to ten youthful guests. Proud Alice had prevailed. Her dream had come true. She was a good Irish mother and here was the proof: her daughter in a cap and gown with a high school diploma in her hand. And now Polly was talking about going to college to become a nurse, but before she went to college, she needed to take care of her brother and sister.

Polly did not understand why Bud left the Home to live with some people in South Charleston. She wrote this verse on page 155 in "The Girl Graduate":

> "My brother of the harrow and hoe
> What make you love the farm life so?
> It is not a family trait.
> If it is, I'm sorry it came so late
> As you know, without a doubt,
> It left your roving, restless sister out.
> But some must hammer, and some must hoe.
> And some must use the pen.

> So wherever we are, whatever we do
> Tho' our honors be many, or our honors be few
> With the world's goodness may our actions blend
> And bring peace and happiness in the end."

More puzzling was Alice's behavior toward her youngest child, Elizabeth. Alice did not take her youngest daughter, her baby, out of the Home.

In 1920, Elizabeth was only ten years old. Polly would have watched Elizabeth if she had not wanted to get her nursing training at Lincoln University in Pennsylvania, the nation's first degree-granting institution for black students. She probably never talked to Bud about watching Elizabeth because in this era, men did not watch children. Alice set a standard when she refused to turn eleven-year-old Polly into a Little Mama, and by that standard ten-year-old Elizabeth was too young to be a latch-key kid. Elizabeth was an angry little girl who did not know any home except the Home. Besides, in the 1920s, only married women's husbands were in the position to sign custody papers. So Polly had to appeal to her fathers' sisters: Nellie, Mrs. William Browning or Lucy, Mrs. Ray Culberson.

The temperature rose to 84 degrees in the last few days of August 1920. Polly was consumed by the heat and the plan with the Culbersons to get Elizabeth out of the Home. Lucy and her husband, Ray Culberson, arrived in Springfield about the same time of Polly's friend Emma Jane Harris' wedding on August 24. Her marriage to Mr. Raymond Spillman was solemnized at Emma Jane's parents' home on Southern Avenue. Emma Jane introduced Polly to a boy in the neighborhood, James Leigh (pronounced Lay). He was the next generation of a prominent colored business family. But Polly was too distracted to be interested at the time.

Lucy and Ray stayed at the Buxton Street house. That was where Polly told her mother that she was planning to leave Springfield to go to Detroit with them, and they were taking Elizabeth. Ray had agreed to sign, and the four reference checks required by the Home with their friends and pastor back in Detroit had been completed. The references attested to the good character of the Culbersons, and their ability to support a child. The Culbersons signed the Agreement Relative to the Care of a Foster Child, Ray's name first then Lucy's, under her husband's signature. Polly could not sign, but everyone knew that this was the doing of the girl graduate.

As with most of these volatile emotional situations, Polly did not record the way this happened, or what her mother said. Polly and the Culbersons arrived at the Home on August 31. It was a warm August day, with high winds blowing north. Polly had intellectualized the situation in a way only an eighteen-year-old would and thought she had it all figured out. She had lived in the Home and she had been put in an advantageous situation that allowed her to finish high school and now she was the most educated person in the whole family. Yet she arrived at the same conclusion that her father's sisters came to years earlier: do not put the children in the Home. Let the oldest daughter watch the youngest daughter. This is why Lucy and Ray went along with it. Polly was not a child anymore and had decided the Home was not the place for Elizabeth, contrary to her mother's beliefs.

Before noon on August 31, Polly, Elizabeth, Ray and Lucy were on the train to Detroit.

℘ ℭ ℛ

Detroit
THE PEOPLE IN THE Michigan Central Depot lobby looked like the scrambling legs of a centipede on its back. People crowded shoulder to shoulder, pushing in every direction to get out of the station and onto the streets of one of the richest cities in America, where there was something for everyone. It was Ford country, with five dollars a day pay and more work than most men could stand. Detroit was a city of immigrants, particularly Eastern Europeans, and by 1920 the black population had increased five-fold. The Culbersons and their Johnson nieces waded into the crowd and fought their way to the exit of the T-shaped building, heels tapping on the terrazzo floors that echoed from the high ceilings. Competing with three thousand people who arrived each week in Detroit, they dodged the massive

columns, trailing behind a porter transporting the sisters' bags containing everything they owned.[5]

During the taxi ride to Lucy and Ray's home in Black Bottom by the Detroit River, one could see how Detroit developed into the city it had become and how it had layered onto itself. The industrial neighborhood from Michigan Avenue to Gratiot Avenue and including a part of Rivard Street, had small shops such as Tessmer Machine. When the driver turned onto Clinton Street, Polly recognized the street name from the return address of her aunt's postcards. The taxi stopped in front of number 178, next to Tricky's Coal & Wood. Across the street was a warehouse. The 1920 U.S. Census (completed by James W. Gaskill) recorded that eighty-four families lived in fifty-nine dwellings; nearly 30 percent of the families counted had no home of their own.[6] Lucy and Ray shared their home with her niece and nephew—Lucille Hall, a dish washer, and Walker Williams, a hotel porter. An additional four people, called "lodgers" in the census, lived in the house: street laborers Oliver Roberson, and Joe Johnson; Eleanor Campbell, a laundress, and Vern Johnson, a restaurant janitor. Lucy and Ray accommodated these eight adults from Virginia, Arkansas, Kentucky, and Ohio, all black. These relatives and lodgers rented sleeping space, meaning a bed for eight hours a day. When one got up, Lucy changed the sheets and another person's rented time began. Polly and her ten-year-old sister Elizabeth became occupants nine and ten.

They arrived in Detroit in time for the opening of the Detroit Public Schools' fall semester of 1920. Elizabeth was a fifth grader. Polly needed a job because Elizabeth was her responsibility; her $24.50 was not going to last forever in Detroit. Someone suggested that she go to the Urban League because they offered good job opportunities. The Detroit branch of the National Urban League was founded in 1916 by the National Urban League and the Associated Charities of Detroit. The agency's mission was to meet the needs of Black Southerns flocking in great numbers to Detroit.[7] Beulah Carter, an Urban League volunteer welcomed Polly and directed her to J. M. Ragland's office. He was the director of the Negro Branch

Employment Department of the Employers' Association of Detroit. Mrs. Carter wished Polly luck in finding something matching her education, skills and talents, and invited her "to come back, let me know how you're getting along. I am here most days, right here at the door." Polly went to see Mr. Ragland, and left with his card but with not much hope of finding an office job.

While the Detroit Urban League had helped thousands of people, including many women in the four years since opening, the organization received very little call for office workers, with the major call for domestic help.[8] Polly accepted a job in a home in Grosse Pointe, a suburb full of houses like the Rodgers. The little city was built with the profits from the automobile industry. Polly did not like her job. When she wrote about it in "The Girl Graduate" book, all she put was two words: *Grosse Pointe*. She wrote, *overnight,* when she stayed to help with a dinner party because the bus service ended early in the evening.

Perhaps it was Mrs. Carter, or the Grosse Pointe job, or her mother, or the Rodgers' influence, that helped Polly make a goal to start college in the fall of 1921. In the meantime, there was nothing to do but work, make sure Elizabeth did well in school and have a good time.

Polly's light skin and soft hair attracted admiring glances all over Black Bottom. Prentiss Walker was one of her admirers. He lived on Detroit's North End with his brother and frequented the Black Bottom. The Second Baptist Church was the center of social life. It had been the last stop on the Underground Railroad, the network that helped enslaved people escape across the Detroit River to Canada. By the time Polly arrived for Thanksgiving services in 1920, the church had two thousand members, four-hundred of them in young people's societies.[9] Besides church, Detroit also offered its black residents entertainment sometimes at odd hours. For instance, Polly went to her first breakfast dance, an event for black people at Detroit's Arcadia dance hall for the Negroes. It started after midnight and went until dawn. The dancers would go out for breakfast, and then return at 9:00 a.m. to dance until noon.

Polly did not return to Springfield for Christmas in 1920. Alice sent a small card with a tiny green cord at the spine of folded cardboard and tissue paper. Inside was the verse, "Tis Xmas Day and in my heart, Sweet thoughts of you do rest. And wishes that with happiness thine every hour be blest. Civis Mondi. Best Wishes From Mother." Polly went to the Arcadia with a group that included many folks just in town to celebrate the Yuletide. One was that fellow she met on her way out of Springfield at her friend, Emma Jane's wedding. He was a tall, slim fellow with dark eyes and wavy black hair. She wrote in her book, December 23 "Dance Arcadia Mr. James Leigh. Fine time."

James William Leigh Jr. (called Jimmy) was something of a legend among Springfield's young black people. He was the next generation of a successful business family. Born August 22, 1901 in Chattanooga, Tennessee, he was orphaned young when his parents, Ella Brison and Henry Leigh, died. He and his older sister, Tina, were sent to Springfield, Ohio, to live with their father's sister Bessie, and her husband, William H. Patterson. Springfield was where most of Jimmy's father's family lived, including an uncle, James William Sr. who owned an ice company. He started it in 1908, financing it from his wages as a Pullman porter and from other jobs. He selected Springfield because of its well-publicized reputation as a business mecca. Senior brought his brother-in-law, and two younger brothers, Ernest and Ivory, and their father, Wilson to Springfield. Wilson was a blond, blue-eyed white man. Their mother was a dark-skinned woman with jet black hair.

The ice business was capital intensive and hard work. Senior bought a building by the river, a wagon, a horse, saws and later on, sawdust. In the harsh months of winter, January and February, the men gouged ice from Springfield's Mad River, then stored the ice in sawdust in a riverfront building. In the summer they sold the ice to housewives to keep fresh food from spoiling in their ice boxes. Senior needed all the men he could get. When Jimmy turned twelve, he dropped out of seventh grade to work full-time in the family business. Senior later sold coal in the winter to keep the crew busy year round. He diversified further to buy houses for his relatives and employees to live in. That is the kind of hard-toiling family Jimmy came from.

In 1920, Jimmy was looking for a new line of work in Detroit but could not find any due to an economic downturn.[10] When his uncle promised that he could work in the office, Jimmy returned to Springfield in January. On February 3, Polly received his first letter. She noted in "The Girl Graduate": "it was very newsy & nice; for a boy who seldom says anything it was a wonder."

Detroit might not have been everything Polly thought it would be for her and Elizabeth, but it offered things she could not have imagined. She turned nineteen on February 7, 1921 at Lucy and Ray's new place, 1530 St. Aubin Street. She celebrated it with a card party at her aunt's house, telling Jimmy she was sorry he had left not stay in Detroit. One year passed before Polly returned to Springfield with Elizabeth and Lucy in early August. Polly was looking forward to the trip, but it turned sorrowful on August 5 when her aunt returned Elizabeth to the Home. No reason was given to the Home and the family did not talk about it. Polly was crushed. On page 69 of her book, she penned this verse:

> To E.J.
> Like a sudden ray of sunshine
> That comes, brightens and is gone on its way,
> Your smile came when I was lonesome and drove the blues away.
> The day may be weary, but we remember the ray,
> So your smile, like the sunshine, in my memory will stay.

The backdrop to Polly's life in Detroit and relief from her job in Grosse Pointe were the parties. They unfolded with an urgency, as if nothing else in life mattered. Of course, life did stall in place for colored people, and that made the parties seem all-important. With a party, life was carefree, and Polly ceased worrying about Elizabeth for a while.

She joined a church in Detroit. Since her mother rejected the Catholic Church Polly rarely attended except when she went a few times with the Johnsons. She chose the Macedonia Baptist Church for her baptism in the spring of 1921. Its membership rolls swelled to more than eight hundred people. Nearly one hundred people enrolled in Sunday school, and another hundred in the youth group. She joined the flock of people at dawn on Sunday for an immersion baptism, probably at Belle Isle, the island park.

Polly returned to the Children's Home in Springfield on November 1, 1921 to pick up her sister, Elizabeth. Nothing would have pleased Home officials more than to release Elizabeth to her sister, the first inmate to graduate high school, a true Home success story. Elizabeth was a pitiable case: put into the Home in May 1913 when just a toddler. Taken out by her mother in June and returned in July. Taken out by her aunt in August 1920 to live in Detroit, and returned in August 1921. Now they wrote "Replaced 11-1-21 with sister Mrs. Leigh of Detroit." That was Polly. No reference check necessary for Elizabeth's sister, but her new husband needed to sign an "Agreement Relative to a Foster Child." The problem was Polly and Jimmy were not married.

Polly was doing everything she could to get Elizabeth out of the Home where she was so unhappy. Alice had saved Polly from becoming an eleven-year-old Little Mama, so in 1920 Polly was willing to put her future on hold to care for her baby sister. She and her mother could not come up with a solution, and her aunt could not deal with Elizabeth, who was a handful. But Polly could not move forward and save Elizabeth because only a married woman could take an inmate out of the Home. It was the law. Elizabeth did not leave the Home in November 1921

Then fate came knocking. In March 1922, Polly visited Springfield. She wanted Elizabeth to know she loved her, and was doing all she could to get her out of the Home. While she was there, Jimmy Leigh came to visit, and they attended basketball games and recitals at the YMCA. As their relationship became serious, Jimmy introduced Polly to his family, and she could see how Detroit might become part of her past. Then Jimmy asked her to marry him and Polly said yes. The plan was to marry in the summer, when Jimmy became twenty-one. He had his eye on a taxi business his uncle proposed opening for him. His uncle had given him a car as a gesture of support. Jimmy wrote to Polly soon after she left Springfield:

> My Dear Little Girl,
>
> I've been thinking so much about you, but six months is not so long and we are going to write. I suppose you certainly know that I miss you....
>
> Mrs. Gazaway is leaving our employ in about two weeks for two months. She is on the verge of a nervous collapse, so I am going to take her place until she returns. I do everything except shorthand, but this is not necessary. In about three weeks we are going to have a drive your own taxi, all Fords. You pay 15 cents per mile for them. Of course if you cannot drive, you are out of luck.
>
> I was reading an account in Saturday's paper about the Home. They told of housing conditions for the girls. If it is all so, I do really feel sorry for your little sister. They say they have to sleep in the halls....
>
> From Your Future, James Jr.

Jimmy was a decent man and Polly was right about him. The future looked so bright for them. But there was a twist of fate. Jimmy's uncle decided to launch the rental car business, and operate it himself. He wanted Jimmy to stay in the ice and coal business, but it was a dying business.

Stunned, Jimmy went to Detroit and asked Polly to marry him now, immediately. Her aunt, Lucy said, "June. Give us a few weeks to get it together." She had to sort out the lodgers in the house first. The lovebirds married on June 10, 1922 in Detroit. They were both twenty years old.

After Polly's marriage, Jeanette, a friend from Detroit who had moved to Ithaca, New York, extended her congratulations, saying that Polly now had "someone to love her." Confronted with Jeanette's words, did Polly realize her good fortune? That she had the love of her mama and papa, who spoiled her? Love of her grandfather and her aunts? She had friends in The Home, and teachers with her best interests at heart. And when she was put out of The Home, she landed with the Rodgers family. Rich people who adored her, and let her be a high school student in all ways. And now she had married this good, handsome man. Her sister Elizabeth had none of that. She had only ever known The Home, and an itinerant mother, coming and going. Maybe Jeanette's words spurred Mrs. Polly Johnson Leigh to action, again. It was entirely possible.

At some point, Springfield City Schools allowed children living at the Home to enroll. Almost one year to the date of Polly's marriage, Elizabeth's Permanent School Census Card noted that she was withdrawn in summer 1923. On Friday, June 9, 1923, the Home inventoried Elizabeth's clothing. Clothing inventory was code for leaving. The last notation on Elizabeth's Home status card recorded her last known whereabouts, which said, "sister Mrs. Leigh Detroit," and it was dated 1921. But we all know that did not happen. It appears that Elizabeth left the Home and Springfield in June 1923, never to return. Two years later, in 1925, the Detroit Public Schools recorded Elizabeth in the tenth grade at Northwestern High School. An apparent two-year gap in her education, or an error in the records? If it was a school suspension, it seemed to say that someone thought school had overshadowed Elizabeth's life for far too long. Was it Polly? Or Pauline? Polly's daughter said Elizabeth lived with them.

The young couple lived with Polly's Aunt Pauline for a few years before moving into their own home. Polly inherited her mother's aptitude for good housekeeping. She made Irish soul food in those years: boiled white potatoes and lima beans, the blandest and greenest of legumes, boiled with a little salt and pepper until the jacket fell away from the mush inside. At the Rodgers home, Polly had watched Mrs. Johnson, the cook, truss up a leg of lamb, roast it and serve it with mint jelly, and could not wait to wrestle with a big piece of meat in her own kitchen. Her aunt, on the other hand, viewed it as a luxury and an oddity. But these dishes, along with pot roast and boiled root vegetables, were what Polly knew how to cook. She used a cookbook, as her high school cooking teacher, Miss Hullinger, instructed. New dishes appeared regularly in front of Jimmy, dishes such as corn relish, more pretty than tasty. The smell of sugar from baking cookies, cakes, and puddings boiling on the stove permeated their home.

Jimmy had skills. He could drive a truck and he went to work for a dairy as a delivery man. During Prohibition in the 1920s, whiskey was smuggled into Detroit from Canada over the Detroit River and delivered around town. Jimmy was one of the delivery men.

With all of these sources of income, Jimmy was a good provider. On December 9, 1923, Polly gave birth to a girl she named Alice Cecilia. Polly's cousin chose the nickname Mary Jane for the baby because it sounded classy. Jimmy liked it. After Mary Jane, the babies arrived regularly like clockwork: Ellen Elizabeth called Patty in 1925, James William Jr., called Sonny in 1927. Elmer Preston called Buddy in 1929. Pauline Ruby in 1931, and Harriett Marie in 1933.

After their first two daughters were born, the family needed a new place to live. Polly did not want to live a nomadic life like Lucy and Ray Culberson. Polly's aunt and uncle moved every year, sometimes twice a year. She wanted more for her family: a home, but home-building required more money. Jimmy was already working hard and she did not want to pressure him, so she went to see Mrs. Carter at the Urban League. Mrs. Carter could see the younger woman was in some distress and asked her where she went to church. Polly told her about being raised with no church home, even though her mother was Catholic, and her father and all his family was Baptist. She was already baptized in the Macedonia Baptist Church and thought about returning.

"A good church," Mrs. Carter agreed, but maybe what Polly and her husband needed was a change of venue. If they were moving their home, why not look on the West Side? There were apartments and schools, and when the time came, plenty of houses. They could catch the Grand Belt bus and easily transfer to other buses around the city. Mrs. Carter said that she was raised Baptist but in 1917, almost ten years earlier, she helped start a little mission church on the West Side, with her husband and other families. It was St. Cyprian's Protestant Episcopal Church. The church had come about because a woman who was having trouble taking her crippled son across town to worship at the black Episcopal church, was not allowed to worship at the white Episcopal church on the West Side. How could Mrs. Carter look away from that?

This is the story Polly told her young husband and in 1926 the Leigh family moved to the West Side with her aunt Pauline and her husband, Cleo. It was a vibrant community with stores, restaurants, dry cleaners, drug stores and schools, everything a family needed. The neighborhood was segregated, but the white residents were moving north, east and west further from the city center.

Polly started taking her girls to St. Cyprian's for services and Sunday school where she saw Mrs. Carter every Sunday. The church was growing, and her daughters made friends. It had many groups and Polly joined the Episcopal Church Women, the Altar Guild, and the Trians, and the Soroptimist Guild, an international group for improving women and girl's economic lives. St. Cyprian's Episcopal Church had a membership of luminaries and connections.

Polly and Jimmy's first son, James William Jr., called Sonny, was born on June 1, 1927, and Polly became pregnant again in 1929. They did not have a lot of money, but Jimmy believed money was not everything, so his concerns were minimal and he did the best he could. The money he earned from driving the bootleg whiskey up from the river and around the downtown hotel district helped. Sometimes a tavern barkeep gave him extra money for helping to carry the cases of hooch inside.

Jimmy worked as a waiter and busser at the Statler Hilton Hotel in downtown Detroit. He was a calm and quiet person. His wife called him the "sphinx," but as his household grew, he needed more money.

One day a few police force commanders came to the hotel and were seated in his section. They had a problem: Black Bottom needed more policing. The force had added a few black officers here and there, but where to get more? One of the men knocked his elbow into another to gain his attention, and pointed to the tall black man standing nearby. How about him? It was not the first time they had seen him. They requested the restaurant manager and asked him, "How about him?" The manager nodded, "He's a good boy." They then signaled Jimmy over to the table and asked, "Do you want to be a police officer, a cop? You can be." The prospect of steadier paychecks with bigger numbers was attractive. Jimmy nodded yes. He attended the police academy to learn how to shoot a gun, and was measured for his uniform. He raised his hand and was sworn-in to the Detroit Police department on September 29, 1929.

He and Polly's fourth child was born in October, Elmer Preston, who they called Buddy, named for Polly's brother Bud, and the third in the string of her fabled father's many names. John Henry Preston Lewis Taylor Johnson. The family was very lucky. It was the start of the Great Depression, and Jimmy had a job all the way through it.

In 1931, another child was born and named for her mother, Pauline Ruby. Another daughter, Harriet Marie born in 1933. Jimmy and Polly were good together, and the family prospered. The children attended the West Side neighborhood school Sampson Elementary, and people like Mrs. Carter kept the teachers and administrators on their toes. However, in 1935, Polly and Jimmy's daughter Harriet Marie was stricken and not getting better. Polly's cousin Laura stayed with the children when the couple took the baby to the hospital. The two-year-old girl died from pneumonia for which there was no cure until antibiotics were ed later in the twentieth century. The sad memory of Levy's death came back to haunt Polly. It was the third generation in Polly's family who succumbed to a respiratory disease.

Polly and Mrs. Carter, who had known each other since 1920 became even closer friends during this time of sorrow. In the following years, Alice started visiting Polly every year. Bud also followed his big sister to Detroit. The neighbor called Bud "Chinaman" for his skin tone and narrow eyes. Already living in Detroit, Elizabeth had grown into a beautiful young woman, so much so that Jimmy had to remind the fellas he possessed a firearm and was entitled to use it.

Jimmy enjoyed his high status as a police officer, and the people on the West Side appreciated his presence. His salary, combined with his status, helped to make ends meet. People in positions of power offered him things. Polly and Jimmy's family lived rent free in the house on Williams Street. The owner was leaving Detroit to return down south but was not ready to sell the house. He wanted a tenant who would keep it nice. Who better than a police officer from the neighborhood to oversee it? It was a big house where the family gathered for holidays.

Jimmy did not mind if they tipped their glasses on Christmas or any day, because he once made money on liquor. Unfortunately, with Polly's family the holidays could end pretty badly. Bud and Elizabeth drank until they got drunk, then they rehashed the past. They were mean drunks, Mary Jane recalled. They hollered and cursed; still mad at Alice after all those years, and she was not even at the gatherings, she was living in Canton, Ohio. They were still livid with their father for dying, and irate at their aunts for not stepping in. They were outraged because it looked like their older sister, Polly got the better part of the rotten deal. She lived in that big house with those rich people, graduated high school, and forgot about them. It went on and on until all of them got their coats and went home and the holiday was ruined. Bud and Elizabeth's grudge upset Polly and her children immensely. Polly's daughter Mary Jane remembered this went on until Jimmy told his brother and sister-in-law the next time this happened they would no longer be welcomed to come to his house. It stopped.

As the Great Depression strangled the nation, Polly and Jimmy's children had a comfortable childhood. Then they got a gift that money could not buy: their grandmother Alice started visiting her black family in Detroit. Sonny, the third born and oldest son, described their grandmother's visits to their home:

> "My grandmother was a visitor unlike other family visitors. She would appear, stay a while then disappear. There was no certain time for her arrival although my mother must have known she was coming. A taxicab would drive up to the house. We children would run

to the front windows and gaze out to watch my grand-mother exit from the taxi, a suitcase in one hand and a shopping bag in the other. We looked at a woman of small stature, gray haired, pale skin and a humpback. She would pay the cab driver and we would yell out to my mother, 'Grandmother is here!' Mother would remind us to not make noise and not to bother grand-mother. Upon entering the house, grandmother briefly greeted us all, reached into her bag and handed out a package to each of us without a smile. We chil-dren were silent as we gazed upon her white face. This face made her real and revealed who she was: A white person. We were a black family, or were we? I remember that while she was visiting, she focused on her son, Elmer and her daughter, Elizabeth. Rarely on us grandchildren. In fact, my mother would warn us not to bother her. When she was ready to leave, a taxicab was called and she would say goodbye.

What prompted my grandmother to be so distant? Was it race? How did she manage it? My grandmother was Irish American and white in America where race was such an issue."

These unusual visits described by Polly's son, was a way for Polly to return to a time when her birth family was whole, not shattered by illness and death. As a woman, wife and mother, Polly was trying to shorten the distance between her and her mother, and to help bridge the gulf between her mother and siblings. Polly's daughter Patty also remembered her mother giving money, food and clothes to the neighbors, because people were cast out of the city's econ-omy by the Depression, and lost their jobs. Polly went to visit those afflicted with illness. It was a Christian duty but also her way to go back in time and pay back the kindnesses extended to her when her family was in disarray. There is a saying for it, "There but for the grace of God, go I," and it had been Polly at one time. Her stability had been hard won, and she did not forget that. She and her husband did not have much, but he had a good job and her surviving children were healthy. She was grateful.

In 1937, it was time for Jimmy and Polly's first daughter, fourteen-year-old Mary Jane, to go to high school, and Polly looked to Mrs. Carter for guidance on where to send Mary Jane. Mrs. Carter's daughter, Catherine, who was four years older than Mary Jane, had attended Northwestern, the neighborhood high school. When Catherine graduated from Northwestern, she went to St. Augustine College in Florida, the college of her mother's choice.

But Polly was more in step with Daisy and Albert Somerville. Mr. Somerville was a waiter, one of the finest at the Detroit Athletic Club, an exclusive, executive members-only club that sat back off Woodward Avenue. Its well-heeled members guaranteed him a steady, living wage, and generous tips. Mrs. Somerville was from the South and she had taught down there. She knew what happened to uneducated black people; Jim Crow was no better than slavery, but an educated person had a better chance of survival.

The Somervilles had two children, Gladys and Albert, Mary Jane's friends. They sent their daughter, Gladys, who was two years older than Mary Jane, to Cass Technical High School downtown. She wanted her children to have the best education she could get them, especially her daughter who wanted to be a nurse. The Somervilles wanted Cass Tech for their children because they knew both would graduate prepared for a job.

The school's downtown location drew students from every zone in the city. Each ethnicity built its own community inside the school building and did not welcome strangers. In 1937, the black student body was so small, their coming together created something much smaller, a clique. Regardless, the most important thing about Cass Tech was that the students came out as something. They were trained as well as educated. "You went there to get a skill, and come out and get a job," Mary Jane remembered. But for Jimmy and Polly, the carfare was a long stretch and they had five children to send to school. Still, Polly wanted Cass for her daughter.

Carfare was not going to stand in the way of Polly sending her daughter to the school she felt was best for her to attend. But it was an issue that needed to be considered and resolved. She found a job at Awrey Bakery within walking distance from her house and was able to give Mary Jane fifty cents each week to ride the streetcar to school. So like Gladys Somerville, Mary Jane enrolled at Cass and studied nursing. Alice also helped with this project. Mary Jane remembered every time Alice visited, she asked her granddaughter, "What do you need for school?" And she would send Polly money to buy whatever it was. Polly would follow the Somerville family model and send three of her five children to Cass.

If a baby was ever going to walk, they needed to grab onto something, hold on and pull up. For most people, family is the steadying rod. Alice's Irish family gripped onto education. Alice put school first for Polly. And Polly was strongly influenced by her mother's belief that school was worth the extra effort. It might have seemed a step too far in the direction of family separation, but when her daughter reached school age Polly had Mrs. Carter as a model of how to put family and school together in a healing way. Mrs. Carter confirmed for Polly that school and black people need not be mutually exclusive, and the combination was not just for rich black people.

St. Cyprian's and the West Side fit Polly and her family, and provided the type of consistent push that only a community can. Every time Polly went to Springfield she visited the Rodgers. They were the ones that helped Polly get through high school. Along with the Clark County Children's Home, these people convinced Polly of the necessity of school, and the importance of sending children to school, especially the daughters. But it was Polly's black aunts who consistently and over the course of her lifetime loved her unconditionally. Perhaps, as Polly became older, she had become a little embarrassed and ashamed she had not trusted her mother more about Elizabeth, who after all, was Alice's daughter. Up until then, Polly had trusted, or rather obeyed, her mother. School turned out to be her saving grace in a family turned upside down by illness and death. In school, Polly had been distracted from her sorrow. Saved from the heavy burden of caring for a child, she had been able to preserve her lively personality. She had learned about a world beyond her own, and school helped her to survive. And she finished school because her mother kept pushing for that.

In most cases, women's opportunities were limited by the location of their families, including their location in geography, and society. She could marry and have a family. She could earn her own money in the world's oldest professions for women: become a nurse or an elementary school teacher. But the issues remained—paying tuition and rearing the young. Polly was the oldest daughter of a woman in a disadvantageous situation, but not more so than any other woman of her time. The obstacles generated from being in the wrong place (Lawrenceburg), marrying the wrong man (a black one) and him dying early (before their last child was in school) were the makings of a woman who faced limited choices, which Alice did not want for her children.

Retrospectively, Pauline Lucy "Polly" Johnson Leigh lived a long and fruitful life. She became an award-winning flower arranger, a skill developed as a member of the St. Cyprian's Episcopal Church Altar Guild. She was a club woman, with three memberships including the Entre Nous club. In 1940, she represented the Diocese of Michigan at the convention of the Episcopal Church Women in San Francisco, a meeting that paralleled the National Episcopal Church convention to which women could not be delegates. She had been married for seventy-four years when her husband James W. Leigh Jr. died in 1996 at age ninety-five. Polly was ninety-six years old when she passed two years later in 1998. Five of her six children survived her. Her family grew to include eighteen grandchildren, thirty-two great-grandchildren and seventeen great-great-grandchildren. Funeralized at St. Cyprian's, her church home for seventy years, she requested that no photograph of her be included on her funeral program, and it was not. ⌘

NOTES

1. Carter, Darnell "The 1904, 1906, and 1921 race riots in Springfield, Ohio and the Hoodlum theory." Electronic Thesis or Dissertation. Ohio State University, 1993. https://etd.ohiolink.edu/, 22.

2. Carter, 22-30.

3. Carter, 46.

4. *Proceedings*, 199.

5. David A. Levine, *Internal Combustion: The Races in Detroit 1915 -1926* (Westport, CT: Greenwood Publishing Group Inc, 1976), 54.

6. *United States, Bureau of the Census. The 14th United States Census.* Detroit city, Ward 5, January 6 -7, 1920.

7. Biography. Detroit Urban League Records: 1916-1992. Summary Information. Bentley Historical Library. The University of Michigan. Online.

8. George Edmund Haynes, *Negro Newcomers in Detroit* (New York: Arno Press, 1969), 12.

9. Haynes, Table III.

10. David Lee Premba, ed. *Detroit in its World Setting: A Three Hundred Year Chronology, 1701-2001* (Detroit: Wayne State University Press, 2001), 233.

Industrialist Robert S. Rodgers of Springfield,
Ohio. Rodgers and his wife Edith benefited
from a quid pro quo relationship with Polly
over education. *Courtesy of 63 Years of
Banking.*

Beulah Draper Carter helped black women
like Polly who relocated to Detroit in the
1920s. *Courtesy of the Catherine Carter
Blackwell Estate.*

Polly graduated from Springfield (Ohio) High School in 1920. *Courtesy of Andrew J. and Mary Jane Humphries Foundation. Image by David R. Barker, The Ohio Historical Society.*

Polly's husband, James W. Leigh, came from Springfield's black merchant class, but he left the money for Detroit, where he found love with Polly, and in September 1929, a career as a Detroit police officer. *Courtesy of The Andrew J. and Mary Jane Humphries Foundation.*

In Detroit, 1924, Jimmy and Polly took each other's photo with their first born, Mary Jane. *Courtesy of The Andrew J. and Mary Jane Humphries Foundation.*

James W. Leigh (l) with his and Polly's younger children,
Elmer (standing) and Pauline Ruby (sitting) in 1932, Detroit.
*Courtesy of The Andrew J. and Mary Jane Humphries
Foundation.*

Polly and Jimmy's daughters, Patty (l) and Mary Jane (r), with big, white dolls, a gift from Grandmother Alice, in 1928, Detroit. *Courtesy of The Andrew J. and Mary Jane Humphries Foundation.*

Polly Johnson Leigh (l) with her youngest daughter, Pauline Ruby Leigh (r), circa 1930, Detroit. *Courtesy of The Andrew J. and Mary Jane Humphries Foundation.*

In 1938, in Detroit, Polly's youngest son Elmer "Buddy" reprises the 1908 photo of his namesake Uncle Bud on a pony. *Courtesy of The Andrew J. and Mary Jane Humphries Foundation.*

Polly was able to climb socially on Detroit's west side through her membership at St. Cyprian's Episcopal Church. Polly (l) with Beulah Carter's daughter, Catherine Blackwell (r), who developed the Detroit Public Schools' African and African-American studies curriculum, in 1960. *Courtesy of The Andrew J. and Mary Jane Humphries Foundation.*

Polly (l) and James W. Leigh (r) at granddaughter Dedria Humphries' wedding at St. Cyprian's Church, Detroit in 1980. *Courtesy of The Andrew J. and Mary Jane Humphries Foundation.*

Polly in her Detroit home with some of her great-grandchildren. Back row (l-r): Terri Barker, Charneise Newton, Keyontay Humphries, David J. Barker. Front row (l-r): Ian Tukes, Briana Stuart, Polly, and Kailea Humphries, 1991. *Courtesy of The Andrew J. and Mary Jane Humphries Foundation.*

Polly with her grown children in 1993 in Detroit. Back row l-r: James Jr., Pauline Ruby, Mary Jane. Front row l- r: Elmer Preston, Polly, and Ellen Elizabeth. *Courtesy of The Andrew J. and Mary Jane Humphries Foundation.*

CHAPTER 5

Mary Jane

THERE WAS NO WAY FOR ME to have known what happened to my great-grandmother because in my family they do not tell children about grown folks' business. In 1961, when Alice was mugged and broke her hip, if my mother said anything about her grandmother's situation it was, "Grandma Alice is in the hospital," or "Grandma Alice is sick." She shared that much because for black people, hospitals were synonymous with imminent death. In the case of Alice, her broken hip was, and is, the kiss of death for a woman with brittle bones, medically known as osteoporosis. Alice's hunchback was a tell-tale sign of it.

It is easy to remember when she died. I was in the living room with my mother, Mary Jane. She stood at the ironing board, not ironing, but waiting. Behind her a telephone stand cradled the black rotary telephone. At the telephone's first urgent jangle, she snatched up the receiver. "Hello," she said, and after a brief pause, she cried out and shrieked, and shrieked. The Irish call it "keening," the sound of a banshee. I remember it as bird calls across a midnight sky. Alice had passed from this life, but for me her story had just begun.

The next spring, maybe summer, I was nine years old sitting in "The Girl's Bedroom." That was the bedroom across from Mary Jane and Andrew's (my father) where the oldest four girls, Marcia, Paula, Alice and I slept. It was a small room stuffed with two sets of bunk beds, four beds in total. The one window was on the north wall and just to the right of it was a small closet with a four-foot rod for hanging clothes and four shelves, one for each of us. I was perched on one of the two lower bunks when Mary Jane came in the room holding her new baby, child number ten. That was Pamela Eileen born in January 1962, the prettiest black white-looking baby ever. She was fair-skinned and rosy-cheeked, with light brown ringlet hair and hazel eyes. She looked like she was 85 percent angel. Mary Jane was pregnant with Pamela when her grandmother died. She had not been allowed to attend the funeral because it might have been too upsetting for her. She loved Alice.

I picked towels out of a square basket sitting on the bed because it was too large to set in the narrow lane between the beds. Mama sat on the other low bunk. We were close. Most likely, I thought she was there to make sure I got my work done before running outside, but that was unnecessary. I did my work or got hollered at, or smacked, or it was waiting for me when I got back. Girls' work was never done. The day of the telling she held her new baby girl, patting the soft ringlets of her hair. Mary Jane did not have much time for each child, unless you were a baby, so her sitting here with me was different. I eyed her as my hands put one fold in a towel.

"You know," she began, "Grandma was in an orphanage."

She was talking about my grandmother, her mother, Polly. I folded the towel twice. No, I did not know.

"Her mother put her there," she murmured.

That was Alice. And that was news. I wanted to know more; I always wanted to know more, but afraid she would shut down, I kept my curiosity in check. I smoothed the towel and whispered, "Why?"

Mary Jane tightened the yellow blanket around baby Pamela against the cool spring air sifting in through drafty windows. She pulled under the baby's arms to sit her straight.

"After her husband died, she couldn't get a job because she had black children. People wouldn't leave her alone."

"*Uhmm*," I said, picking up another towel. I had questions, but the conversation evaporated. Perhaps one of my sisters barged into the room, or a brother came near the door. I did not press her for more details because just her telling me someone else's business was unusual. Mary Jane was the ultimate confidante. She started talking about something else, perhaps a story in the newspaper about city government, about Councilman Billy Rogell, who had parlayed his status as a former Detroit Tiger baseball player to get elected. Having run for City Council herself, she had an interest in local politics. Perhaps Mary Jane thought she had said too much about what she knew so little of, her grandmother Alice. She could have switched to any other subject, anything but Alice.

But somehow I knew she was trying to figure out the puzzle of her only grandparent, her white grandmother, the woman who mysteriously showed up to spend time with the family and then left, only to come back again the following year. Or a few months later, like a bad penny, or a boomerang. That was Alice. Mary Jane loved Alice and she was going over this piece that made little sense. I do not know if it made sense to any of my elders, but I do know they never talked about it, tried to understand it, or turn a wrong into a right. I do not know when or how Mary Jane was told anything, but after Alice died, she told me this simple fact: Alice put her children in an orphanage.

My initial thought was that Alice must have been the kind of mother who put her children in an orphanage, probably a drunk or dissolute, unable to meet their responsibilities because liquor meant more to them. I was working with so little information that I envisioned a Miss Hannigan from the comic strip *Little Orphan Annie* meeting Alice and her three children at the door and asking her, "Who are you?", because orphans do not have parents. How had Alice come into our family if she had once declared her children had no parents? But she was my grandma's real mother. This I never doubted. In the final analysis, as far as I knew an orphanage was for kids like Orphan Annie, no parents, no mother or father, but Grandma Alice died an old and bent woman surrounded by her children and their children. All I could do was narrow my eyes at Mary Jane in frustration at her incomplete story, and think, "Alice had a secret." That's what it seemed to me. *She had a secret.*

80 C8 C8

MARY JANE WAS THE FIRST CHILD and the oldest daughter of Polly and James Leigh. She was born in Detroit, December 9, 1923. Her original name was Alice Cecilia after her grandmother, Alice. The story was Polly's cousin, Laura preferred the name Mary Jane because it was high class unlike the name Alice. Laura did not like Alice and thought she was low-class, and even lower for putting John Henry's children in the orphanage. Why name a child for her? But history repeats itself: it was the same battle from a generation ago. Alice and her black sisters-in-law differed on a nickname for Alice and John's baby. Alice preferred Polly, and John Henry's sisters called the child Little Pauline. In an era where many people in a family had the same name, nicknames were necessary to know who was who. However, Mary Jane was not a nickname for Alice Cecilia; it was an entirely different name. Polly did not protest too much about the change, and the new name caught on. In a letter to Polly dated June 19, 1924 written while she was visiting family in Springfield, Jimmy called their six-month-old baby Mary Jane:

> "My Dear Wife,
>
> I sure do miss you two especially now as there is no one here to hug. I went to town yesterday for the first time, since you have been gone. I hope you are enjoying yourself. I hope all the people like the baby and tell Bud not to buy her too much.
>
> Hold yourself for I am going to tell you something. Helen took sick Monday night and passed away Tuesday night while in Thelma's arms. It was the same thing she always had, cold upon cold on top of cold and developed into pneumonia. Everybody in the neighborhood is sad, especially me for I would hold her and think she was Mary Jane."

Mary Jane never answered to any other name except Mary Jane, even in school. People, even teachers, had to learn this name and use it, though her legal name on her birth certificate was Alice

Cecilia. Any fight light-skinned Polly had over what her baby was to be called, happened early and was settled with her black cousin as the winner. None of the back and forth that Alice suffered with. It was the price Polly paid when she chose family over mother, black over Irish, concern for her twelve-year-old sister Elizabeth, and her deplorable situation over the child she made with her husband. Mary Jane was new business, while Elizabeth was the unfinished business of Polly's birth family.

Mary Jane's childhood was unremarkable, but that must have been remarkable in itself considering how volatile her parents' lives were when they were children. Her early years were spent on the lower east side of Detroit in Black Bottom because that was where black people lived. A woman always washed and braided Mary Jane's thick, soft hair. Her grandmother, Alice, spent some of her wages on gifts, including a huge white doll, as big as Mary Jane herself, with thick hair. Mary Jane looked like one of those white dolls but her sister, Patty did not. Patty was brown-skinned and her head was covered with long gorgeous midnight hair. In 1926, when the family moved to the West Side, four-year-old Mary Jane was pushed to their new apartment in a double pram with her sister Patty. Her father had a good job as a milk-man, then he was a hotel waiter or porter. Five-year-old Mary Jane's education started at the West Side's William T. Sampson elementary school on Begole Street. For a Depression-era child, her childhood had advantages. She barely noticed The Great Depression because the first decade of her father's police career corresponded with the economic collapse. He worked every day from September 1929 until his retirement, providing his family with a steady, if modest, income. The unemployment rate in the city of Detroit was in the double digits and higher among black people. Living on the West Side, they did not see the worst of it. The worst was in the Bottoms. Some people ate the refuse collected from the Eastern Market, the big open air market that served wholesalers. Polly and Jimmy knew some of those people,

"Elite" is what Mary Jane's kind of black people were called. She was in the inner circle of Detroit's black striding class—people willing and able to work to create the life they wanted. Growing up on the West Side, she maintained a close circle of friends, the earliest of them being Albert and Gladys Somerville. Mary Jane met them when they were around eight years old. Their families lived one block away from each other on Northfield Street. Wesley Edwards was Mary Jane's best friend. She was also a light-skinned black girl. Her parents died when she was young. That made her a real orphan.

The year was 1929 when the U.S. and the whole world plunged into an economic abyss that showed no sign of relief because Congress did not understand the economics. They thought the free market could handle the crisis, but international economies do not work that way. The American presidency changed over this issue and Hoover was out, and in 1932, Franklin Roosevelt was in. His "nothing to fear but fear itself" mantra encouraged Americans. His New Deal program of federal government programs gave them hope. His Works Progress Administration (WPA) put people to work in their communities. Still, there was little lucrative work available, because the Depression wiped it out. People were glad to have a job because most did not, at least most in the automobile industry. The number of hourly employees—those were the ones who worked in the factories—dropped 32,000 in one year, from 1929 to 1930. Another 44,000 lost their jobs in 1931, then another 20,000 hit the bricks in 1932. By 1933, the ranks of hourly employees were reduced from a high of 170,000 to 46,000 people.[1] When in 1937, Mary Jane started Cass Technical High School, the premier public high school in Detroit, with a core group of black students from the West Side, she gained her agency, that is, freedom to act for herself. She rode the streetcar to Cass Tech downtown, leaving the neighborhood with her friends, and getting away from her mother. Yet, Cass Tech was an unfriendly world for black students. They were not welcomed or encouraged to join the clubs. Though the boys were accepted in sports, the black girls were isolated in their own social circles.

At Cass Tech, Mary Jane socialized with a group of kids from the West Side —Wesley, the Somervilles, and Mabel Wright, Augusta Cason, Bernice Finley—and met more like-minded black students from all parts of the city. The school did not offer a lot of social activities that were open to blacks. Mary Jane and her friends partied a lot at St. Cyprian's church. She remembered the dances. The church mothers, including Polly, sat at the door admitting young people, casting stern eyes on the kids they did not know, especially the boys and in particular the boys loping in from the North End. Mary Jane needed clothes for these events. Since her parents were strapped for cash, the extra money came from Alice. Mary Jane became accustomed to talking with her grandmother. Alice was interested in hearing about classes, school activities and friends. On one of Alice's visits, Mary Jane remembered showing her grandmother a magazine picture of a skirt and blouse she wanted. Alice nodded and when she got home to Canton, she sent the money back to Polly with instructions to buy the outfit for Mary Jane.

Cass Tech had one interest: education and getting ahead. There was no distinction between education and training; every student who attended Cass Tech shared the goal of finding a better life. Vocational education consisted of class offerings such as a health care curriculum with nursing and pharmaceutical; home economics with cooking, sewing, tailoring, and millinery; and an industrial arts program that included tool and die making, auto mechanics, and foundry, printing, typesetting, electrical and so much more. Most of the instruction was hands-on-training, so graduates could go into the world and get jobs. Students understood that preparation was necessary to avoid having to sweep and scrub floors for a living. Mary Jane and her friend Wesley studied nursing education and took science classes, biology and chemistry. Mary Jane planned to become a college-educated registered nurse. It was a goal her mother Polly had in mind for herself until a school error was made, and then her sister and brother needed her. There was no reason for Mary Jane to take the practical nursing course and become a LPN (licensed practical nurse), since none of the hospitals hired black nurses. There were some jobs with black physicians in the small hospitals they operated, but those jobs were limited.

When the Japanese bombed Pearl Harbor in Hawaii on December 7, 1941, the U.S. economy geared up for war. It angered Americans beyond belief that half of the U.S. Navy Pacific fleet was lost, and hundreds of American servicemen were killed. Volunteers flocked to the military. And women, who would become known as "Rosie the Riveter," took men's places in the factories that had been converted for munitions production.

Mary Jane graduated Cass Tech in January 1942. She would have gotten out in 1941 but she was set back one semester by a bout of bronchitis treated with, on a German doctor's advice, rest at home. She completed high school in January and her plan was to go to nursing school. During the early years of World War II, which was the two years after her graduation from Cass, she had two jobs, one after the other.

First, she worked as an elevator operator at J. L. Hudson's. It was the signature department store downtown. Every city in the U.S. had one of these so-called carriage trade stores. It offered wares and goods from the bargain basement all the way up to the twelfth floor. Customers ate at the formal restaurant, or the buffet on the mezzanine. Each Christmas Santa accepted wish lists in a wonderland on the fourteenth floor. Some said Mary Jane was Hudson's first black elevator operator, but she contested, "No, I wasn't, and I wish people would quit saying that." But an elevator operator was considered a good job, and black Episcopalians got most of the good jobs reserved for black people. This is why going to church in Detroit mattered. There was no better pew to sit in than the one that was once attached to the Anglicans of the Church of England. Henry Ford was an Episcopalian. Two prominent black Episcopal churches were St. Matthews, and St. Cyprian's.

St. Matthews sat up on Woodward Avenue, the median of the city of Detroit, in a ritzy neighborhood of mansions. Clara Ford, wife of Henry Ford I, would worship there at least once a year. One of Ford's high-up black employees attended St. Mathews as well. It was known that if a person wanted to work at Ford, you had to pass his inspection, but Woodward Avenue, lined with monstrous edifices of every denomination, intimidated people. And black Episcopalians could be as snooty as white Episcopalians, maybe more so. An Episcopal church that was more friendly was St. Cyprian's on the West

Side. It was six or so blocks past the corner of Grand River Avenue and West Grand Boulevard where the white Episcopal church with the granite bell tower sat. The black Episcopal church nestled in the neighborhood attracted hordes of young people, like Mary Jane, who enjoyed themselves there.

The head of the parish was a savvy priest from the East Coast, The Reverend Malcolm Dade. His other title was "Father." During services Father Dade wore a biretta, a type of religious pill box hat, with lace on his white cassock and a cape in the winter. He had political ties, so job applications to the City of Detroit, and pretty much anywhere else proved most successful with him as a reference. St. Cyprian's also had an indirect tie to Henry Ford. That was Dr. Austin Curtis, who traveled on business to Detroit from Alabama with Tuskegee Institute President Booker T. Washington. When Washington visited Henry Ford I in Detroit, Dr. Curtis worshipped at St. Cyprian's. After Washington died in 1915, Dr. Curtis moved to Detroit, opened his own laboratory and became a member of St. Cyprian's. Thus the church where Polly and Jimmy were raising their family became influential in the fortunes of young Detroiters.

No black person got a good job in Detroit without passing through some similar test. Good character references determined who was going to the next level. Regardless of who *the first* black elevator operator was at Hudson's, Mary Jane enjoyed good working conditions with no heavy lifting, and no dirty work. The downside was that she had to learn to navigate racial and sexual harassment while earning low pay. When it became known at St. Cyprian's that the U.S. Rubber Company was hiring, she went there.

The U.S. Rubber plant made tires. It was located on East Jefferson Avenue, along the river, before the bridge to Belle Isle, the island park. Mary Jane was hired as a quality inspector and was assigned to the midnight shift. Her father said she would not like it, and how dreadful it was spending the entire night inspecting new tires for imperfections, the smell of hot rubber filling her nose, but Mary Jane enjoyed her co-workers. Sometimes, after getting off work at 8:00 a.m., she hung out with her crew and partied until noon. She loved that. But her behavior irritated her father. One time she came home from work at noon, he said, "If you are going to live here you need to come home after work." So she did. Getting to know her city was a sign of her adulthood: black parents kept their children close and occupied. She learned from Alice that the races were segregated. Mary Jane recalled that when her grandmother visited them in Detroit, she often journeyed to Corktown, the Irish section of Detroit near the old Tiger Stadium, because she was uncomfortable as the only white in the black community.

In time, Mary Jane earned enough money for college. She quit the tire company, and enrolled in Wayne University. This was the university that grew up from the various programs offered at Detroit City College. She still wanted to be a registered nurse. Her plan was to take a few classes at Wayne, then transfer to a black nursing school because Wayne's nursing school did not admit blacks. She planned to transfer to Howard University in Washington, D.C. There were other schools—Bernice Finley went to St. Louis—but, Mary Jane's mother was on board with Howard because that's where Gladys Somerville went. Best friend Wesley used her nursing studies to land a rare job in a doctor's office. To get into Howard, Mary Jane had to get a chest X-ray. The test result showed scared lung tissue. She had tuberculosis.

Tuberculosis, also called consumption, was a disease caused by bacteria that multiplied in the lungs forming tubers, which were growths and damaged the tissue, making it difficult to breath. Mary Jane thought maybe someone she worked with had tuberculosis and that constant exposure, her breathing the same air they sneezed or coughed into, together with her bout of bronchitis, and her late nights, were her undoing. She was worn down and her immune system was compromised. What a shock and fright that must have been for her mother. Three generations in a row the family had lost a child from a respiratory disease. In 1879 and it was whooping cough. In 1935 it was pneumonia. Now tuberculosis had struck.

Mary Jane convalesced at Maybury Sanitarium, the recuperation facility for blacks who did not have the huge amounts of money necessary to pay for a private clinic. Maybury was outside of Detroit in Northville. Sending Mary Jane off on a bus from Detroit, Polly told her to do what she had to do to get well. Polly visited infrequently, and Jimmy never took the long bus ride from the city to visit. Mary Jane was alone in the world of the sanitarium. She did not like it, but, "I just had to grow up," she said. She also had to take financial responsibility for the small cost of being in Maybury. The facility tried to charge her father, but he said she was an adult and could pay it herself. She presented her birth certificate to prove her age of twenty-one. "Who is this person, Alice Cecilia?," the Maybury bureaucrats demanded. They pushed her to legally change her name to Mary Jane.

As was her mother, although older, Mary Jane was sent away from her family. She was alone with no close family or friends, with medical authorities telling her what to do. It was the same thing that happened to her mother, but in this case, it was for the good of her health. But does the reason matter? She was by herself. She had to make her own way, find her own people, make her own judgments about who to spend time with and who to avoid. Did she feel orphaned, too?

Mary Jane recalled that the sanatorium was "boring as heck." The treatment protocol called for meal after meal of gooey food, like oatmeal, and lots of rest and sleep. That was the daily routine. She told me she gained twenty to twenty-two pounds that year. "Some of the people complained that they did not like the food, but I ate it. I wanted to get out of there. A lot of the people rode the bus back to the city to get food they liked, like barbecue, but I never did. I did what the doctor said to do." She occupied some of her time tutoring a woman younger than her, Marilyn Bryant, who was diagnosed and sent to Maybury when she was a ninth grader. Mary Jane told Marilyn, "I don't know about you, but I am getting out of here." She missed her friends, and appreciated those who wrote to her. She prized loyalty. One of the people who wrote to her was a Cass Tech classmate who was in the same boat as Mary Jane: away from home and lonely. His name was Andrew John Humphries.

Andrew was in the U.S. Army. After graduating from Cass Tech in 1942, he enlisted in 1943. He served in the European theater of combat and the Army of Occupation in France and Germany. In 1946, the Army sent him to command school at the University of Vienna, in Austria. He learned to command, and speak German. He spent his free time learning to play the piano, writing poetry and sketching. He was a North End boy, one of the perceived interlopers to the West Side elites. His neighborhood was to the north of West Grand Boulevard as it crossed Woodward Avenue, and ran up to Clairmount Avenue. His family lived in an apartment building at the intersection of Leicester and Brush streets. The streetcar made it possible for him to attend the dances at St. Cyprian's church. When the car stopped running, or he did not have a nickel, or he did not want to put it in the fare box, he walked the four miles. He did the same thing when attending school at Cass Tech. He could have attended his neighborhood high school, Northern, but his widowed mother wanted him to go to the best school and meet the best people, so they could have a chance. He was tall, handsome, and smart. He was her oldest son of four children and she needed him to help his family. His father had died of pneumonia in 1936 when Andrew was twelve years old. The Humphries family story is cut straight from the master narrative of how black southerners came to Detroit: in search of work in the auto factories.

Andrew's father, A.C. Humphries, was from Savannah, Georgia, and in 1924 he was a student at Savannah College, a school established for black people. He was the father of one son, Lester B., whose mother he did not marry, and the father of an infant son, Andrew John, born on October 21, 1924. A.C. married the second mama. She was Lula Mae Orr, tall and slender, with golden skin and a fiery personality. She was sixteen, a descendant of the Geechees, an African people who never lost the old ways. They lived on the Georgia sea islands and spoke Gullah. In the summer of 1924, A.C. came to Detroit, ostensibly to earn money to finish college. His new wife and son were supposed to stay down south, but Lula was anxious about him in Detroit alone and, perhaps more so, anxious about living with his mother, Louise, so Lula joined her husband in Detroit, bringing their six month old son. In that way, A.C.'s summer job turned into a full-time gig with Ford Motor Company. They made it work. His older brothers and sister lived in Detroit and they had families he, Lula and their son could be a part of. In time they had other children in Detroit: Lorraine born in 1926, Theodore born in 1929. Life was good.

Like most black men employed in the auto industry in the 1920s, A.C. worked the dangerous jobs. Ford's River Rouge plant designed by local architect Albert Kahn, was lauded as a masterpiece, but the working conditions inside the plant were far from being world-class. The foundry, where A.C. earned his living, ran hot and cold in extreme temperatures and was wet. Pneumonia was a major risk. Facing the furnace, the employee was hot on his chest, and with his back to the windows, he was cold. In 1936, A.C. contracted pneumonia. It was only three days from the moment he felt sickly to his untimely death. A stunning turn of events—Lula was pregnant. And while she knew the Humphries family and everyone had a job, no one was rich enough to take on their dead brother's family. And there might have been some animosity toward Lula because if she had stayed in Savannah, A.C. would have returned to school, finished with a trade and had a solid start in life providing for his family. Their oldest son, twelve-year-old Andrew, became his mother's right hand. Lula delivered her last child, a girl, named Laura, later that year.

Lula Mae Humphries supported her children as best as she could—she was a skilled seamstress—until Andrew finished high school and was drafted into the Army. He sent his mother money back from Europe. The Army gave him a good assignment because of his draftsman skills. His mechanical lettering techniques were exceptional, a skill he learned at Cass Technical High School. While he was at Cass, he met this pretty, yellow-skinned girl from the West Side, Mary Jane Leigh. And now she was sick and wanted to receive letters, so he wrote to her from Europe:

"Alice Cecilia

Although you've gone and changed your name
Love will always be the same
I know it hasn't changed a bit
Could be I like your ready wit,
Else I surely would have quit.
Could it be you changed shape, too.
Even to your fine hair-do.
Can say you haven't made a change,
It's you I want in my arms range.
Lately, we had much to say,
In fact, you're with me all the day.
Alas, I wonder what you weigh."

Mary Jane left Maybury in spring 1946, exactly one year to the day she had arrived. She recalled, "I was so glad to get out of there." She left behind many of the patients who were non-compliant with doctor's orders. Some of them died there. She left Marilyn too, but eventually the younger woman was discharged, and they remained friends.

The Army discharged Andrew Humphries in spring of 1946, and he came home to Detroit. They married on February 15, 1947 in the St. Cyprian's rector's office. Her mother, Polly, was very unhappy because Mary Jane was pregnant. This dynamic delayed the marriage until Mary Jane was seven and a half months pregnant. All, or mostly all was forgiven when baby boy made his appearance on April 3, 1947. He was the first grandchild in Mary Jane's family, and the first grandson on Andrew's side. Mary Jane named her son, Derrick Anthony, after a movie star, or singer.

Andrew needed a job. He enrolled at Wayne University under the G.I. Bill and enjoyed the company of the fellows he went to school with. He wanted to be an engineer, and use his skills to design and make things, but what could he do to earn money right now? He had two families depending on him: his wife and child, and his mother and teenage sister. His best friend, Carl Bruce Huffman, another Cass Technician, had been accepted into Ford's tool and die apprentice program. Andrew went to Ford, as well. He got a job, but he did not stay long. He told people that he left Ford because the shut-downs for model changeover, strikes, and lay-offs to reduce inventory build-ups, meant no paycheck for employees.

His father's death may have also haunted him, and he looked to his father-in-law, James Leigh, the Detroit police officer, as a model. Andrew had never thought of becoming a police officer, but his father-in-law, who inspired him, was willing to speak up for him with the police commanders. Andrew joined the Detroit police in 1948. Now he had a job to pay the bills, and school to work on his dream.

The newlyweds lived with his mother in an apartment building on Leicester Street on the North End. But the following year, one of the state representatives wanted quality people as tenants in an apartment building he had bought, and offered apartments to black police officers. Andrew and Mary Jane stayed on the North End, moving a few blocks away to 7441 Brush Street, Apartment 112, on the corner of Custer Street. The building was a very lively place, more lively than Mary Jane's somber West Side neighborhood of elite blacks. The apartment house was filled with other young couples trying to get a toe hold in the economy. These were regular black people, their parents having come from the south, people she knew nothing about—both her parents were from Ohio. The neighbors Mary Jane encountered brought black southern culture with them. Andrew's circle ate these exotic foods like chitlins. The smell reeked, stinking up the whole building and the flavor of pig intestines was intolerable, even with hot sauce. But other tastier, more pleasant smelling dishes made dinner more fun than it had ever been at home where the bland tastes of Irish food reigned. Mary Jane ate greens and ham hocks, cornbread, and pound cake, which was exactly what it sounded like. The recipe called for one pound each of the main ingredients: eggs, sugar, flour, milk, flavored with vanilla. *It was heavenly.* It was a heavy cake that could be eaten for breakfast or desert. She loved the good times, Friday night paydays, and fish fries with potatoes, peach cobbler and beer.

Mary Jane stayed busy with their children, Derrick and second child, daughter, Marcia Ellen, born on July 13, 1948. Her first name is pronounced "Mar-cee-a," and she was named in part for Mary Jane's sister Ellen. Marcia was like her aunt in that she was a brown sugar babe crowned with hair thick and dark as black strap molasses. She strongly resembled Andrew's sister, Lorraine, a substantial, lovely café-au-lait woman with curves. Marcia was an excitable little girl. She was afraid of the seed pods that grew on honey locust trees. They looked like worms, twisted and curling as they dried and fell to the ground. Her favorite photo of herself was taken at Grass Lake, a recreational area west of Detroit, which Mary Jane recalled, the Episcopal church owned. In the early 1950s, the family held outings at Grass Lake. In the photo, Marcia sat at a picnic table with a brown Pabst Blue Ribbon beer bottle in front of her. One of her young aunts or uncles let her take a sip. She was grinning, although only six years old, she always wanted to be grown, it seemed.

Both sides of the family loved the children, and spent time with them, but ultimately, they were Mary Jane's responsibility. After a five-year gap in children, when Mary Jane was working a job here and there, I was born on December 19, 1952, and Andrew Dwight quickly followed on February 12, 1954. He was called Andy, though not to distinguish him from our father, who was by this time called "Gump." Andy was a big kid whose presence made it clear the apartment was far too small for a family of six. They needed a house, and Mary Jane was hoping to get back closer to her family on the West Side.

Schools topped the list of features Andrew wanted in the neighborhood where he bought his family home. The one thing Mary Jane and her husband agreed on was education for their kids. She might have had in mind that they would troop down to Cass Tech, building on the foundation that she and Andrew had established, but in 1954, Derrick was just seven years old and in second grade in elementary school. That same year, however, the U.S. Supreme Court judgment offered hope. In 1954, it issued the famous *Brown v. the Board of Education* opinion that ordered desegregation of public schools in the entire United States. Thurgood Marshall argued that landmark case, and he would go on to the Supreme Court at the next vacancy in 1967, appointed by President Lyndon B. Johnson. In response to the *Brown* decision, white people in Little Rock, Arkansas violently protested integration of high schools. Eisenhower sent in federal troops to escort the nine black students to class. They were called The Little Rock Nine — black teenagers brave enough to risk injury or death from people whose souls were distorted by racism.

With integration of public schools under way, Mary Jane and Andrew decided that the neighborhood schools in Detroit would suit their kids. One reason they attended Cass Tech was because in a era when racism was alive and kicking, mixing different ethnicities, namely, the Polish and the blacks, had made neighborhood schools in Detroit abhorrent. In addition to good schools in their new neighborhood, Andrew also wanted bus stops, stores and libraries.

He was entitled to a mortgage under the G.I. Bill, but bought a house on Wykes Street in the Springwells neighborhood on land contract. There was a large 1920s red brick school one block away from the house. There were two bus routes, and the intersection of Tireman Avenue and Wykes Street offered many conveniences, such as the Tireman and Prairie Grocery Store, Shelly's Drugstore, Finley's Beauty Nook, and Hughley's Barber Shop. There was a bar and a few churches, the biggest being Berea Lutheran and Unity Baptist. St. Cyprian's was four miles down the way, a walkable distance in sensible shoes. The library was at the end of the next neighborhood, but it was okay because that neighborhood was where Polly and Jimmy lived. Andrew and Mary Jane's new house was a two-family flat. Mary Jane, Andrew and the kids lived downstairs, and Andrew's mother and sister lived upstairs. Lula did not want all those children's feet tapping over her head.

Like Alice's house, Mary Jane's house was a modified shotgun style with decent sized living and dining rooms and a kitchen bright from the south facing windows, but the three bedrooms and the bathroom were small for a growing family. Andrew's vision was to rent out the upstairs unit until the house was paid for and then his family could spread out in both units. And that is where Mary Jane and Andrew raised their family. Their fifth child, Paula, was born on Wykes Street, in the house, on February 20, 1955. The entire brood in order by birth year was:

Derrick Anthony, 1947
Marcia Ellen, 1948
Dedria Ann, 1952
Andrew Dwight, 1954
Paula Georgette, 1955
Alice Susanna, 1956
James Nathan, 1958
John Charles, 1959
William Duane, 1960
Pamela Eileen, 1962
Gregory Bryant, 1963
Mark Christopher, 1965
Kimberly Ann Marie, 1967

Before the pill became available in 1965, birth control was crude and ineffective. The only sure prevention to making a baby was abstinence. Poor birth control could also be attributed to a number of factors, such as the 1873 Comstock Act and various state Comstock laws that outlawed the distribution of information about safe sex and the use of contraceptives.[2] There were also religious restrictions to contend with, notably the Roman Catholic Church, which remains opposed to artificial contraception. Perhaps the most important factor is that women were historically viewed as a creative source of human life that was intellectually inferior and without legal rights whatsoever. It was during the nineteenth century that a cult of domesticity was established that restricted women to stay home, obey their husbands, have babies and raise them. Even if some women had to work, they were still expected to have sex with their husbands even if it meant having babies they could not afford to have or precipitated a physically painful pregnancy. In some cases, the unreliability of birth control is why wives who refrained from sex often looked the other way from their husband's infidelities. The women in my family were not activists, but each of them did what they could to work around the social mores of the times, on their own terms. Polly and Jimmy had separate beds for as long as I could remember. Maybe it happened after their youngest child died in 1935.

The people at St. Cyprian's were astonished at Mary Jane's fecundity. It was not the Episcopalian way to be so reproductive. But, one of the church founders, Mrs. Beulah Carter, was a social worker, the first black one with Women's Hospital in Detroit, and the third black social worker with the City of Detroit Department of Public Welfare. She saw many women with fewer children than Mary Jane struggle to carry them, birth them and raise them. When she saw Mary Jane's accomplishment, she pronounced the woman she had watched grow up in the church, "Amazing Mary."

Similarly, there was much Andrew did not know about his wife. He knew her father was a police officer. He knew her mama was light-skinned. One day in 1961, while I washed dishes or dried dishes, or both, and Mary Jane cooked at the stove, Andrew sat at the kitchen table humming, a mechanical pencil in hand and a piece of paper on the table in front of him. It was filled with numbers. He knew his way around calculations and measurement from his training in high school as a draftsman. That day he was figuring out how white Mary Jane was.

When Alice came to live in Detroit in 1961, it was perhaps the first time Andrew found out about his wife's grandmother being white. Though it is difficult to know what people see when they looked at her, he had to know some white person was in her mix. Mary Jane is yellow-skinned with white undertones, her hair black and soft. He appreciated that because he was color-struck. Color-struck means that there are black people who care what color skin is. While black people come in all different hues and colors, for the color-struck, dark-skin was off limits and you did not bring home anyone darker than a brown paper bag. It is called the bag test, and the lighter the skin, the better. Oddly enough, the color-struck did not like white people, even though they lusted after their white privilege.

But on this day in 1961, while Andrew was humming and doing his calculations, he figured out the equation of his wife's black forebears and this one white woman. Finally, he looked up at Mary Jane and exclaimed, "why, you are 23.67325 percent white." Or some preposterous number.

She looked at him like he was crazy.

Today, Henry Louis Gates Jr., the host of *Finding Your Roots*, a television series researching the family history of well-known Americans, and commercial DNA tests do pretty much the same thing: deconstruct cells to deliver surprising results to equally surprised people, black and white.

My father, the Negro widow's ambitious son, was pleased to have married Mary Jane, the 23 whatever-percent white-Negro girl. What surprised him was that her white relative was a living woman who came to visit and eventually lived with her black family. The Big Mama of his wife's family was a very old white woman who had climbed over the color line.

The Springwells neighborhood worked for a time for Mary Jane and Andrew. It maintained the character that first convinced them this was a great place to raise their children. The neighborhood school, Edwin S. Sherrill School was one block north of Tireman Avenue on Wykes at the next cross street, Garden. The school had a crossing guard, Mr. Fears, to ensure students' safety. Parents did not have to worry about their young children walking through the Polish neighborhood to Munger Junior High because Sherrill went to eighth grade. Mary Jane and Andrew's oldest, Derrick, graduated eighth grade in 1960. His father slotted him for the neighborhood high school. This surprised Mary Jane. She had their children pegged as Technicians. What was going on?

Actually, Andrew did not enjoy attending Cass Tech. He found the racism disheartening, including the snubs from white students, and not being welcomed to do more than go to class. The only open social avenue had been sports, where the black and white fellows got acquainted. It had been enough of an upward climb making friends with the black West Side kids, enduring their mothers looking down their noses at guys from the North End. And then he was faced with doing it all over again with white people.

By the fall of 1960, Mary Jane and Andrew had nine children. Andrew called us Princess and Handsome. In 1967, their brood would grow to thirteen, and supporting thirteen children ceased to be a mere notion. The pressure of keeping them fed, clean, clothed, and calm was very real. Sometimes in winter, the house got too small for us and we fought. Our father was glad when he was home and could walk us, especially me and Andy, in the cool night air. He would walk us far south on Livernois Avenue to the Ford Expressway, known in the larger world as I-94. He would stop on the land bridge overpass where the street lights dimmed, and the Big Dipper blazed.

In addition to Andrew's personal feelings toward Cass Tech, there was no way on a police officer's salary that he would be able to pay carfare to Cass for all of his children. It had been difficult for him to always find carfare to Cass Tech for himself. Doing that for Derrick at the price of providing for the rest would be unfair. Sometimes, Andrew worked double shifts, sixteen hours straight as a cop on the streets of Detroit to make ends meet. But finally, change happened. Because of *Brown v. the Board of Education,* the neighborhood high school administrations were forced to quell racial hostilities and openly integrate. As a result, white families that preferred not to deal with an integrated school fled to the suburbs with the help of post-World War II federal housing policies. Mary Jane saw their friends and family, particularly those who lived in northwest Detroit, sending their kids to neighborhood high schools. She followed the trend and sent Derrick to the neighborhood high school, Charles E. Chadsey.

Derrick started at Chadsey in the fall of 1960. The school was located north of the Ford Expressway in the Polish neighborhood, two miles from his home. Andrew's brother, Ted, had joined the police department and he was on duty at the McGraw sixth precinct police station across the street from the school. That neighborhood also had a Catholic high school, St. Andrews. Just like the Sherrill

school, Chadsey was named for a Detroit Public School superintendent from the early twentieth century. It offered an assortment of
trades programs, like commercial cooking, sewing, auto mechanics,
and a strong college preparatory curriculum including classes in
Latin, for aspiring doctors. The teachers and administrators were
Polish. Dr. Joseph Wytrwal taught math, and Mr. Yost taught Latin.
Mary Jane and Andrew started to breathe easier when Detroit police
officer Mackey Johnson's wife, Pearl, was appointed to the faculty.
She taught sewing.

Derrick played football at Chadsey, but as a student in the college prep curriculum, he also had to hit those books, and he did.
Away from school Derrick was a Boy Scout platoon leader, and an
altar boy at St. Cyprian's. He also played baseball for the Mohawks, a
team our uncle coached. Derrick was helpful, funny, handsome, and
popular with all the students. In 1963 he ran for senior class president, and was elected co-president, which stirred some controversy.
Derrick, along with Mary Jane and Andrew believed he polled more
votes, but the administrators refused to declare him the president
outright, so they named him "co-president." The effect of *Brown
v. the Board of Education* sifted down slowly. As he moved toward
graduating summa cum laude from Chadsey High School in 1964,
Mary Jane and Andrew considered various next steps, like working
for the police department, or getting an appointment to West Point
Academy. Finally, Derrick accepted a Board of Regents academic
scholarship to the University of Michigan in Ann Arbor, the "Harvard
of the Midwest."

Derrick was seventeen years old when he started at the University of Michigan. How proud Mary Jane was to ride forty-five minutes
west on I-94, exit at State Street and arrive to the lofty Ann Arbor
campus. Both she and Andrew had started college at Wayne, but she
did not return to class when she was released from the sanatorium,
cured from tuberculosis. Andrew was still working on his degree,
but it was slow going with a full-time job as a police officer and a
growing family. But Mary Jane put all her young mother's energy into
Derrick with great success. Then one day, her husband said to her,

you better go see about that boy in Ann Arbor. They are going to put him out of school. Derrick was failing a math class.

Without a working family car, Mary Jane boarded the Greyhound bus to Ann Arbor. "We were not going to let Derrick flunk out of the University of Michigan," she told me. She spoke to Derrick and the professor. Later, Derrick told them that meeting made the professor take an interest in him. The professor said, "Anybody whose mother would come to see me has to succeed." Education was a long-standing tradition in Mary Jane's family. Polly was an attentive mother; with her school a must-do-well activity like her mother Alice, who had little enough to give her children except a better future through education. That was their inheritance.

In 1975, nearly thirty years after Mary Jane and Andrew married, they still lived in the Springwells subdivision. The house was paid for and their family had spread out to both flats. Andrew was eligible for retirement, but he had not done it yet. They were working to get the second half of their baker's dozen out of Chadsey and into college, like every one of the Humphries children had done since 1964. One day, Mary Jane was visiting Chadsey High School, attending to something or the other. When she rounded the corner to the back hallway, who did she see but her fifteen-year-old son William. He was number nine, born October 19, 1960. William reminded me of "Baby Huey," the cartoon character of a big whale-sized duckling. William was always big. He was six feet three inches tall and looked too big for his clothes, which might have been hand-me-downs. William had beige skin, hazel eyes, dark blond hair and was more than a little rough. He irritated Andrew almost every day by being late to school. And William was well aware that he did not have as much as some of the other kids in the neighborhood whose fathers, and some mothers, worked in the auto plant earning a lot more money than his father, the police officer. What bothered William the most was not having money for McDonald's hamburgers and fries.

That one day Mary Jane rounded the edge of the lockers in the back hall of Chadsey she saw William with his paws on this smaller boy. He had this kid pinned up against the locker so high the boy's feet dangled in the air. "William," Mary Jane barked, and hearing his mother's voice, he dropped the boy to the floor. The kid scrambled away down the hall. "Don't you ever do that again," she told him in her stern, no-nonsense voice. But Mary Jane relearned this that day: School was more than a place to learn. It was an entire biological environment with a pecking order. Mary Jane cared about the academics. She made sure her kids were always at the top of that heap. Now she knew her son ruled the pack.

In 1983, the last the Humphries' sons was graduating Chadsey. That was Mark Christopher, born on May 13, 1965. If Derrick was the model son, then Mark was the "uber-Derrick." Taller than his oldest brother, Mark was six feet four inches, dark featured which means his hair and eyes were black, and when he closed his eyes, his black eyelashes rested on his cheeks. Mark was too smart for Chadsey, but he was comfortable there with his best bud, one-year-older brother, Gregory Bryant, born on October 8, 1963. They went to Chadsey together but everything they did was in direct opposition to each other. Mark went out for football and made the team, Greg went out for football one day and the next day he gave his helmet to Mark to return to the coach. They were in some of the same classes. Mark was on time, taking a front row seat, homework crisp on his desk. Greg came in late, walked across the room in front of the teacher in the midst of her lecture, took a seat at the open window and threw spitballs at kids outside in gym class. The teachers were puzzled as to why Greg never had his homework done when all he had to do was copy Mark's.

Greg told all these stories about him and Mark at Mark's funeral.

In 1983, Mark graduated Chadsey and went straight west on I-94 to the University of Michigan in Ann Arbor, the fifth Humphries to be accepted. Greg had come out of high school the year before, and was admitted to Eastern Michigan University, which is located in Ypsilanti, the community next to Ann Arbor. He only stayed for his sophomore year because Mark was coming to Ann Arbor. When Mark got busy at Michigan, Greg went home to Detroit. Mark was perfect for University of Michigan. He worked hard to go into the science field, but when he saw what his classmates did to get those great grades necessary for medical school the pills known as uppers and downers—he was outdone. He kept up, however, and he tried to keep up socially too. He wanted to move out of the dorm to an apartment, like his brothers and sisters did. But the Humphries were such a conservative family, my response was, "Naw, Mark. Stay in the dorm and keep the main thing the main thing." He moved out anyway. That was his prerogative.

Interacting with landlords, negligent ones in particular, can be a challenge. Some take care of their property, and others do not. This one morning during spring semester, Mark came out of his new apartment building and slipped on the ice that the landlord did not salt or remove. His six feet four inch frame went straight down, like a felled tree, and he hit his head. Mark was never the same. One time I was over at Mary Jane and Andrew's house sitting upstairs talking with Mark and our youngest sister, and Mark got up and turned off all the lights. We were sitting in the dark. It was weird and scary. Another time, he locked himself in the bathroom upstairs and they had to take the door down to get him out. He was on medication, which made him gain weight and he hated that, so he stopped taking it.

Mark was under doctor's care for schizophrenia, but it seemed likely that he suffered from an internal head injury. He would have no choice but to be admitted to the hospital when he stopped taking his medication. His condition would improve when he resumed medication. He would continue studying only to relapse with worry about his grades at the end of each semester and end up in the hospital again. He came back to live with Mary Jane and Andrew in the Springwells subdivision, but Mary Jane is only five feet two inches tall and he towered over her by more than one foot. She could not take care of him so she sent Mark into a half-way house on West Grand Boulevard near St. Cyprian's.

This decision challenged everyone. Every day he came to his parents' house, but at night he returned to the half-way house where people could manage his needs. It evoked the same challenge Alice faced in 1913 with her children. Two-year-old Elizabeth was just too young to stay by herself while her mother worked, and Polly deserved to go to school.

Physical illness was one thing Mary Jane could deal with. She took her children to the free clinic for well-checks to be examined by an anonymous doctor who would not be there the next time because he was in training. But any time one of her children got sick, she took us to her doctor's office and paid his fee. But mental illness was far more complicated and out of her wheelhouse. Afflicted people can hurt themselves, or hurt others, which we had not experienced until Mark got sick.

So Mark was like a mouse on a running wheel: school, semester-end crash, hospital. When he could no longer attend the university, he returned to Detroit to recover, which was primarily a tough love approach that failed. Then he was in the hospital smoking cigarettes and chain eating cupcakes. No one can continue living like that, and he did not. Mark died in 1990 at age twenty-five.

Having known about the family's childhood vulnerability to respiratory illness, Mary Jane must have been terrified when she contracted tuberculosis, and thereafter, every time one of her children caught a cold, she was nervous. She may not have known how early the pattern of child death began. The 1879 death notice for Alice's brother Elmer was locked up in Alice's mother's prayer book and stowed away with Alice in Canton, Ohio. Only her death would spring it open. Polly's efforts to have a smooth family life may have stopped her from talking about her dead brother, Levy. The emotional wound of her youngest daughter's death from pneumonia scarred Polly and Jimmy so badly they hardly visited Mary Jane in the sanitarium. The thing was, home was the only safe place for our family and sometimes it was not even that. Alice had to leave her home in Lawrenceburg to get her life started. Still home had to be preserved.

Mary Jane always put her children first, before herself certainly, but this one time finding Mark another place to live was the correct decision. I knew a well-off, very highly educated and respected historian, a black woman, who let her mentally ill adult son live in her home. One morning he stabbed her to death. Mothers must make tough decisions. Little is said about those grueling decisions except that, unfairly, maybe she could have done more. Mary Jane scratched her head at parents who put their own interests ahead of their children, especially when it happened to advance material acquisitions, like cars and houses, so it was with much disdain one year that she relayed to me what my brother James was doing. It was one of the few times she complained about one child to another.

Her number eight son, James Nathan, was born on February 15, 1958 on her eleventh wedding anniversary. If Mark was an "uber-Derrick," then James Nathan was a "miniature-Derrick," imitating all those great qualities in a body that more resembled Mary Jane's Uncle Bud. James was about five feet ten inches tall and round. He graduated Chadsey and matriculated at the University of Michigan. He played football, walking on to the team coached by Bo Schembechler in the 1970s. Those were the years when the Wolverines played in the Rose Bowl every year. James tutored his teammates and in a show of appreciation, when he graduated with his bachelor's degree, the coach helped him land a highly-coveted seat at the University of Michigan Law School. He continued to tutor the football players while in law school. He graduated and passed the bar, and started his legal career. Ultimately, James was tapped to lead the Detroit Public Schools government grants department, federal grants in particular. James had a lot of responsibility and his salary reflected that. Now he needed the house to go with it. He was married to his high school sweetheart, Diane Rogers, and three of their four children lived at their home.

In 2001, James and Diane decided to put their house on the market while they were looking for another house. They had a very nice two-story brick house on the East Side of Detroit, and it sold quickly. But they did not have another house to go to. Mary Jane, who had lived in the same house for nearly forty-seven years in 2001, was fuming. "That was so stupid! Where are they going to live now? Well, I tell you what, the kids can live here with me, but those two, they can sleep in the van."

What was best for the kids came first with Mary Jane. Not having a house was a form of orphaning those three Humphries children because where there is a house there can be a home. No house, no home. The house was the stabilizing place for family. At the root of Mary Jane's impatience with her son was Alice and Polly.

When Alice became widowed, she managed to keep her house on Irish Hill that her husband and father-in-law built. Home was the family touchstone, one of the last vestiges of married family life. Even when she surrendered her children to the orphanage, she kept their home intact so Polly and Bud were able to return to it. But it was the greatest sorrow of Elizabeth's life that she was unable to return home.

$$\wp \, \wp \, \wp$$

Little Mama

THERE IS A SAYING: Mothers love their sons but raise their daughters. The story of Mary Jane, the mother, cannot be told without the story of Marcia Ellen, her oldest daughter. In 2013 when Mary Jane turned ninety years old, all of her children were involved in planning her birthday celebration. Marcia more than anyone else wanted it to be the best ever event for Mary Jane. But at the height of the party she acted strangely.

We were a polite, courteous family. We have a public persona, and a private one. We might shout at each other, but your name has to be Humphries for you to hear it. We are clannish, like the Irish. That night Marcia forgot to act like everything was hunky-dory. We were all sitting in our order, more or less, on a dais for the program honoring Mary Jane. The room was packed with 300 family members and friends who had been on this journey with her. People from St. Cyprian's, from her YMCA water aerobics class, her long-time friends, people from the neighborhood, kids she had watched grow up and who she advocated for with her activity in the schools. Each of her children was going to say a little piece of love about our mother. There were confessions. I thanked Mary Jane for raising my oldest son until I could help my new husband do it. Then Marcia spoke. She looked down the line of her siblings, and she faced the crowd, and said, "Just so you know, these people are all my children too." She pointed at us, her sisters and brothers, of whom she had taken charge of so many decades ago.

As Jacob Riis pointed out so graphically in his book about late nineteenth century European immigrants living in New York City, a Little Mama is a stand-in. She is there when mama cannot be. She is usually a silent senior partner in the business of raising a family, but at Mary Jane's party, Marcia spoke up. She realized perhaps how she wanted public appreciation from the siblings she gave so much of her time and love to help raise. She had carried out her duties, imposed on her by her parents, particularly by her father and certainly by American society at the time. The oldest daughter is the mother's first line of aid. And the oldest daughter also compensates for the father's absence. For Mary Jane the lost history of the secret of why Alice put Polly, Bud and Elizabeth in the orphanage would have helped in understanding Marcia, our Little Mama. Perhaps prevented her from becoming one.

Marcia followed her brother's footsteps. At the Sherrill school, she was a Service Girl, part of a group of seventh and eighth grade students who helped the younger students with their coats and hats. She was a Girl Scout, selling cartons of cookies directly to her family after we ate them. At Chadsey, she played basketball. Girls played half-court because it was believed we lacked the wind to sprint the length of the court. Marcia took Latin, and piled on the home economics courses, learning to sew and to cook from a Betty Crocker cookbook. She was independent, hard-working and reliable. The winter of 1962, there was a major snow storm. Marcia got up extra early to get to Chadsey on time. She walked. Marcia walked all the way to school to find the building closed. No school that day. She was on time, ahead of the Polish administrators who had not declared school closed yet. She walked all the way back through the streets in the freezing cold. Two feet of snow covered the sidewalks. She also graduated high school with honors, and did it all the while being a mainstay helper to Mary Jane with her children. Her accomplishment was like that of Ginger Rogers who did everything Fred Astaire did, but backwards and in heels.

There were plenty of opportunities for Marcia to be useful as Mary Jane's family grew larger and larger. Mary Jane was the commander-in-chief, and Marcia was the general. She was groomed for this job of keeping underlings in their place from early on. Mary Jane passed the baton of authority in clear view, so the rest of her children knew what was up: obey Marcia. The adored oldest son, Derrick, was in on it early on. One day Mary Jane and Andrew left them both in charge and upon their return home every corner of the house was filled with a child.

Marcia became old enough at eleven years old for the Little Mama role in 1959 when John Charles was born. Born thin, and with long, spindly legs, he also cried a lot, Mary Jane recalled. She would leave him crying, but Marcia picked him up. Mary Jane worried when her one-year-old son could not crawl or walk. Children usually start walking at about ten months old, so he was on the late side. Mary Jane took him to see Thomas A. Brown, M.D., the general practitioner who took care of her pregnancy after pregnancy, and delivered all of Mary Jane's babies. After the six-week check-up, he rarely saw her children because she took us to the free clinic operated by the city health department. But she took her stationary son to Dr. Brown, who was also a member of St. Cyprian's church.

In 1960, many doctors had their office in a part of their house. They lived above, behind, in front or beside their medical office, but Dr. Brown's office was on Warren Avenue on the West Side of Detroit, near St. Cyprian's. The doctor himself lived in a fine house on LaSalle Boulevard, nearby the Reverend C. L. Franklin, Aretha's father.

Dr. Brown might have fussed at Mary Jane because she was pregnant with her ninth child, and it was not good for her body to have so many babies so fast. "Yes, Dr. Brown," she said, setting her little son John on the exam table. Perhaps Dr. Brown was worried because Mary Jane had already birthed so many children, this one was affected by being one of so many. He examined John Charles. The boy was on the thin side, but lots of healthy kids were. That did not stop them from walking. He asked Mary Jane to set the child on his feet. The tissue paper on the table crackled. The doctor watched for any abnormalities, unusual weakness in the limbs that might indicate a problem with the boy's bones. Something that might keep the baby from becoming a toddler. But with his mother's fingers under his arms, John stood up on his little feet. A might unsteady, but that was from disuse. Puzzled, the doctor asked Mary Jane, what does he do at home? She told him, "Cry in his crib. Cry until Marcia picks him up. When she is home from school, she carries him around the house on her hip."

Mary Jane said, "I told Marcia to let John cry." She did not enforce the rule since she was always preoccupied with her other children and her household duties. Dr. Brown snorted, "Ain't nothing wrong with this boy. Tell your daughter," he might have said "that girl" — Dr. Brown was blunt like that — "Tell your daughter to put him down. Leave him on the floor. He'll get up and walk." And John Charles did just that.

In 1963, one summer Sunday, Andrew was on special duty at the Detroit Zoological Park. The Detroit Zoo was ten miles up from the river on Woodward Avenue in the community of Royal Oak. Detroit police officers received special patrol assignments at the Zoo, Belle Isle, Tiger Stadium and the State Fair as a thank you and appreciation for their service. It was a fun day for the officer to be out where people were enjoying themselves and problems, if any, were minimal and quickly solved. The zoo was a self-contained family space with a train running through it. Officers with family made it an event where their children could see their uniformed father "working." It reminded me of Polly talking about going with Isaac, her grandfather, when he "ushered" at the Billy Sunday tent revival.

So this one Sunday, Andrew was assigned to patrol the zoo and he took us along. He was having fun riding a bicycle around the zoo "working." Mary Jane was with the ten or eleven children. Marcia, who was fifteen-years-old, was the oldest present. We had a picnic — imagine carrying the food to feed all those people — a basket, an ice cooler, cookies and no special treat from the refreshment stand because there were too many of us for our father to afford to purchase food. Toward the end of the day, four-year-old John Charles went missing. He was child number eight and son number four, a tall, skinny kid, white-skinned with blond curly hair. He wanted a snow cone, one of those summer treats of shaved ice with red, blue or green syrup drizzled on it. The zoo was closing, and we needed to get packed up to go. This was not the time to lose one of her children. Mary Jane was frantic and as she charged back to the refreshment stand, Marcia was left in charge. She was the leader, the caretaker her younger siblings needed.

At the refreshment stand, Mary Jane said she was looking for her little boy; was he there? The refreshment stand worker, a white woman—they were all white working for the city in the suburbs—told her, "No little boy." What she meant was, no little *black* boy. Mary Jane left more worried than before, and suspicious.

She found Andrew. He was really working now, during the hour before the zoo closed, herding thousands of people moving to leave the park. This was what he will be doing for the next hour or so. She told him, John is missing. I think he was at that refreshment stand; get him. Andrew told his supervisor and the police shut down to one lane for exiting through one gate so they could see each person leaving. They were trying to keep John from wandering out of the zoo in the crowd, or someone taking him out. Andrew hightailed it to the refreshment stand like Mary Jane asked. He spoke as a man in blue with a badge, and a gun. He said, I am looking for a lost little boy. Have you seen him? The woman said, we have a little boy here, and she brought out John Charles, his little hand clutching a blue snow cone.

The woman did not believe the little white-skinned, blond boy belonged to the light-skinned dark-haired Negro woman. The refreshment stand lady thought John Charles was one of those Ashkenazi Jews with the blond hair of a curly, coarser texture.

Even though Marcia was not directly involved, her presence and the trust her mother instilled in her made it possible that the other children were safe and no other situations came out of this one. That is what a Little Mama does. Now add race to this need of a mother for help with her children. Being on the same side of the color line in America had clear advantages. Mary Jane had one of her children withheld from her because he did not look like he belonged to her. John Charles was a throwback to some white person in our family, a little whiteness here, a lot of it there. The advantage of being on the same side of the racial divide with your children was something most mothers fail to appreciate. Mary Jane and Alice could not take it for granted. Alice being with her son in public when he was a child was something she could do in Springfield because he looked white. She could be the mother to her young children in public. But when Bud, as a young man came to visit her at work in Canton at the Aultman hospital, she denied knowing him—like Peter denied Jesus. Alice essentially orphaned him again, left him standing there alone. She would not claim him. There was something very real at risk: her job. Here is where education came in again. Color can be mitigated with enough smiles and education.

In 1966, at the Chadsey commencement, colorful honor ropes fell over Marcia's bosoms onto her graduation gown. I remembered that about her graduation, but what I did not know was she only earned a C in Latin; it was the home economic classes that spiked her grade point average. As a result, no university enrollment in her immediate future. Marcia matriculated at Highland Park Junior College in the city of Highland Park. Highland Park had been an auto boomtown since when Henry Ford built his first assembly plant on Woodward Avenue, and then Chrysler made Highland Park their world head-quarters city. There were block after block of beautiful homes, some brick, all impeccable examples of the finest architectural design and the sturdiest construction offered in the state. The junior college was a grand limestone building that stretched an entire city block.

In defense of Marcia's accomplishment, it was said that High-land Park Junior College "was harder to get into than Wayne State."[3] Highland Park Junior College had its own radio station and a nursing program, but by 1966 half of the student body were black students. It was a good school in a rich community. After two years, Marcia transferred to Wayne State. She wanted to be a dietitian and a sorority girl. She got on a big pledge line of twenty-nine women. She led her line sisters in doing all the stuff the pledge club was asked to do, and did more than her share. The pledge period went over the term, and when grades came out hers were too low to qualify for membership. Marcia did not know where to draw the line and when to stop taking care of other people. She graduated from the university with a degree in accounting, but it did not happen in four years, it took much longer.

In 1968, while in college Marcia was hired at the National Bank of Detroit in the Cash Services department. That was where they counted bills and coins deposited each day. She worked the afternoon shift, 3:00 p.m. to midnight. Early on, Marcia was made supervisor. She knew how to tell people what to do, and had the demeanor to let them know she expected them to do it. She was comfortable with authority. She took care of her people. On Friday after work her people played cards, often at their supervisor's place. She ended up working at National Bank of Detroit for thirty years. When the bank was sold and in the process of closing, she was asked to stay on the job until they locked the doors for the last time. They needed her. The term they used was "essential personnel."

How patient my ninety-four-year-old mother was with my questions about our family dynamics, but sitting and talking with her, I got the impression that she had this conversation about Marcia before. Mary Jane's answers did not seem rehearsed, she just seemed resigned to the conversation, as though she knew the direction it was going. Mary Jane said she did not press Marcia into the Little Mama role. The situation, she said, was Marcia loved to cook. This was no doubt a big help to Mary Jane. The daughter of a half-Irish mother, Mary Jane cooked the same way. Three generations of women who only knew how to cook bland food married to men from a soul food world. Mary Jane was in the same situation at home as her grandmother, Alice, offering plain Irish fare. Marcia would be in a starring household role since people gravitate toward delicious food. Having been a fledging cook in the midst of Andrew's Georgia family, Marcia was nurtured with a taste for food with taste, and she was learning how to cook it. Even when she cooked white potatoes, they were not mashed. One time, Marcia cooked a five pound bag of potatoes into French fries for us.

The kitchen was on the way to everywhere else in the house: to the bathroom, to two bedrooms, to the basement and out the back door outside. She stood at the stove, over a cast iron skillet of hot grease frying potatoes. Our family did not have a deep fryer where a basket of potatoes could be lowered into a hot oil bath and lifted up to let the oil drain off before dumping the mess of them onto a paper towel-covered plate. What Marcia had to work with was a flipper utensil to turn the potatoes to brown on the other side. This was the same utensil used to flip pancakes, except pancakes cook in a smidgen of the hottest sizzling grease, unlike French fries. I know she burnt herself standing over the stove frying potatoes, so we could all sit down together and enjoy them like we were at McDonald's. We never went there because there were too many of us and we could not afford it.

Every time someone came past the kitchen, they took a French fry. Brown fingers, yellow fingers, white fingers snatching a fry or two or three from the plate. This went on for two hours. In the end all Marcia had to show for her time was one plate of French Fries. Maybe twenty fries in all, not enough to even uncap the ketchup bottle for.

Marcia babysat us while our parents went out every other Friday to take care of some business. The business was to cash Andrew's paycheck and pay bills. So who fed us lunch those Fridays? Marcia. Marcia popped popcorn and poured melted margarine over it. In winter, she stood over the stove stirring and stirring a pot of sugar, butter and chocolate to the hard-ball stage to create a pan of fudge. She baked a lot of Snickerdoodles — the round cookies rolled in cinnamon — during Christmas season and stored them in a tin. They were usually gobbled up before Christmas Eve. Many Christmases she spent her whole paycheck on gifts because the money Andrew budgeted was for food, clothes and the tree. Every year Mary Jane would try to temper her children's expectations for Christmas by saying, it will be a small Christmas this year. That meant gifts of slipper socks, then Marcia would start tying the festive bows on stacks of boxes, signing each gift tag with, "From Ms. Claus."

Today, mothers who can afford it have such help. They are called nannies, governesses or au pairs. Women who are paid to care for little children, a figure that has been captured on stage and film. Think of England's *Mary Poppins* who used magic to entrance the children into obeying, or *The Sound of Music* set in Austria. There an Austrian maid uses music to captivate the kids, and their widowed father. Think about Calpurnia in Harper Lee's novel, *To Kill a Mockingbird*.[4] Calpurnia is the housekeeper and cares for the children while the widowed father, Atticus Finch, works as an attorney. Childcare was a paid job in the home of wealthy people and it costs. Sometimes the helper can be encouraged with a good wage into staying with the family for the time it takes to raise a child to adult.

However in the U.S., society forced women into such roles, and in particular, black women, who were confronted by both sexism and racism. Besides facing employment discrimination, they were not allowed easy access to educational opportunities; or if educated, they were relegated to low-paying and often dirty jobs, so being a mother to someone else's child was considered a good job. It had benefits: Calpurnia's job provided her nephew access to a lawyer when he needed one. Ironically, in Alice's time, women who needed to work for money did not want to watch kids, they would rather be laundresses because they made more money. Childcare was a girl's job and through the years in black families it has continued to be a girl's job. Even on the television show *Black-ish*, where money is not an obstacle for the upper middle-class family with an advertising executive father and physician mother, the idea of a nanny was not introduced until season two.[5] What matters to black people is to know their caretakers personally; strangers not accepted.

Mary Jane needed help with her eleven younger children. It so happened that Marcia had her boots on the ground, to adopt an Army saying. She knew when and how to fulfill her duties as the oldest daughter.

In addition to Marcia and husband Andrew, Mary Jane's sister Patty and her husband Nathan, and her brother Sonny helped with the children. Neither Patty and Nathan, or Sonny had children of their own, so time with the big family of children was welcome. Holiday meals and fellowship bonded the family. Polly and Jimmy held Christmas and Easter dinner at their house every year, and after dinner, the kids trooped up the street to Patty and Nathan's house to listen to jazz and play pool. It could be said that, in total, Mary Jane's children had seven adults and one teenager raising them.

My father Andrew's siblings were responsible for an extensive family of their own. Consequently, we were not as close to them as my mother's family, but we had our traditions. Andrew's sister Lorraine took a special interest in Marcia, and in particular, for the Cinderella Pageant of big, beautiful black women. Mary Jane and Lorraine's daughter Amoret rented a hall for the whole family to have Thanksgiving dinner. Andrew and his brother decided that weddings and funerals should not be the only two regular avenues for family members to unite. So Uncle Tedde started an annual Humphries Family picnic. It was on the first Sunday in August on Belle Isle. The southern food for the picnic was delicious.

In 1994, thirty-three years after Alice died, Mary Jane's sister took inventory of the family heirlooms, including Alice's belongings. For the missal, Patty penned a note: "This prayer book once belonged to Ellen Stark Donlan — my great-grandmother." Alice left a legacy of love and determination that cast a halo over her mother as well. With the help of family, a mother can achieve great things with her children, even in the midst of racism and sexism. Following Polly's example of graduating high school in 1920, and aspiring to college, all of Mary Jane and Andrew's sons and daughters completed high school and went to college. Altogether, we earned eleven bachelor's degrees, and six advanced professional degrees. We worked in the areas of law, finance, education, health care, journalism, psychology, music, business, and politics. Mary Jane and Andrew would never have had that success with their offspring if they had not had a Little Mama in their oldest daughter, Marcia.

Fortunately, Marcia's advancement was not compromised by family obligations. She was able to go to college, and worked a job that she liked. She married twice and traveled the world, but she never had children of her own. She had already nurtured eleven younger siblings. Mary Jane's success as a mother stemmed from Alice. In 1913, she made a point about education and upheld a value many felt did not apply to little girls, especially black little girls. ⌘

Notes

1. Allan Nevins and Frank Ernest Hill. *Ford Expansion and Challenge 1915–1933* (New York: Charles Scribners & sons, 1957), 587.

2. Jone Johnson Lewis, "Comstock Law. *ThoughtCo,* June 14, 2018. Thoughtco. com/history-of-the-comstock-law-352947.

3. Aaron Foley, "From state-of-the-art to state takeover: The rise and fall of Highland Park Public Schools." MLive.com, February 2, 2012.

4. A popular vote judged it the "#1 Best-Loved Novel" in "The Great American Read, Results." PBS. Pbs.org/the-great-american-read/home. 2018.

5. *Blackish*, Season 2 episode 18, "Black Nanny" directed by Anton Cropper, featuring Tracee Ellis Ross and Anthony Anderson, aired March 23, 2016 (Los Angeles, CA: ABC Studios).

As young adults, Bud and Elizabeth found stable family life with Polly's children Mary Jane (left) and Patty in 1920s Detroit. *Courtesy of The Andrew J. and Mary Jane Humphries Foundation.*

John Henry's sisters were mainstays for Polly's children. Back row (l-r): Nellie and Pauline. Front row (l-r): Polly's children, Mary Jane, James, Jr., and Ellen Elizabeth. Standing: Nellie's son, William Browning Jr. *Courtesy of The Andrew J. and Mary Jane Humphries Foundation.*

Mary Jane was an outgoing and popular teenager on Detroit's West Side in 1940s Detroit. *Courtesy of The Andrew J. and Mary Jane Humphries Foundation.*

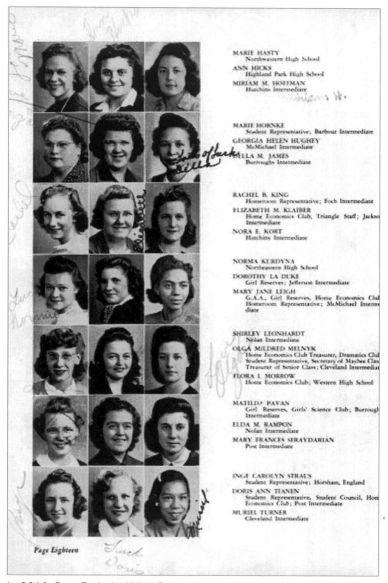

In 2014, Cass Technical High School honored alumna Mary Jane Leigh, class of 1942 (fourth row down). *Courtesy of The Andrew J. and Mary Jane Humphries Foundation.*

Mary Jane (l) spent the year 1944 in a tuberculosis sanitarium where she made friends with Marilyn Bryant (r). One year later Mary Jane's younger brother Sonny was admitted to the sanitarium with the same diagnosis. *Courtesy of The Andrew J. and Mary Jane Humphries Foundation.*

Mary Jane bragged that her beloved, Andrew John Humphries, was one of the best-looking young men living in Detroit's 1940s north-end neighborhood. *Courtesy of The Andrew J. and Mary Jane Humphries Foundation.*

In 1947 in Detroit, Mary Jane's marriage brought her into the Humphries family. Left to right: Lorraine, Andrew, Mary Jane, Theodore, sister-in-law Mary Lois, and mother-in-law Lula Mae. *Courtesy of The Andrew J. and Mary Jane Humphries Foundation.*

Mary Jane's growing family spent every Christmas at Polly's house. In 1959, from left to right: Derrick, Andrew, Dedria, Alice, Paula, James, Mary Jane, Marcia and John Charles. *Courtesy of The Andrew J. and Mary Jane Humphries Foundation.*

Mary Jane and Andrew J. Humphries and their brood in 1985 in Detroit. Back row (l-r): John, Mark, Kimberly, Alice, Pamela, Dedria, Paula, Gregory, Derrick, Andrew D. Front row (l-r(: James, William, Mary Jane, Andrew John, Marcia. *Courtesy of The Andrew J. and Mary Jane Humphries Foundation.*

Mary Jane at home in Detroit with her CT (Cass Tech) afghan, 2013. *Courtesy of The Andrew J. and Mary Jane Humphries Foundation.*

Mary Jane (r)with her personal NBA star, grandson Kristopher N. Humphries (l) in Detroit, 2015. *Courtesy of The Andrew J. and Mary Jane Humphries Foundation.*

CHAPTER 6

Dedria

CONSIDER THIS STORY ABOUT FAMILY TRADITION: A woman grew up seeing her mother cut off both ends of the beef roast before lifting it to put in her spacious pan to cook. One day, she asked her mother why she trimmed the ends of the roast. Did trimming make the meat cook faster, juicier or more flavorful? Her mother quickly answered, "I trim the beef before cooking because that's what my mother did." Not satisfied with that answer, the younger woman asked her grandmother, "Why do you cut off both ends of the roast?" Her grandmother replied, "I only had one pan that would fit in my oven, so I cut off both ends of the roast so it would fit in the pan."

This is the thing about families: we do what we see, no questions asked until we realize we do not know why we are doing what we are doing. That was true of the women in my family: we ate bland food, with the exception of sugar, a flavoring we craved. We also lived in cities, raised our children to read books, and relentlessly pursued a college education for them. But we did those things for the same reason as the mom cooking the roast, because our mothers did it. As for her daughter, that ultimately became an unsatisfying answer. And when I understood that I did not know why I did some things, I went back in time to a great-grandmother I hardly knew. It was a curiosity built up over many years, from the time I was a little girl until I became a mother. I found these women—Alice, Pauline, Polly, and Mary Jane—lived their lives in a way that benefited me.

A great part of myself is a culmination of their stories. I received the best of all the worlds they lived in: white and black, family and school, north and south, city and riverfront, and from horse and buggy to the automobile. I am an aftershock to the earthquake event of American race mixing. I am shaped by Pauline, who lived a black woman's life in a black family in Kentucky, Ohio and Michigan. I am the result of Polly, who tried to untangle a childhood of family dynamics complicated by race and economics. I am in part Mary Jane, known for her commitment to her thirteen children and their education. And while I did not dedicate a chapter to my oldest sister, Marcia, I benefited from her when she assumed some of the traditional responsibilities of Little Mama.

And then there was Alice, who my family rarely spoke of. Alice, who wrangled, politely enough, over culture with her colored sisters-in-law because they were the only family her children had. Her family did not want them or her. The mystery of Alice gnawed at me ever since I was a little girl because I needed to know her. When I found out about Alice leaving her children, my search for Alice's story was one way to validate my own story of leaving my children to pursue my education and career. I needed to know more about my family's matriarch, and how she affected my life.

ℰℭℛ

I WAS BORN THE THIRD CHILD and second daughter to Mary Jane and Andrew John Humphries on Friday, December 19, 1952. Ten days earlier, my mother had turned twenty-nine years old. My appearance was like the sun in that I was yellow-skinned, and my pate was smooth because I did not have any hair. My twenty-eight-year-old policeman father was happy because now he had a yellow-skinned child, and I remained a favorite his entire life. I was baptized at St. Cyprian's Episcopal church, and the photos taken that day show me wearing a long white christening gown. Both of my grandmothers, my mother's and my father's mothers, were delighted. Father Malcolm Dade sprinkled water on my bald head.

Growing up in the 1950s and 1960s, I was tall and skinny, petulant, unpredictable, and excitable. I was prone to accidents. I had to have my foot cut open to drain an infection after I stepped on a nail; I almost hung myself rushing down the basement steps into a wire clothesline. I burned the inside of my knee reaching for some thing behind the radiator, and burned the back of my hand reading a book on the ironing board. I got my front tooth knocked out when I ran into the back of a friend's head playing tag. During a game of hide and seek, I fell in the alley and cut my wrist. The shadow of a scar still falls across the tendons there.

Most things my parents wanted me to do I resisted, like piano lessons. After three teachers, my father gave up on me. I did not want to learn to play because my older brother and sister played. I never was a good Little Mama like my older sister Marcia, maybe because I was the selfish, second oldest daughter and was spoiled into thinking I could do what I wanted because I was light-skinned in a mostly brown family. If only I had gone along with the program, things might have been better for Marcia—as the saying "many hands make light work" leads us to believe—but I did not because I knew Marcia would do it all. I did not dare say "no" to requests that started, "Dedria, can you, would you," but I whined a lot because I did not understand why I had to help with the work of our large family. Mary Jane would direct me to watch my ten-years-younger baby sister Pamela. I protested and grumbled. My mantra was, those are not my kids. When I took that sweet child out of the house on what I considered to be "my time," I often marched her down the block to my best friend's house and left her with my friend's little sister who thought Pam was cute. "Effie," I would say, "when you tire of her, take her home," and off I went with my friend. Mary Jane needed help, but I was not it.

I was child number three, with my ten younger siblings born after me one and two years apart, like stair steps. I just wanted to do what I wanted to do, namely read and entertain people. I could do these things as long as I got my work done. I did not mind doing housework, but because of the competition for my mother's attention, I felt a bit like a half-orphan. My father paid attention to me, but when he felt testy, he would say, not directly to me but to all of his children, "You want attention? I'll give you attention," and he would threaten to get out his razor strap. In retrospect, it seemed harsh, but that was the way the Greatest Generation parented us Baby Boomers. Finally, one of my brave siblings made that black belt disappear.

Time with my mother was precious. Not only did Mary Jane have thirteen children to care for, she had friends and family she needed to help, whenever she could. She never missed being present in time of death. An occasion fraught with emotional landmines, she secured and maintained bonds by showing up to the bereaved home to clean the kitchen, washing and drying and putting away dishes, and taking the dish towels home to wash. I do not know how I started going with her on these compassionate visits (maybe I was invited because I was no use at home), but I continued because the travel gave me time to be alone with her. Even if as a little girl I did not know how Polly, Bud and Elizabeth suffered from their mother's absence, I understood. Only Polly realized they needed to cooperate with Alice because refusing to make the best of it made a bad situation worst. Their mother only could do so much.

One early death that reached the depth of our familial bond was that of my cousin, Michael Humphries. He was the oldest son of my father's brother, Theodore, called Tedde, and his wife, Mary Lois High. There is a cute photo of the two Humphries brothers standing on the steps of the Detroit Institute of Arts on Woodward Avenue with their two toddlers, Derrick and Michael, both born in 1947. In 1964, when Derrick was riding up I-94 to the University of Michigan, Michael enrolled at Wayne State University in Detroit. Michael had dark hair. His piercing eyes examined the world from behind his glasses. He created big canvas paintings and polished wood sculptures. During the 1960s, the Vietnam War era, Derrick joined ROTC at Michigan, and fulfilled his duty with Army camp two weeks each summer, and after graduation gave the Army a few months of active duty. Michael joined the Navy, and went into the world to die. The news put our household in a tizzy and my mother was at Aunt Mary Lois and Uncle Tedde's house every day doing what she could to help and comfort them. I went with her. It took the Navy forever, it seemed, to get Michael's body back to Detroit. When it arrived with an escort of seamen there was glass or clear plastic over the opening of his casket. Mary Lois was living a mother's worst nightmare, burying a child.

Mary Jane was a talker, but in these death situations she said as little as possible because death was a minefield of fear and anger. It was far too easy to say something terribly wrong, or something right that was interpreted terribly wrong. There really was no way to walk back words spoken during a time of death. People cling to them as they would to a life jacket. I wonder if something like this happened at John Henry Johnson's death; if the issue of the baby's care was prematurely introduced and the echo of those words kept Alice and her sisters-in-laws from finding peace.

During my childhood, communication was a void in a family that mostly did not "kiss and tell." But to not know Alice, a woman who lived amongst us, who my mother wailed over? How do I account for that? Why did I not long for her?

I was squarely on the black side of the family. I knew Pauline. I would go to visit her with Polly or Mary Jane. Pauline lived a few blocks away from St. Cyprian's on Stanford Street. In my lifetime, she was always old. Like most old people's homes, hers was suffocating. Visitors crossing the threshold smashed into a heat wall. In her greeting, she referred to herself in the third person the way that U.S. Senator Bob Dole made famous. Her voice grown reedy with the living of four generations, she said, "I'm so glad you came to visit Aunt Pauline." She kept the furniture covered with plastic and to preserve monuments acquired from hard, humbling work. I sat on the sofa, my legs stuck to the plastic, and stared at the cut glass candy dish. My hope was someone had replaced the stale hard mints since the last Sunday. I never thought to bring any candy as a gift. My job was to sit. Within earshot, she never said anything about Alice. Pauline was not a story-telling old lady. If the conversation drifted that way, there was always something on a high kitchen cupboard shelf a tall girl like me could be sent to get. I do not remember Alice and Pauline ever together in the same room. And because one was white and the other black, I never connected them.

Polly's cousin Laura was very close to our family. She renamed Alice Cecilia as Mary Jane. Laura lived in the same Springwells neighborhood as our family, and Mary Jane often sent me with my two younger sisters to give Laura something or the other. She called my mother frequently, but did not seem to understand how super busy a mother of thirteen children was all the time. Laura wanted to talk, not listen. Sometimes, the phone handset would be off the base and as one of us started to hang it up, Mary Jane would say, "Don't hang it up, Laura is talking." And sure enough, when you put the receiver to your ear, you could hear this woman chattering. When the phone rang at our house, and I answered it, my "Hello" was met with her high-pitched voice. "Hello, Debbie?" My name was not *Debbie*. Debbie was the daughter of the white people Laura worked for. I knew this because the white blouses and navy shorts I wore in summer were hand-me-down camp shirts and shorts labeled in hand stitching with the name, "Debbie." My name is *Dedria*, a form of Deirdre, a Celtic, that is, an Irish name. It means sorrow. There was no more direct reminder than my name of Laura's uncle's Irish American wife. It could have been why Laura avoided my name.

I was part of a cohort of school children in Detroit bussed to school out of my neighborhood for racial balance to fulfill *Brown v. The Board of Education*. I caught the bus at the corner and rode twenty minutes through the neighborhood to other stops picking up kids, and then out of the neighborhood and past Chadsey High School on up to Clippert. I did not like it there and the Polish students did not like me and my friends. It was the only place where I got called a "nigger." It happened on the playground, and came out of the mouth of this white girl. After one year, I was released from that hell and I walked to Munger Junior High across the street from where my uncle worked at police precinct six, McGraw station. In time I went to Chadsey, which was next door to Munger. I was elected vice president of my senior class, won the Betty Crocker Homemaker of Tomorrow award for my graduation class. It was a recognition program my mother was responsible for installing at our high school. Me and all of my sisters won it by acing a written test.

I had always wanted to be a writer. I wanted to write books because I read a lot of them; but at the time I did not take my book writing goal seriously. As a grade school student, I entered a writer's contest and won tickets for my father and me to see *One Hundred and One Dalmatians* (1961). He was so pleased he bought tickets for the whole family. When I wrote to my uncle in Cincinnati, he said my letters sounded like I was sitting next to him talking.

Polly showed my writing to her friend, who thought I was a good writer. Was it Virginia Hamilton? My grandmother knew her, but I never met her or communicated directly with the celebrated children's author. As a staff writer of my high school newspaper, I won an award for humorous writing. On the SAT college entrance examination, I scored high in verbal ability and small liberal arts colleges outside of Michigan, mostly in Ohio, wrote to encourage me to look at them. But that was a type of college my family was unfamiliar with. No one knew how to help me get there. People did not want to interfere if my father was not for it, and he was not. We were a big public university family, meaning Wayne State University and more recently the University of Michigan, 45-minutes west on I-94. Going away to college was a new thing for our family and it did not include the daughters. I did what I could to make the best out of a bad situation, but my next stop was motherhood.

If black boys are adorable until they grow tall, black girls are clever until they turn curvy. I was eighteen, graduated from high school in January 1971, enrolled in a Wayne State University Upward Bound program set to start in summer, still living at home, working as a receptionist for a small family-owned business where the patriarch commented every single day about my breasts. That happened every day, twice a day. I could not quit because Humphries do not quit, so I lost my voice, could not do the job of answering the phone and got fired. After that I was a volunteer at the Head Start program, and then I quit that. Next was a terse conversation between me and Mary Jane. We talked standing up. I was pregnant. She wanted to know what I was going to do. Get married?

No. I barely knew the man; my family did not know him at all. We met at my brother Derrick's apartment on Wayne State University's campus when my brother was in law school. I was a high school senior, and that night I was out with Derrick and Marcia. I wore a peach colored dress, a girly style that had a tie string belt looped a couple of times around my waist, Grecian goddess style. The man was a friend of a friend of my brother's, and the two of them stopped by my brother's apartment that night. He was older than my brother, who was six years older than me. I gave him our home phone number and agreed to no particular kind of a date.

If it had been the nineteenth century, it would have been a match. He was older and could take care of me. He took care of me alright, in a motel room rented by the hour. Never a concert. Sometimes dinner and a screw. He worked at a General Motors auto plant in the next county and lived in that same county with his mother. I never met her, but I was at their house once and met a school teacher friend of his who could not understand what his friend was doing with this girl half his age. I was young enough to be my lover's child. He told me that.

We were never a match. I knew that. And he went away as soon as I started college that summer. But by then I was pregnant, and the procedure I underwent to end it did not work. They did not call them abortions back then; it was against the law. A physician could lose their medical license and go to jail. The procedure I had was meant to cause a miscarriage, a "natural" abortion.

"Well, what then?" Mary Jane wanted to know. I was about six months pregnant.

"Give it up for adoption."

Silence. Mary Jane just looked at me.

Maybe I said it a little cavalierly, maybe I was like one of those bad women from the nineteenth century. Back then, the government and church officials punished unwed mothers by making them suffer the world, but there I was, a college student who could not support myself, not to mention a baby.

Perhaps somewhere in the back of my mind, I clung to the romantic notion of an orphanage and orphans rescued by rich people (Little Orphan Annie and Daddy Warbucks; or Heidi and Clara). Perhaps I was thinking that since my great-grandmother put her children in an orphanage (at this point that basic fact was all I knew) that might work. I was in a better position than Alice; I was in college. Later I would know my child, visit it, and get to know their children. Just like Alice.

Stupid innocence, borne of ignorance. I would have been repeating history. My father also knew the saying, but maybe he knew it as philosopher George Santayana said it, "Those who cannot remember the past are condemned to repeat it."

My father had his own family history that he regretted. His younger sister became pregnant before marriage, and her first daughter was born and raised by a grandmother in Georgia. When the granny died, the baby, now a teenager, came to Detroit to join her mother, her mother's husband and three other children. I remember how my soft-speaking southern cousin simply showed up, a stranger who looked just like my aunt. Now my father was faced with a similar situation with his daughter. My father said, "Everyone should know their family," including this little baby boy, his first grandchild and first grandson. My parents decided my child would come home from the hospital with me. What a gift from my parents. My son was born November 30, 1971. He was healthy at birth, weighed more than seven pounds. The abortion inducing procedure had no effect, though it was a wonder he had all his fingers and toes. I named my baby boy from a list of names presented by my dashiki-wearing brother. I picked Diallo Kobie, which is African for "straight-forward warrior."

In 1971, with their thirteenth and youngest child four years old and almost in school, my father, Andrew, provided me and my infant a home, and my mother cared for him while I went to college. She took him into her heart as a baby and she was his center. It was clear to Diallo that she was "Mama" and he called her that. Me, he called "DD." But my youngest brother, Mark, who was six years older than Diallo, could not tolerate the confusion. One day, Mark pulled Diallo aside, and pointed to Mary Jane dressed in a sensible housedress. He said, "This is *my* mother." And he pointed to me wearing the gray and white hot pants jumpsuit. "And, that is *your* mother." Diallo has never called me Mama, but he started calling Mary Jane, "Grandma."

I started Wayne State University in summer of 1971, in an Upward Bound program called the Project 350. Project 350 divided 350 students into two groups: 250 were students who might have gone to college, but needed support. Maybe education was not a core value in their family: their grade point average was marginal, or test scores a little low, or money to pay tuition scarce. I was in that last category. The other 100 students had the potential to go to college but had not proven it. They lacked academic accomplishment in most areas, but at the last moment wanted to go to college. The university called our admission, "Experimental." I was there despite having scored well on the SAT, so excellent in the verbal section that small liberal arts colleges tried to recruit me. So instead of me taking a spot at a college where my talent and aptitude and attitude may have fit in better, I repeated what had already happened in our family. People may have thought that I stayed home because I had a child, but the truth of matter is that I was home because Wayne State University was my only choice. My father did not want his daughter to go away to school. At the big public university, I caught the bus to class, scuffled to pay tuition, pledged a sorority, lived at home. The Project 350 director, Marjorie Edwards, and her staff, gave me the support I needed. I worked in her office editing the Project 350 newsletter, and I pledged Delta Sigma Theta sorority, which gave me a lesson in humility and inducted me into a community of black college-educated women.

Early on I had some tortured feelings about my family situation. I truly resented at one point Mary Jane's dear relationship with my son. So I went to see a psychologist at the university's counseling office. I did not mention this at home. Seeing someone about your feelings and other unseeable processes was tantamount to admitting to being crazy. One could be physically ill, but the inability to deal with reality by cursing it, and seeking help to sort out feelings was verboten. But I went because I was grown and did not have to ask anyone. They assigned me to this mental health worker, a white man. I told him about my problem. What he was most concerned about was that I was not married and had a child. He said, "Let's consider that you have been married, let's approach it like that." Then he said to remember that the current situation was not forever, my mother was helping me get to another place in life. But it bugged me that I was counseled to believe that had I been married to my son's father. And then it made me think: while women around the world have made great strides toward equality and opportunity in the past century, prevailing social attitudes still mirrored historical values and behaviors. I did not go talk to him again.

I had some interesting jobs as a college student. The most interesting was a science demonstrator at the pilot of the Detroit Science Center. This pet project of Dexter Ferry, scion of the Ferry Seed Company, was located in a former car garage on Forest Avenue nearby to Wayne State University. My uniform of a light blue jacket sported a big question mark on the back and two words, "Ask Me." I roamed the space filled with science presentations, facts, experiments in biology, chemistry, physics, geography and geology, but nothing pointing out the misnomer of the Detroit River. (It is a strait, a deep water channel between two great bodies of water.) There was a chicken incubator where fertile eggs hatched under a heat lamp. In the science center theater, I demonstrated scientific principles, showing for instance, the properties of laser light. The show happened in a darkened theater with me spraying aerosol hair spray in the air, and pointing the laser gun at that. The laser light showed up as a red line as it reflected on the particles in the air. The job was within walking distance of Wayne. I loved that job, and they loved me. Dexter Ferry told me one time I reminded him of his wife. I do not know if that was a veiled invitation, but I did not take it as such and continued to enjoy my job. I thought I was being hired for my skills, which I worked very hard to attain. Years later I ed that one of those skills was appearance, my "light" skin.

At Wayne, I was an English major. I took literature classes, especially African American literature classes. I had studied French from junior high into high school, reading Alexandre Dumas' *Le Comte de Monte-Cristo* (1844) over and over again, but at Wayne State University I switched to Kiswahili, a language of eastern Africa. I lived at home for college because I was a mother, but I still came alive to myself and a world outside of my family when 1960s militancy settled into 1970s normal: frustration with the government, natural hairstyles called Afros, names changed to multi-syllable African ones, and a switch in focus from European studies to African. I had a lot of fun back then but I needed to start thinking about how to earn a living for me and my son. I was a senior, I still loved writing, and I still wanted to write books, but first I had to learn how to write. Journalism was the quickest way I could earn money while writing every day. So I enrolled in a journalism class as an elective.

To get information, I had to talk to people and I was shy. I did not like the class, but I muddled through it. And then I took a second journalism class and dropped it. I quickly realized I did not like journalism as a topic to study, but as a job it was interesting. I became a freelancer for the weekly newspaper serving the black community, the *Michigan Chronicle*, where Longworth Quinn Sr. was the editor-publisher. I wrote interviews and event stories, and was paid ten dollars a story. Later, Mr. Quinn let me work production for an hourly wage on Saturday mornings. I took Diallo with me and he watched cartoons on the television in Mr. Quinn's office while I wrote party stories and read page proofs. Mr. Quinn refused to hire me full-time saying, "You will go on to do other things." I had to because I needed to make money, but in order to do it, I needed to get into big newspaper action. Detroit was a major media market, but I was not good enough to get on with the *Detroit Free Press* or *The Detroit News*, plus I had an English degree, not a journalism degree.

After I graduated Wayne in 1976, I wanted to go to work for the City of Detroit. During college, I had been a seasonal employee within the city, working over term breaks for departments with peak workloads, like the Elections Commission and the Water Department.

One year after graduation I worked steadily for the City, and applied but was not offered full-time employment, so I went back to school. I thought I would switch from English and go into business school, but at the last minute I did not take the entrance examination. Instead, I applied to the English program's two-year master's degree program. One day, realizing that I had not heard "yay" or "nay" from them, I went to the graduate advisor's office to inquire about it in person.

The director told me, "I just sent you a rejection letter."

"Pardon me?"

"Yes, you do not have the qualifications for the master's program because your foreign language was Swahili. You need a Romance language, French, Spanish, Italian, or German."

"What? Kiswahili satisfied the English department requirements to earn a bachelor's degree, and now I cannot be admitted to the English master's program with that same degree? That does not make sense."

After talking about it for a while, the graduate advisor agreed with me. He admitted me on the spot, with the understanding that I would have to pass the language examination in some other language. I said, French, naturally. By the time I was going to graduate school, I had two children. I mentioned my plan to my uncle, my father's brother. He said, "Your job is to take care of your children." This came from the son of a widow who worked as a seamstress in a dry cleaner to support her four children. Perhaps he misunderstood the depth of her struggle, with help for widowed mothers being only slightly better during the 1930s than in 1913, because social progress moved slowly after Teddy Roosevelt 's White House conference on children, and the Great Depression came on fast.

As a graduate student, I continued with the *Chronicle,* getting better as a writer and earning grocery money. I got my biggest raise ever from Mr. Quinn, 50 percent, going from a fee per story of ten dollars to fifteen dollars per story. I was rich! At Christmas 1978, I was busy making arrangements to move me and my son from my parents' Springwells house. I had applied for an apartment in one of Wayne's few residential buildings, the Chatsworth Annex, a beautiful three story brownstone in the post-war New York City-style, next door to a tall blond brick building, the Chatsworth, where faculty lived. They accepted me. In a rare move, Mary Jane was in Pasadena, California, enjoying watching one of my younger brothers play for Michigan in the Rose Bowl football game. Derrick and Marcia went. I had been left behind because I was broke. I stayed home with the little kids and introduced them to kiddie wine on New Year's Eve. I never had any money. Before I was a true adult, my earnings were already allocated to the care of my child. I needed more money, and my brother set me up with an interview with Congressman Charles C. Diggs, of the Thirteenth Congressional District. Diggs was a long-time congressman. He beat an incumbent and won his first election in 1954. He went on to distinguish himself as a staunch opponent of apartheid in South Africa, when he was the chairman of the sub-committee on Africa of the Committee on Foreign Affairs. And he was a founding member of the Congressional Black Caucus.

I was hired as a part-time communications director at his field office on Woodward Avenue on the North End. I went to a fantastic orientation at the Library of Congress in Washington to learn how to use the library for information. I represented him at meetings in the district, and at a speech by Black Muslim Minister Louis Farrakhan. I collected information, so I could tell him how he should think about an issue, but the most important information Diggs wanted, I could get just by calling the City-County Building to the mayor's office. Diggs always went along with Mayor Coleman Young on district issues. I knew the Mayor's position by re-reading the stories I wrote about him because I was still writing freelance for the *Chronicle*.

By the time I went to work in the Thirteenth Congressional District, Diggs was under indictment for mail fraud. He was accused in March 1978 of taking kickbacks from employees' salaries. I came on board a month or so before he was convicted on October 7, 1978. He gave one interview before going to the federal penitentiary, and it was with me. His part-time communications staff person was the only news reporter he talked to. We talked in the Woodward Avenue office, if the whispering Mr. Diggs did could be called talking. When the story appeared in the *Chronicle*, the *Detroit Free Press* editors were so angry over the scoop, they called me out by name on their editorial page. Obviously, the editors did not know or care about how the black community worked because the *Chronicle* readership had no problem with the story at all. After Congressman Diggs went to prison, the whole staff worked for the Speaker of the House of Representatives. Then former Recorder's Court Judge George W. Crockett Jr. won election to the seat in November 1980, and he let me go.

In January 1979, one semester into my master's program, I moved away from home at age twenty-six. That fall, I finished one year in the master's program and applied for the Publishing Institute. This was a month-long summer course in book editing offered at the University of Denver in Colorado. It was directed by Elizabeth Geiser, who worked in New York City for the Detroit-based publishing company, Gale Research. Gale paid all Publishing Institute expenses for a Detroiter, and provided a paid internship upon completion of the course. I was admitted and with Gale's support went to Denver. I loved the city, the private university, the mountains, and the people from all over the world who attended the course. My sister Paula brought my son Diallo to Denver, and we all went roller skating in the park. Their photo was taken and published on the front page of the *Denver Post* newspaper. Diallo enjoyed the perks of being the child of a working mom. Neither I nor Alice forgot our children.

I remember telling a new friend at the Publishing Institute, a woman who had just graduated from Pomona College in California, that I thought I would be getting married when I returned home. My beloved was a man I had met three separate times already.

Michael David Barker was born on August 28, 1952 in Detroit, the first child of Sudie Eliza Jane Davis and her husband, Jesse James Barker. Michael's mother was a native Detroiter, while his father was originally from Chicago. They met in Detroit at Miller High School. Sudie's father, George Davis, was run out of the south by some good ole white boys who did not like his "bad" attitude toward them. Jesse's folks were from Chicago. Jesse was killed in the Korean War as a U.S. soldier when his wife was pregnant with their second child, and Michael was one and a half years old. She delivered a girl on December 14, 1953 and named her Janet Jessica. Sudie bought a house on Detroit's West Side with her survivor's benefit from the U.S. Army.

As Sudie's children grew older, she took a job at General Motors' Cadillac division where most of the adults in their large extended family worked. Michael was smart, but a poor student in high school which was not helped when the State of Michigan Department of Transportation condemned their house and the entire neighborhood to build I-96. The city already was cut east-west by I-94 and north-south by I-75. This new freeway shadowed Grand River Avenue. Michael was a student at Northwestern, the Detroit high school with its military tradition signified by the cannon out front. Unlike in Mary Jane's era, the Northwestern student body was almost completely black, but this was not the case with the high school nearby to his mother's new house. She moved the family to northwest Detroit nearby to the suburb of Southfield and Northland, the new shopping mall. The move put Michael and his sister in the district of Henry Ford High School. Michael balked on enrolling. He stayed at Northwestern until he got kicked out for instigating a black power activity. He spent junior and senior year at Ford and graduated in 1970. His SAT scores prompted several colleges to contact him about attending, and he matriculated at Ferris State University in Big Rapids, Michigan, way northwest of Detroit where it was very cold, real Michigan. After one year, he returned to Detroit and enrolled at Wayne State University.

I first met Michael hanging around with the campus newspaper editor and black politicos we both knew. Our relationship took shape over talks about books and writing. I graduated and lost contact with him, then met him again at a Christmas party, lost contact again, and finally during the year when I was trying to get a job with the City of Detroit, we reconnected. We were both working for the Water Department at the Water Board building downtown. I was still a temporary employee, but he had a full-time job. We married on June 28, 1980. I married him because I loved him and I was pregnant, again.

Our daughter was born November 19, 1980. A beautiful brown girl child. We let Diallo name her, Terri Nicole.

And I got these children. First child at age nineteen. So stereotyp ical for working-class people: graduate high school, get pregnant; support yourself with a job that was dead-end for all but the most determined. Because when a young woman has a child sucking on her breast, society says, all is right with the world. Then I was mar- ried with two children, but if I had to be a homemaker, I was going to be Mom Manager. I did not have to always be there to make sure my children were okay. My husband's trusted cousin, Lucille, took care of one-year-old Terri, and my mother continued helping to raise ten-year-old Diallo, who spent weekends at her house in the Spring- wells subdivision. I went back to school in 1981, got an academic teaching assistantship, and finished my course work in 1983.

At the end of the academic year, in June 1983, I went to California for the summer, leaving my children at home. It was an opportunity for me to spend summer in San Francisco, but also to get on firm footing to do the work I wanted to do: writing. My mother, nor her mother had ever left their young children. Mary Jane could not take a bath without one of us asking, "Where you going, Mama?" But my Irish great-grandmother put her young children in an orphanage, so she could work, a move never discussed in our family. In some ways she was so modern, and there was so much I did not know.

I was going to Berkeley, California to attend the Summer Program for Minority Journalists (SPMJ) at the University of Berkeley, Califor- nia. This was a ten-week program funded by major American news media organizations and run by the esteemed African-American journalists Robert Maynard and his wife Nancy Hicks, and LeRoy Aarons, with a rotating staff of other prestigious journalists, like Les Payne, Vern Smith and Jeanne Fox-Alston. The purpose was to train journalists of color and counter major media's claim that the pau- city of journalists of color was due to not being able to find anyone qualified. During the summer training program, I would go through a placement and interview process and start a job with a newspaper in fall 1983. I had sent in my clips from the *Michigan Chronicle,* and filled out the application. It asked, how many dependents do you have? When I stopped to think about it, the answer was obvious. I wrote "0." My two children were not my dependents. They depended on my husband. He worked full-time for the City of Detroit. I was in graduate school. The training program gave me a stipend, so we could afford it. Later someone asked me about that "0" and I said, the competition was steep: twelve applicants for each slot. Would they pick me if they knew I had two children? People worry about kids. They fret about who is going to care for the children. They are skeptical if mom can do her job and care for her children. They do not understand how a mother can find someone to manage their care while she worked. They did not "get" mothers like me and Alice.

Young people dream of California, land of perpetual sunshine and youth. Cali. "Look at California," crooned Frankie Beverly. "It never rains in southern California," sang the R&B group Tony! Toni! Toné!. Most people attribute this phrase to author and newspaper editor, Horace Greeley, "Go west, young man," a seeker's journey, what new-agers held as the ultimate path. I was already on the mother-hood path, squarely on it and yet, I was jetting off to California. My husband, son, daughter and my mother came to see me off. This was back in the day when visitors could go to the gate. We walked through the terminal, and made small talk while, behind the plate glass window, a tractor tugged my plane up to the jetway. The silver jet outside was going to wing me to San Fran, and then after a short jog across the Bay, I would be at the University of California, Berkeley.

At the airport departure gate, my mother looked a little stern, a lot worried. I was leaving two children to go to California, a far-away, fun land. Mary Jane had been to Pasadena. She was not thrilled to see me board the jet to "Cali-funland-fornia," leaving my husband and children behind. My husband of not quite three years must have wondered, why is she going? Is she coming back? Our toddler daughter hung on to her father like a little monkey. She probably cried when I boarded the plane. I do not know. I took my seat.

My husband and his mother took care of our girl, and my mother and father took care of my eleven-year-old son; he was more her son than mine. It worked out, as far as I could judge from the vantage point of Berkeley, California. The year 1983, was the era of Michael Jackson's block-busting hit album, *Thriller*. It was well before the age of cell phones, so I was not in contact 24/7. Thank God. I loved my family, but I had other dreams. Was my fate to be the same as my mother's? Her rather routine dream to be a nurse deferred by one bodily condition, and then another. First, at the physical for admission to nursing school she was diagnosed with tuberculosis and sent off to the sanatorium for one lonely year. Then upon emerging, her boyfriend was back from Europe and World War II and she got pregnant and married. That was the end of school for her.

Mine was a young person's trip, but at age thirty-one I was a young wife married less than three years, and mother of two, the youngest one two years old. Perhaps I was unfeeling toward my children, but consider Alice Walker, author of the novel, *The Color Purple*. (1982). Her daughter, Rebecca, told radio show host Diane Rhem that in her divorce decree, Alice Walker negotiated custody on a yearly basis. One year "on" as a mother, and the next year "off." During the "on" year, if Rebecca got sick and could not go to school or camp, her mother set her up on the sofa with blankets, water, juice, whatever, and television. Author mom headed out the door to her writing shack, bidding her child adieu. "See you at lunch."[1] It seems even one-half child of one's own can be too much for some writers.

The Summer Program for Minority Journalists set me up with an interview with a newspaper in rural Illinois, one hundred miles south of Chicago. That was a first for me. I flew to Chicago's O'Hare airport in a jet and then I rode the bus around and around and around, for so long I thought they were driving the six of us passengers to this town, Danville. Danville? It sounded like a place where I might meet Barney Fife; it sounded like the place Jed Clampett had left behind. In enough time to have driven to Danville, the bus pulled up to a small airplane with propellers. The captain greeted us, and the co-pilot carried my bag on board. I was assigned a window seat, but then I noticed every seat was a window seat. The fuselage was so narrow that from the center aisle I could stretch both arms and touch either side. The plane took off and it felt like the first attempts at Kitty Hawk. Then it started raining and storming. Thunder and lightning rocked the little plane from side to side. That was flying. That ride convinced me I do not like that kind of flying. I prefer sitting in big living room jets with cushy seats, and watching a movie with earphones on. Back on the ground, I had a good interview with the publisher and editor of the *Commercial-News*. The only problem was when it was over, I had to do the trip in reverse.

After that I returned to California and watched my colleagues land jobs with the *Sacramento Bee, Santa Ana Register, Bakersfield Californian* in California, and with the *Oregon Statesman Journal,* the *Des Moines Register, Middletown Times Herald-Record, Milwaukee Journal, Colorado Springs Sun, Hartford Courant,* and the *Greensboro News-Record.* I was disappointed to be going to, by my standard, a po'dunk town. With a 30,000 population, Danville was only as big as my neighborhood in Detroit, but it was, I learned during my research on Alice, six times bigger than Lawrenceburg's population of 5,000, which she left to go to work as a maid among 300,000 people in Cincinnati. In one way, I was living her life, in reverse.

In September 1983, I started my first professional writing job as a staff writer on the *Commercial-News* daily newspaper in Danville, Illinois, an eight hour drive from Detroit. Outside of my husband and two children, my co-workers comprised my entire community. My neighbors, and my friends were my black colleagues. All of us lived in the same apartment complex away from the core city, one mile past the last cow pasture. The managing editor, Chuck Carpenter, directed us there. He was a good ol' boy from West Virginia, a self-avowed redneck. Six of us journalists of color from all over the nation arrived about the same time to work on the *Commercial-News*: one black man each in photography and sports, one black woman on the copy desk, an Asian woman worked on the news desk, and me in features. The newspaper's bureau was located in a farming community and that was where the Mexican-Arab guy worked, among the migrant workers, because he spoke Spanish. Chuck spread us around, one to every section. Our Affirmative Action group could have put out the paper ourselves.

I usually ate in the lunchroom where I watched a skinny white guy eat his sandwich of thin white bread spread with a strip of peanut butter, or at the downtown Chinese restaurant, always ordering wonton soup. One day, however, Alvin Reid, the black sports writer from St. Louis, said, "Let's do lunch." I piled into the car with my friends. Getting around downtown Danville could be a trial, especially in the fall, during harvest time. The 1920s limestone newspaper building sat off the main downtown artery, which was blocked in an attempt to create a mall. To get to the restaurant we had to skirt around that and then cross six sets of train tracks serving the grain elevator. Those tracks were wider than the street they crossed. Crossing the tracks, we were jostled to the sound track of "phoo-towel, phoo-towel, phoo-towel," a breath escaped from my body each time the tires hit the track. Returning from lunch, traffic on the street slowed and then stopped short of the grain elevator company. We sat there watching cars stacking up from behind and to the side. Ahead a train departing the grain elevator property blocked the view. It was a long freight train that had delivered corn for storage. The track cleared. I felt the car shift forward in readiness, but the gates stayed down. Then another train appeared. It was going in the opposite direction as the first train. This second train entered the grain elevator property.

Editorial staff were salaried, but I could hear a mental clock ticking. This is how I imagined it would look when our black contingent trooped in late from lunch: irresponsible darkies. Plus, Alvin hunched over the steering wheel, anxious about being on time for an interview back at the office. Click, click, click, his fingernails danced on the steering wheel. The second, long freight train cleared, but the gates stayed down. And next I was seeing freight cars again. A third train. Alvin rolled down his window, pitched his head, shoulder, arm and hand out the window, shook his fist and exploded. "Call your congressman. There's a law against that. They cannot hold up the road for more than eight minutes. Keep us waiting like we have nothing else to do." He gestured to other drivers to let him through and when enough space in the next lane opened, he pulled the car out of the lane into a careening u-turn.

My surprise was monumental. How did he know that there were laws regulating trains blocking a street? An education in St. Louis included that? I was from Detroit, and did not know about power struggles between the grain elevator trains and cars on the street. I did not know this about the Midwestern United States, the bread basket of America, where I had lived my entire life. That was added to knowing nothing about rivers. I bet Alice was surprised by some things in the Ohio River Basin where she lived her entire life, as well. Things such as how marriage between blacks and whites could be legal, but not accepted, so no marriage license for her and John Henry.

In Danville, police officers did not know I was a police officer's daughter, unfortunately. One Saturday afternoon I was driving my family in my 1980 Honda Civic, an early model of what is no longer a tiny car. At the intersection, I intended to turn right, but my husband said, "You might want to go straight across." He jutted his chin to the police car across the intersection facing us. Because I am from a Detroit police family, I laughed. "I'm macho. I'm not afraid of the police." And I turned right. The cop car fell in behind me. Immediately, the lights burst on. I pulled over.

I am nothing if not courteous to police officers. When the officer arrived at my window, I looked up to see a beefy white man in blue. "What is the problem, officer?"

He explained that our car had a Michigan plate on the front and an Illinois plate on the back. I mentioned the new law allowing for only one license plate on the back and whatever you wanted on the front. "Not a state plate," he said. The front was only for vanity, or fun plates, like "I Love (heart) Michigan." He showed me his pink palm. "May I see your driver's license?"

When he came back to my window, he asked me to step out of the car. There was a warrant for my arrest; Detroit said I had an unpaid speeding ticket.

I protested. I paid that ticket. Really, I did. He put me in the car anyway. Now, I needed bail money.

ATM cards were new, and wo did not havo ono. Miohacl found Leisa Richardson, my friend the copy editor, at home down the street. She had an ATM card and $50 in her account that she loaned me so I could get out of jail.

Monday morning I had to tell Chuck. He said thanks; that explained why my name was on the police blotter.

At about the one-year mark, in May 1984, I got pregnant. We were still in Danville. And I was disappointed since finally it seemed that I was at last on my way with my career. Michael loved spending time with the kids and seeing how far he could stretch my meager paycheck. He bought beer, Milwaukee's Best, that cost $1.50 per six pack. That was 1984. I did not earn much, but we had decent health benefits. I could go to the doctor. She was an Asian woman. I told her I wanted an abortion and speaking softly, she advised me not to. "It will be alright." And I listened. I made it through fine because I was healthy and strong. Toward the end of my pregnancy, maybe seven or eight months along, I was obviously, apparently pregnant in my maternity shirt of royal purple. I had interviewed someone at my desk. I do not remember who it was. The subject of my story had left my desk, walked the length of the newsroom, passed Chuck's glass-walled office and was descending the stairs when I remembered a question I wanted to ask.

"*Ohhh,*" I breathed out loud. I jumped up from my desk and dashed across the space trying to catch the person.

When I returned, Chuck was waiting for me in the middle of the newsroom, red-faced.

"I thought something was happening," he said. "You scared us all." I looked around the newsroom and found every face turned toward me, every pair of eyes trained on me, and some people on their feet. Friends, even those at work, showed their concern.

I went home to Mary Jane to have my third child. It was a boy, David James Barker, born on January 14, 1985 in Detroit. I remained on the *Commercial-News* payroll until June 1985, but I never returned there. It was an excellent decision to go through that pregnancy. I remember asking myself, "Was I going to give up my baby in order to stay with this small chicken dinner newspaper?" However, I did have my fallopian tubes tied. There would be no more babies, I told Mary Jane while sitting in the smallest bedroom of her Springwells subdivision house. She said she understood. Birth control was unreliable back when she was having babies. Wives could not shut down reproduction without their husbands' permission. She said it was good I was taking control, and that I lived in a time when I could.

I interviewed with a couple of newspapers. It looked like I was going to get on staff with the *Detroit Free Press,* but someone realized I was the same *Michigan Chronicle* freelancer who had beat them out of an interview with Congressman Charles C. Diggs on his way to the pen. A bigger Gannett newspaper with an 80,000-circulation and located just 90 miles from Detroit offered me a position. Over the next four years, I was a county government reporter, a police reporter, business writer, editorial writer and opinion page editor at *The Lansing State Journal.*

When I first started working, Mary Jane advised me to remember, "You don't go to work to make friends." It was good advice as long as I was in Detroit where I could not get a start because there was always something wrong with me, my qualifications or experiences. But my mother never worked as a professional. As soon as I left home, I learned that the recipe for success called for a good measure of friends. They strategize with you. They keep you informed on what is happening in your workplace. They go to lunch with you. They worry about you. But what Mary Jane meant is that they also can stab you in the back and it could mess up your job too. Even the maids in a Cincinnati Great House found friends useful. Alice definitely made a friend at her Great House job. He became her husband.

In 1989, my oldest son, Diallo, graduated high school. He was seventeen and I was thirty-five. Mary Jane came with my siblings for his commencement from East Lansing High School, held by tradition on the first Sunday in June. When she left, he was in the car with her.

I remained with my husband and these two little kids. At least once that summer, I walked the streets sobbing because I still had these two little kids, Terri and David, to raise. Terri was nine and David was five. If I did not have two other young children, in 1989 I would have had my life back, however, I did have them, and it was not so bad.

In the years after I learned about Alice putting her children in the orphanage, I was young, and I did not question it much. Besides, I knew white people and the racist part of Mary Jane's explanation made perfect sense. White people did not like black people, and they did not like the white people who liked black people. The violence was in all the newspapers and magazines about Emmett Till, the Little Rock Nine, the Freedom Riders, lunch counter sit-ins, dogs and water hoses trained on black people wanting to register to vote. Hundreds of thousands of people attended the March on Washington in 1963 and heard Martin Luther King Jr. speak his dream. He practiced his "I have a Dream" speech in Detroit first. I was ten-years-old in 1963 and did not attend that rally, but Viola Liuzzo, a white mother of five, did. After hearing him say that civil rights were everyone's responsibility, Liuzzo drove to Alabama to help in the civil rights protests. She was murdered. This all stayed with me until I became a mother myself and realized the orphanage part of Alice's story did not make much sense: orphans do not have parents except Polly and her siblings, and their white mother, Alice. This mystery of my family seemed key to who I was, and what made me, me. What turned up the volume on the silence surrounding Alice, was an adage I learned in college, "those who do not know their history are doomed to repeat it."

∞ ☾ ☾

Visiting Polly

LIVING IN A NURSING HOME is like being on prison lock-down, which has its advantages for visitors. I could drive from my home to Detroit 90 miles away pretty much anytime and visit Polly. She was a resident of the Boulevard Temple Retirement Community on West Grand Boulevard. She lived there from when she was about ninety-two to her death at age ninety-six. In the early 1990s, I visited her many times during the week. These were the *Take Care* years. *Take Care Multicultural Health* magazine was the magazine I founded, owned and published from 1993 to 1997. It was a health magazine from a colored people's point of view, people who did not get much information about health care until they had to make serious decisions. Then, I realized, it was far too late.

My father Andrew was asked to make a major medical decision quickly, and he could not do it. A diabetic, he had dropped his Underwood typewriter on his foot and the wound did not heal. He delayed going to the doctor, and when he delayed on making the decision to amputate his gangrenous foot, his leg had to be amputated above the knee. He was in a wheelchair after that and died in July 1993 from complications of diabetes. I dealt with my grief by starting a health magazine. I had two editions, *Take Care Lansing* and *Take Care Detroit.* The Detroit edition allowed me to go to the city and see family. When I visited Polly on weekdays, we were alone together.

We sat in chairs along the wall. She was not getting any sharper, so most days I had to be satisfied with just sitting close. One time I fell asleep with my head on the frame of her chair. Sometimes she cried for Alice, "Mama, Mama." Another time she asked me, "If Mama was white and Papa was black, what am I?" It seemed a curious question. Polly had two races to pick from, white and black, and she picked black, because that is what her family was. Her choice might have seemed disloyal to her mother. The only sense in which Alice could be considered black was as "Black Irish," that is, Irish Catholic.[2]

Alice was white, yes, after a while. Yet, her daughter, Polly, chose to be black. She lived in a world of black people. With the exception of her mother, all Polly's people were African-American: her aunts and cousins, her husband, the ladies at the beauty shop, her friends at church came in all colors of an autumn rainbow. Her cultural heroes, Langston Hughes; acclaimed children's book author Virginia Hamilton, and Jack Johnson. She loved Leontyne Price, if not the opera. She collected post cards with Caribbean palm trees. She cried in 1958 at the announcement that Detroit's Black Bottom, where she had lived as a young woman new to Detroit, was to be razed In urban renewal to put up Lafayette Park, a district of high-rise apartment buildings designed by renowned architect, Ludwig Mies van der Rohe.

We were all black except Alice, but what Polly was asking was who she was at her essence? Regular Americans might see her as either/or but every census until 1930 recognized her in-between racial status. It was based on appearance, so it did not matter if your white look came from generations ago, like my brother John Charles' look, which is called a "throw-back," or if your mama was white, you were what you looked like, or more accurately what the census taker thought you were. They categorized light-skinned mixed-race people like Polly, "mulatto." Elizabeth Dowling Taylor explained in her book, *The Original Black Elite* (2017), that black people distinguished further into a subcategory called "mulatto nobody."[3] As implied, the essentiality was knowing who your people were. Appearance meant nothing without a pedigree of some sort. Knowing one's lineage mattered. The real shame lay in how little Polly knew about her mother and her Irish family. What she did know came in bits and pieces, and that often came from keepsakes offering silent and incomplete testimony. Polly rarely talked about what happened, and never to me, because she did not know much. But what she did know, she told. One story was that one of her Irish grandfathers gave the church a piano.

On either side of her family she knew about the men, not the women, not her mother.

Polly practiced a sort of shorthand when talking about her mother. When talking about how she went to work in a bakery to earn the carfare for her daughter Mary Jane to go to Cass Technical High School and then for her children's college tuition, she apologized, "We've always been poor people." "We" were the women. And it was a source of shame that in her family the women worked. They earned money because they did not have a husband, or their husband did not have money, or had not left it. The reason to work was to take care of the children. It was always for the children, and in some ways my bird-dogging Alice's story was that as well. There came a point where I could not ignore my ignorance. In 1998, my daughter, Terri, was a college freshman with a bright future at the University of Michigan, where controversy raged. A widely publicized lawsuit questioned Affirmative Action's effects on enrollment. She told me white students would challenge her place at the university, never mind that she was from a family that had been going to Michigan since 1964. This bothered Terri. She needed to know where she came from, what influences continued in her life from our family's earliest traceable days. Ultimately, she was why I needed to know the "whys" and "wherefores" of Alice's life.

I realized I was inoculating her against herself, and me, and my Irish great-grandmother. If Terri ever found herself in the unfortunate position of no care for her children, of course, her father and I would support her, but I wanted her to know she would not be the first to need others' help with children. I wanted her to embrace not ignore her need for as much education as she could get. She would know the story of Alice. I would find our history.

Not knowing was a form of orphaning, wrote Azar Nafisi, in her memoir, *Reading Lolita in Tehran: A Memoir in Books* (2003). Nafisi's book is set during the 1978-1981 Iranian Revolution that resulted in creating the Islamic Republic of Iran. During the era when the regime restricted women's rights, behavior and appearance, Professor Nafisi gathered a group of women students to read and discuss western literature featuring controversial women characters. *Lolita,* a 1955 novel by Valdimir Nabokov, was one of the books.[4] *Lolita* is a scandalous novel with a pedophile protagonist, Humbert Humbert, who goes to extreme lengths to make a twelve-year-old schoolgirl, Lolita, his mistress. Of *Lolita,* Nafisi wrote, "Despite Humbert's attempts to orphan Lolita by robbing her of her history, that past is still given to us in glimpses."[5] That is what I had of the past, glimpses. I needed a full frame look at my woman-family history.

Leaving full-time employment to publish my health magazine meant I had more time to do my own work. My two younger children were getting to the point where they did not need me all day long, so I was able to start researching Alice's story in earnest. Finally, I was a working writer of history, doing my research. The day I regretted that my family did not tell stories was when I found myself in another serious library.

Michigan State University's library, just down the street from my house, was the first place I thought to research. But first, I needed basic information about certain people in specific places, so they referred me to the Library of Michigan in downtown Lansing, the state repository for the census. It was a modern building of white limestone with colorful glasswork spanning the floors. Inside on the first floor, glass walls circled a tree trunk. The rest of the tree, a white pine, which is the state tree, grew up out of sight into the sky. Separated into two wings, the building housed the library and archives on one side, and the historical museum on the other. As does the Library of Congress, this special library serves the information needs of the legislature as it makes law. It is supposed to ensure that decisions are based on fact, expert opinion and sound reason though too often that seems not to be the case.

I skipped the elevator in favor of climbing the intriguing rough-hewn granite block staircase. The second floor Genealogy section opened in a space of library tables, comfortable chairs and the banker-style table lamps. As modern and bright as the building design was, I spent most of my time in the gloomy microfilm room with reels and reels of census reports. Alex Haley's book *Roots* fired up scores of grey-haired family genealogists to find their ancestors and learn their family identity. They crowded into microfilm rooms across the nation. Microfilm machines had not changed since the technology was developed, and I felt like I had crossed over to the museum side of the building. I leaned into the great hulking machine to get a clearer view. Captivated, I became a fixture of the microfilm room.

Census research is a process only for the patient. A census researcher hurries to the section where the Soundex search function said their people were, and then slows to a crawl drawing ever closer line by line to the name. I must admit, it was exciting to find my story. To finally know, and in a sense the story of me. To be able to talk about my family history, so that neither I, nor my children would be doomed to repeat it.

After I had done the census work and learned about the adults who helped raised Polly, and noted their names and addresses, I asked Polly about them. Her face would brighten as she leaned forward. "Do you know them?" It had been so long since she had seen those people, her grandfather, her aunts, and uncles, her father and Alice, even her husband. He had died at age ninety-five in 1996, ending their seventy-four year marriage, seventy-five years if you count the year Polly *said* she was Mrs. Leigh. One time Polly asked me, a bit hesitantly, who had she married? And then with a tinge of hope, she asked, "George?" She meant her handsome high school chum, the one whose friendship, and that of her two girlfriends, Ernestine and Irene, helped her get through to graduation. I laughed. "No, you married Jimmy." She sat back, mused over that a minute, and then she smiled.

I probably had waited just as long as I dared before getting started with the research into how and why Polly was put in an orphanage. In 1994, Polly was ninety-two-years-old. Her mother, Alice, was dead three decades; and her sister, Elizabeth, dead eighteen years. Her brother, Bud, died before both of them, but no one on the black side really knew when Bud died. He was married to an Italian woman at the time of his death, and living on Detroit's far East Side nearby to his wife's family, Mary Jane remembered. He was buried before they called anyone but his mother Alice. Bud's Italian in-laws had not wanted his black family to attend the service.

I found Polly's younger sister Elizabeth in the 1920 U.S. Census of the Clark County Children's Home. Had Polly ever lived there? I had mentioned this to my uncle, Sonny, when he returned to Detroit during the summer from the west coast where he lived. I had shown him the agency's permission slip. I do not think I asked him to ask Polly for permission, but he had asked me to meet him at the nursing home.

That day the security guard at the Boulevard Temple Retirement Community came out of his hut in the parking lot and waved me to a space along the fence. I gladly pulled in off 14th Street. The neighborhood's desirability and safety had faded and become just another inner-city neighborhood. I saw my uncle's rental car parked in the lot. I parked and hurried inside.

I stepped off the elevator into the dining area. Boulevard Temple Retirement Community had that spare-no-cost design that was never found in a nursing home. Maybe at one time it had been an office building. An atrium claimed the center space, and rose to the roof. Natural light poured in. Plants grew around the circle, and over the wall. When our family visited as a group on Sundays and Polly's birthday, we clumped there with cake and party hats. Usually, smells in institutions overwhelm me, but that atrium kept the air circulating.

Three of them waited for me. One I had not expected, and perhaps did not want to see, not today, my other uncle, Buddy, neé Elmer. A common nineteenth century name, it came down from the Irish side of our family. Fastidious in appearance, he was as lean as he had been in the Air Force forty years earlier. His skin was toasty brown and his hair straight, thick and black. He looked Egyptian, similar in appearance to the actor Omar Sharif, and looked exactly like my grandfather. Neither man talked much. My grandfather used silence to his advantage as a Detroit police officer. His son, Buddy was a dentist. I knew that with family he measured his words.

But of course, there had been a good chance Buddy was in town. He always came from New York to visit when his older brother Sonny was in Detroit. I had nothing to feel uneasy about; I was not here to get my grandma to sign away her deed to a gold mine, but I felt a little bit being ganged up on, as if just wanting to know Alice's secret jeopardized my place in our family. I wondered how the secret had affected my life. In a sense I was going through life blind, unaware of what made me. I needed to know Alice.

In all these years, the proffered explanations about why Polly was put in an orphanage were mostly too brief to make sense. We let it go until history almost repeated with me. In my family, when we can, we look away and then we roll on, like a bus driver who does not hear the ping of the pulled cord. Yet, I was an English major whose spirit latched on to Faulkner's familiar quote, "the past is not dead, it's not even past."

Sonny, Buddy and Grandma waited in the hallway outside her room. When the effort to find her a nursing home was underway, Sonny took Polly to look at nursing homes. She knew that Sonny was planning his retirement from the university where he was a professor, and she had pronounced this residence just fine—for Sonny.

The brothers had pulled three big chairs together and put their mother in the middle. She was a short, plump woman, stout. Half-white, she had soft hair with lazy curls. Some years it had been rinsed fashionably blue. In the nursing home it was iron gray and white pepper. Her feet rested on a box because they did not reach the floor. With her two sons on hand, she was happy. It did not matter where she was if her sons were nearby. She doted on them, just as her daughter Mary Jane doted on her sons. Perhaps that came from the Johnson family, where only one son had survived.

"Hello, Dedria," Polly greeted me. Her voice had a sing-song quality, as it cut out the second vowel, to arrive at the correct pronunciation of my name, De-dra.

"Hi Grandma." I kissed her cheek. Her skin felt like reedy papyrus.

My uncle, Sonny, was soft and jovial. He wore a casual shirt, like he was playing tennis later on. We shared hugs and greetings all around. When we hugged, Buddy said only, "Dedria."

The permission slip was in my bag, but I made no move for it. Better to play this by ear. I wondered if they had talked about this before I arrived. We all knew why I had driven 90 miles to meet them, and I was glad Sonny was helping me. I did not think Buddy approved of what I wanted to do. He was a private person, certain in his ideas, when he expressed them. If asked a direct question, his first response was usually, "No." Or he might laugh, while backing away and holding out two hands, palms out. Was my, uncle, Buddy going to leave me stranded without my history? Orphaned?

Sonny leaned over to Polly.

"Mama, Dedria wants to look into what happened in Springfield. Is that okay, Ma?"

His tone was kind, like that used by a professional. He was a social worker by education and profession, and he was the eldest son, the most powerful person there. I kept my mouth shut.

Polly did not answer right away. She looked down at her white hands in her lap, then up at me. At age ninety-two, the skin on her face hung loose, but her eyes shone sharp and clear.

She looked to Sonny, who smiled, and at Buddy, who said nothing.

"Alright," Polly said, finally. Her voice was strong, but not loud.

My anxious ears heard it as, "Alright, I understand," not "Alright, yes."

I gave Sonny the permission slip. It was for the orphanage in Springfield, the Clark County Children's Home. He put the piece of paper on the tabletop in front of Polly. "If you sign this, she can look at records about you."

She would do whatever her eldest son asked of her, the tables having reversed in their relationship. He held out a pen to her. I held my breath, and avoided Buddy's stare. She had researched her grandfather's military service and undoubtedly had her reasons for not researching her own life. What the reasons were I did not know, or knew if she still held them. I watched her with the pen. She gripped it. I kept my eyes on Polly.

She lowered the pen to the paper, and looping the ink, signed her name, Pauline Johnson Leigh. It took strength for my grandmother to weave black ink into a key to the past, and give it to me.

Sonny picked up the authorization and handed it over to me. My heart soared.

℘ ∞ ☙

WHAT A PAY-OFF at The Clark County Children's Home. Records there brought details to the fore. Records of the little black and white, widow-led family with no choice in society except to separate from each other. In comparing documents and dates, I realized that Polly had tried to deceive authorities and the people she loved, or wanted to love, all to help a child. It made me respect her more, but it was more than what she wanted known. On a 1995 visit I let her know

I knew about this one particular incident. The record showed she had arrived November 1, 1921 at the Children's Home wanting to remove her sister out of the Home. She claimed on that day to be Mrs. Leigh, a married woman living in Detroit, but the fact of the matter was Polly did not marry Mr. Leigh until June 10, 1922. Her feet hit the floor then, pushing her chair back away from me. She whispered to my aunt who was also visiting, "She's plotting against me."

It was one of the few times Polly expressed suspicion about people. It was one of the few times I was able to glimpse into the shame that surrounded Alice's secret. Polly had risen above her mother's family abandoning Alice when they realized she was a colored man's lover. She had endured the sorrow of her father's early death, and the distress of that year when her working mother tried to care for her three children alone. The lack of child care, the racial differences, mothering as a widow, being an orphan, and the health crises. All of these challenges had been surmounted one way or the other, but Polly was still ashamed of deceiving others on behalf of the welfare of a child.

By my next visit she had forgotten about being plotted against, and shared some particulars of her life. She was glad I knew the same people she knew. She liked to talk about her father. His name was John Henry Louis Preston Taylor Johnson. He was a social animal. "You'd be talking," she said, "then he'd start talking, and pretty soon he was the only one talking." Her favorite way to describe her father was "a hail fellow well met." It meant that he enjoyed fortune and people's good will. She laughed quoting her mother, "John Johnson was a big fat liar." She hard-stressed his first name, "John John-son," no doubt in imitation of her mother Alice's speech, which I thought carried the hard twang of a hillbilly. For me it recalled the nickname of President John F. Kennedy's young son, "John-John." Polly wrote about some of her early life with her parents: the first day of school; a big Christmas in 1908; how her mother hated the game stew John Henry's father cooked; how her mother baked cupcakes and gave them out to the entire neighborhood.

"Where did your parents meet?" I asked.

Her answer came quick. "At work. They worked at a Great House in Cincinnati. She was a maid." Polly told me little else about that, but this one fact helped me to start imagining the two lives that begat her own.

Now I took my research on the road and went to Columbus, Ohio, to look for more documents in the Ohio Historical Society collection. In Columbus, I took a break to visit with a cousin.

William Browning Jr. was Nellie Johnson, and William Browning's only child and son. He was born in February 1918 when a lot of the turmoil in the family had been settled by Alice's action. He never knew his uncle, John Henry, or his grandfather, Isaac Johnson, but he knew Alice. He called her Aunt Alice. And he smiled when he said that, but said little more about her. Bill benefited from Alice winning the battle over education. Well-educated, Bill graduated from Springfield High School, class of 1935, after which he was admitted to Ohio State University. He stayed at OSU for one year, and then transferred and graduated from Wilberforce, the black college, also in Ohio. Bill received his master's degree from the University of Michigan, in Ann Arbor. He and his wife Portia visited Detroit fairly often. They had no children, but Bill had a daughter by a previous relationship. Bill was a big man, tall and dark-skinned with good sturdy white teeth, good-natured and well-off. Once, he and Portia drove their 30-foot cabin cruiser through Lake Erie and the Detroit River to visit his cousins in Detroit.

Bill was more than happy to meet me in Columbus where he lived, and over lunch, he told me a story about Bud that Bud had told him. Bud was working at a country club or some ritzy place like that when one of his co-workers visited Bud's home in Detroit's North End. Bud lived with his first wife and two daughters. The two men were sitting there drinking beer when Bud's two daughters, Shirley and Sharon, came running through the house. The co-worker looked at them and asked Bud, "Why you let those niggers run through your house?" And Bud said, "They are my daughters." Bud lost his job two days later. It sounded to me like Bud was tired of that gig.

After lunch, Bill and I swung by his church. I met one lady who was working in the food pantry. She came out from between the shelves to greet me.

"This is our family genealogist," Bill said introducing me.

She was pleased to meet me. "My son," she said, "is researching our family. He has found 1,500 relatives." She beamed, so proud and appreciative of the back-breaking, eye-straining work.

"That's quite an accomplishment," I laughed, cheerfully, "but I'm not going for volume. All I'm trying to do is tell a story." Alice's story.

ℰᴑ ᴄᴈ ᴄᴙ

WHEN I WAS A COLLEGE STUDENT, Mr. Quinn, the editor-publisher of the *Chronicle* said I would go on and do more. And I had. My reading and writing career launched me into positions as writer, teacher, editor, publisher, and public speaker. I attended writers' conferences, several on the east coast, the publishing mecca, but after I started working on the Alice project, I decided to go to a Mid-west conference being held in Alice's native state of Indiana. It was Rope Walk, sponsored by the University of Southern Indiana. The conference was being held in the south-west corner of the state, just about as far west of Lawrenceburg as one could get. The town of New Harmony sat at the corner of the Ohio and Wabash rivers.

A historic town on the Wabash River in Posey County, Indiana, New Harmony was founded by the Harmony Society in 1814. Initially named "Harmonie," it was created as a cooperative community based on plans for humanity's salvation through "rational" thinking, cooperation, and free education. Although the community contin-ued to thrive into the 1820s, the decision was made to sell the property and search for land to the east. The community was also discouraged by the lack of integrity displayed when a man stole the unlocked community cash box. In 1825, the Harmonists sold their town to Robert Owen, a Welsh-born industrialist and social reformer, and his financial partner, William Maclure, who renamed the town New Harmony. A progressive and secular Scotsman, Owen based his communal concept not on religious ideology but on education for the masses. Both Owen and Rapp were attempting to achieve what they called a Community of Equality, a Utopian communal life style. Some of their beliefs were, at the time, considered radical. They denounced slavery and supported equal rights for women. It soon became known as a center for advances in education and scientific research. Town residents established the first free library, a civic drama club, and a public school system open to men and women.

Although united by their communal labor, and to the idea of Utopian life, the very rational concepts upon which Owen had based the community on were antithetical to communal life. Because they lacked a strong central belief (like religion), which served to unite other Utopian groups, the members of this community lacked the commitment to carry out the mission that Owen envisioned. New Harmony dissolved in less than three years. It left architecture that ranks among the most creative in the world, including a visitor's center designed like New York's Guggenheim Museum. Today the town is nationally recognized for its unique cultural history and origins as a Utopian community, and remains a functioning, small town that has centered its foundation on its economic, ethnic, and generational diversity that emphasizes the importance of local crafts and artisans, a collective entrepreneurial spirit, spiritual connections, and commitment to live in harmony with one another.

I was accepted to Rope Walk and given a scholarship to attend and work on an imagined story of what it was like when Alice's parents found out that their only daughter's beloved was a colored man. It was full of high emotion and curse words, and a punitive Catholic priest. The people at Rope Walk loved it. The reason I selected Rope Walk to attend that year was because it was situated in the Midwest. I drove the circular highway around Indianapolis and further south, then west to the end of the state where my great-grandmother Alice was born. It was right to work on my Indiana story in Indiana, but the Indiana in my story was not the Indiana I was sitting in. What a sharp contrast. What New Harmony Utopians ed about people was the same thing I ed in Alice's story. People have the capacity to do right, and live with a code of moral behavior, but "right" can mean different things to different people. It depends on a point of view, and decisions to take action, which speaks to character. Did Alice's parents threaten to disown her if she continued to see John Henry, or did they quit the familial relationship the moment they ed she was seeing him? New Harmony got a second chance as a utopia. Was Alice awarded a second chance for perfect Irish behavior, only to thin humans there is no such thing?

I revealed a secret about my own flaws while I was in New Harmony. I took a chance and told my workshop a story stemming from one of my former flaws — anger. I had stabbed a door with a kitchen knife and accidentally cut my hand. I severed two tendons and one nerve, which required surgery and physical therapy to restore the use of two fingers. After I finished telling my story, workshop leader Kim Barnes stared at me intensely. Finally, she laughed and asked, "Haven't we all done something like that?" Everyone around the table chuckled and nodded. I felt so much better, relieved. New Harmony, Indiana, combined with Alice's story reaffirmed that I am human and so was she.

New Harmony gave me a taste of real river life. Traditionally, the last night of a writers' conference celebrates writers. That means a festive dinner party with copious conversation and excessive drinking. I was looking forward to the party in a big tent outside, but also regretted it because I planned to get up early the next morning to drive to Lawrenceburg on the other side of the state. The tent was pitched on the lawn in the middle of the university conference center's property. This piece of land dropped into a gulch, and had two high sides. The gulch could also be crossed by the bridge at the far end near the greenhouses, but all week the gulch was dry, and I used it as a shortcut between The Barn, the writer's residence on one side, and the houses where the workshops were held on the other side. That last night just as we sat down under the tent, a heavy downpour of rain started. It continued all through the party. Since it was raining there was every reason to stay at the party. Not until my feet started squishing in the grass, did I turn to look at the gulch. Now it revealed itself for what is was, a valley cut by water. It was filling up with water coming from the direction of the Ohio River. Around midnight the water in the gulch turned opaque. I needed to go. If I got too late a start in the morning, I would not get to the Lawrenceburg library on time. One guy suggested taking the shortcut, but, I wanted to take the bridge. And he said, it's not very deep. I looked and I could not tell in the dark where the land ended and the water began. I did not know then about the Great Flood or any river flood; I am from Detroit and our river is not a river, not really. "Come on," someone said striding past me. "We'll run across." I watched his back disappear. When I heard the splash, I decided, Oh hell, no. I will never get anywhere but the grave if I follow them. I got soaked walking to the greenhouses and over the bridge, but at least I got there.

The next morning I set out for the state's eastern-edge and Lawrenceburg. I drove toward the sun watching the river as much as I could because rivers are wonder-filled bodies of water.

The thing about curiosity is it grows, and answers only lead to more questions. I knew Alice had put her children in an orphanage. Why? That was her secret. Information I collected pointed to her girl. She did it for her oldest daughter, my grandma Polly. She did it so Polly could go to school.

How did Alice go from being Irish to being white? What did the shift mean? How courageous she must have been in the face of John Henry's death, and especially with pressure from her sisters-in-law who wanted different things for her children. The twists of her life as a colored man's widow surprised me many times as I absorbed its teachings and questioned its truths. This little old white lady I knew as great-grandmother had overcome adversity as surely as any black woman I have known.

In the past, orphans had parents, usually mothers, and orphanages were not always merciless places for little red-headed girls; they were shelters for ordinary kids, the children of women struggling to live as family. Sometimes the moms were drunks, or wayfarers, but mostly they were workers, they were rarely black women. They were among the ranks of poor white widowed women, like Alice.

Marrying across the color line when it was illegal or considered immoral, threw a woman in a world of trouble. American society exacted a price for miscegenation, and ethnic people collected it without mercy. Alice paid a price for loving John Henry Johnson even if it meant severance of her family ties; cut off from those she loved. She sacrificed family support, and missed that mightily when she was desperate for it, only to gain mistrust from her black-in-laws because she was different.

More than just a violation of racial values, women who found themselves in Alice's position gave up their children because they were widows. When husbands died from illness or disease, they left white widows to shoulder the burden of supporting and raising children on their own. Most mothers took their children to another man's home to raise, because they did not have an independent means of support. As a widow, Alice was a white woman with black children; what white man or black man would have her? Her dire situation forced her to surrender daily custody of the most precious gift of her married life, her children.

Had she followed a black code of family values it would not have come to that. Booker T. Washington articulated those mores at the White House Conference on Dependent Children. Washington, the esteemed president of Tuskegee Institute in Alabama and famous self-sufficiency advocate, said at the conference, "In our ordinary southern communities we look upon it as a disgrace for an individual to be permitted to be taken from that community to any kind of an institution for dependents."[6]

In his formal address, "Destitute Colored Children of the South," Washington said, "The Negro, in some way, has inherited and has had trained into him the idea that he must take care of his own dependents, and he does it to a greater degree than is true, per-haps of any other race in the same relative stage of civilization." He cited the $600,000 cost of supporting destitute children in Massachusetts as "more money than is spent for the dependent Negro children in the whole southern country." Of the total Negro population of 900,000 in Alabama, Washington said, Negro children in institutions numbered 301.[7] He was not prescribing black life in the southern U.S., he was describing it. Was he trying to engender respect for black people? Was this his way of calling attention to the disparity of care between blacks and whites? Or was this the point of view of a man who would not in any circumstance be asked to provide that care which was women's work? Washington was a wily fellow who worked diligently to build support from white men for Tuskegee Institute. He built it into the resilient training and educational establishment that survives to this day. At the conference, Washington's comments were contested by one black man who knew the difficulties of caring for dependent children. His story sounded more realistic.

Richard T. Carroll, manager of the South Carolina Industrial Home for Destitute and Dependent Colored Children, told the Conference that "most of the homes of the colored people in the South are amply supplied [with children]; there are very few families who have not as many children as they can take care of. I know some that have from eleven to sixteen more than they can feed, clothe, educate and care for properly and they are always willing and ready to give away those." Carroll said that during his eleven years of experience, he had placed 543 children into foster homes. He supported the work by selling wood, or cows, or clothing "or anything, to keep the work going." He would have elaborated on his experience—his speech was eight minutes long—but he was shut down by the Conference chairman who said the connection of Carroll's remarks to the program topic of foster homes "has not been apparent."[8]

A White House Conference recommendation was to provide direct financial aid to poor mothers with dependent children. Most of the men objected. The priority in a patriarchal worldview was: Whatever the cost, do not let these mothers manage money for their sustenance and keep their children. By 1936, the United States had instituted the Aid to Dependent Children program, known as ADC, or welfare. It took America almost an additional three decades to figure out how to implement that humane idea, and how to treat mothers like adults.

Monsignor McMahon, an Irish Catholic priest, at the White House conference said that the advantage of indoor care, indoor care meaning an orphanage, where the Catholic church housed 100,000 in New York alone, helps control the numbers of those who seek help, "for few wish to part with their children."[9] It was an extremely tough decision to surrender a child, but some did do it. Notably, my great-grandmother, Alice.

Alice gathered the strength to go forward. The option of a Children's Home left children cared for, secured in school, and allowed mother to continue to play her role. It was an option that needed improvement, not rejection. Alice surrendered all of her children to an orphanage, and that gave the oldest, a girl, a chance at her life. This was a seldom-heard story, even in families like mine where educational achievement seemed to come from the use of an orphanage.

I benefited from a family that valued education, and I am grateful. It is the kind of support few mothers receive. In fact, schools can prevent a woman from becoming a mother just as being a mother can prevent her from being a scholar. But I was able to have both, and not everyone can. From 1989 to 1993, I worked as the editor of the Michigan State University College of Human Medicine's magazine. In the halls, at events, I met a great number of highly-educated women, some were already mothers. It took them a little longer to complete school. Many more women who were medical students were pursuing their vocational goals by sitting in the library studying, going to class, when they might have been on the path to a family life. One black medical student told me that once she went home on a term break to that her boyfriend had gotten married. She was so concentrated in her studies she had not noticed.

People around me have called my research and writing about Alice, a labor of love. They were right. It was personal. A white friend of mine suggested I should not openly discuss that I have an Irish ancestor, and a part of me agreed. Like my father, I thought white skin represented a "whiteness" that was out to harm me. Learning about Alice provided me a sense of why and how other groups define people by skin color, culture and language. I also did not know I could sustain a project for so long. What I got out of this experience is a stiffer backbone, a staunch determination to be proud of who I am.

I used to not pay much attention to feminism or the women's liberation movement. I thought that it was a white woman's thing, but through this experience I realized that black feminism has been around since the time of slavery, as exemplified in Sojourner Truth's famous speech, "Ain't I a Woman?" But my curiosity about feminism was the lack of support for childcare, a challenge that persists.

American mothers have always had to invent creative ways to care for their children while they worked. Colonial women placed small children in standing stools to prevent them from falling into the fireplace. Pioneers on the Midwestern plains laid infants in wooden boxes fastened to the beams of their plows. Southern dirt farmers tethered their runabouts to pegs driven into the soil at the edge of their fields. As enslaved people and servants, black mothers sang white babies to sleep while their own little ones comforted themselves. By the late 1890s, as the Industrial Revolution changed the landscape of America, so too did the need for childcare, especially for poor working families. Since many women, poor women, were given no choice but to enter into the workforce, they worked either in factories, or for wealthy families, and were forced to choose between leaving their children home alone, or not working and seeking charity from the community.

What were their choices? What were Alice's choices? Mothers left children alone in cradles and cribs, and locked them in tenement flats and cars parked in factory lots. They had to leave their children with parents, grandparents, play mothers, neighbors and strangers. They took their older daughters out of school to care for their younger siblings so mother could go to work. Some mothers took their children to baby farms, gave them up to orphanages and foster homes, and surrendered them for indenture. Alice's situation was hardly unique; but what was unique is that she did not want her eldest daughter to sacrifice her education to become a Little Mama.

Alice did not make this decision lightly; it is clear to me she gave this significant thought, considered her options before making a final decision, and was able to find a relatively safe place for her children.

At the end of the nineteenth century, American child care had come to consist of a range of formal and informal provisions that were generally associated with the poor, minorities, and immigrants and were stigmatized as charitable and custodial. This pattern of practices and institutions provided a weak foundation for building twentieth-century social services. As women's reform efforts picked up steam during the Progressive Era (the 1890s), however, child care became a target for reform and modernization.

It is why I was thrilled to read the "Proceedings of the White House Conference on Dependent Children," a watershed event in the history of American child welfare. President Theodore Roosevelt demanded the conference consider the care of dependent children—that is, children who depended for support on any person or institution other than their parents or other relatives—and to make recommendations regarding their plight. Considered the most comprehensive report on the needs of children ever written, it framed the first important body of child health and welfare standards to ensure that every child had a fair chance, and would become a foundational text for the then-emerging profession of social work. The report shows how the current American child welfare system started with a policy conceived by men in an age when women were infantilized, meaning it was not perfect, and it would take years to get some their ideas institutionalized.

In Alice's time, women could not help themselves, but that was 1912, more than a century ago. Ironically, President William Howard Taft signed the U.S. Children's Bureau into legislation in 1912, placing the new agency within the Department of Commerce and Labor. Taft's signature made the United States the first nation in the world to have a federal agency focused solely on children. During the height of its influence, the Bureau was directed, managed, and staffed almost entirely by women—a rarity for any federal agency in the early twentieth century. It was most influential in bringing the methods of reform-oriented social research and the ideas of maternalist reformers together to execute federal government policy.

The agency eventually moved to the Department of Health and Human Services in 1989. While the agency has done some good work, key issues remain unsolved. For example, private resources determine what public agencies can do. While a few major corporations offer subsidized daycare, in most cases, companies tend to only offer this benefit at corporate headquarters, which only helps those at the very top of the company's hierarchy, rather than the people at the very bottom, who really need it. When the government doles out meager attention to child care laws and providers, even families who could afford it often find fewer and less dependable providers. Childcare is not a service that should solely depend on consumers alone.

Unfortunately, prevailing political thought holds that child care is a family issue, so our government does not provide the full support that is needed to help every single family's needs. For example, most of a mother's paycheck goes to childcare providers unless she is a highly paid professional or an heiress. When child care expenses exceed the amount on a paycheck, mothers must cobble together care from whomever and wherever they can get it, sometimes with tragic results. In some cases, working poor mothers satisfy a state requirement for government benefits by putting in long hours at minimum wage jobs. They juggle young children in child care arrangements from whoever can provide it, a different person every week, sometimes every day, until she does not know who put that mark on her child, who knocked her child out, or who killed her child. Everybody loses when childcare is unaffordable or inaccessible to poor families.

Because of its long history and current structure, the American child care system is divided along class lines, making it difficult for parents to unite and lobby for improved services and increased public funding for child care for all children. When it comes to public provisions for children and families, the United States compares poorly with other advanced industrial nations such as France,

Sweden, and Denmark, which not only offer free or subsidized care to children over three but also provide paid maternity or parental leaves. Unlike the United States, these countries use child care not as a lever in a harsh mandatory employment policy toward low-income mothers, but as a means of helping parents of all classes reconcile the demands of work and family life.

Alice put her children in the Clark County Children's Home because she wanted her daughters to complete their education, and at the very least, graduate from high school. For all the years that Alice was scorned, her children's education was her greatest achievement: Polly graduated from high school; Bud graduated high school and attended Wittenberg University; and Elizabeth earned a General Educational Development certificate (GED), completed nursing school, and became a nurse. Alice should have had it easier; she did not. Whatever the origin or result of her action to give up her children, Alice became the mother of orphans, which every working mother is in danger of becoming. ⌘

NOTES

1. Rebecca Walker, interview by Diane Rhem, The Diane Rhem Show, Washington, D.C.: WAMU, January 11, 2001.

2. Ignatiev, How the Irish, 41.

3. Elizabeth Dowling Taylor, The Original Black Elite: Daniel Murray and the Story of a Forgotten Era (New York: Amistad/Harper Collins, 2017), 67.

4. Azar Nafisi, Reading Lolita in Tehran: A Memoir in Books (New York: Penguin Random House, 2008), 1 -77.

5. Nafisi, Reading Lolita, 37.

6. [NEED FULL CITE] Proceedings, 115.

7. Proceedings, 114.

8. Proceedings, 136.

9. Proceedings, 97.

Two-year-old me decked out for Easter 1954 in Grandma Polly's backyard garden. *Courtesy of The Andrew J. and Mary Jane Humphries Foundation.*

Fourteen-years old in 1967, and solemn about being bused to school, made me wonder why adults leave the heavy lifting of social change to their children. *Courtesy of The Andrew J. and Mary Jane Humphries Foundation.*

Young, unmarried mother in 1973 with my first child, Diallo. He was the 14th of Mary Jane's children, and the oldest of my three. *Courtesy of The Andrew J. and Mary Jane Humphries Foundation.*

Working for Detroit's *Michigan Chronicle* took me to many a party, 1976. Photo courtesy of The Michigan Chronicle.

Michael D. Barker was a handsome man with deep Alabama roots, but I had to warm up to his talkative personality before we married in June 28, 1980. Diallo felt the same way. *Courtesy of The Andrew J. and Mary Jane Humphries Foundation.*

I looked the part of mother in 1981 in Detroit, but doing "mother" proved to be more challenging with two children, Diallo, age nine, and Terri Barker, born November 19, 1980. *Courtesy of The Andrew J. and Mary Jane Humphries Foundation.*

Me and my sisters and brothers 1978, Back row (l-r): Derrick, Marcia, Andy, Alice, James, John, William, Pamela. Front row (l-r): Paula, Gregory, Kimberly, Mark, Dedria. *Courtesy of The Andrew J. and Mary Jane Humphries Foundation.*

Sandy, my co-worker on the Features desk of the Danville *Commercial-News* (Illinois) in 1983 taught skeptical me how to use the newspaper's computer system. Photo credit: J. Anthony Williams, *Danville Commercial-News.*

Michael picked up some weight after eight years of marriage, but it was not from my home cooking. On vacation in 1988 in Michigan's Upper Peninsula, with Terri, age eight, and David, born January 15, 1985. *Courtesy of The Andrew J. and Mary Jane Humphries Foundation.*

Police and newspapers call these kinds of
photographs, mug shots. Here's my mug shot from a
1980s column I wrote for the *Lansing State Journal*.
Photo by Greg DeRuiter, *Lansing State Journal*.

A family wedding: Mary Jane with her daughters. From left: Pamela, Mary Jane, Dedria, Marcia. Santa Barbara, California, 2011. *Photo by Auguste Humphries.*

In a big family, there's always a wedding to attend. Me (r) and my husband, Michael Barker (l) in Palm Springs, California, 2016. *Courtesy of The Andrew J. and Mary Jane Humphries Foundation.*

One time I loaned my eighty-plus year-old mother, Mary Jane, a blouse, but when it looked better on her than me, I just gave it to her. Front row (l-r): Mary Jane and Dedria. Back row (l-r): Pamela, and Paula. *Courtesy of The Andrew J. and Mary Jane Humphries Foundation.*

ABOUT THE AUTHOR

D EDRIA HUMPHRIES BARKER is a public speaker, journalist and teacher who lives in Michigan. Her essay, "The Girl with the Good Hair," appeared in the anthology, *The Beiging of America: Personal Narratives About being Mixed Race in the 21st Century* (2017). Her essays have been published by The Society for the Study of Midwestern Literature, the Ohio and Michigan historical societies, and the National Trust for Historical Preservation. A Detroit native, Barker holds a BA and MA from Wayne State University, and studied at the Iowa Writer's Workshop with James McPherson. ⌘

OTHER BOOKS BY
2LEAF PRESS

2Leaf Press challenges the status quo by publishing alternative fiction, non-fiction, poetry and bilingual works by activists, academics, poets and authors dedicated to diversity and social justice with scholarship that is accessible to the general public. 2Leaf Press produces high quality and beautifully produced hardcover, paperback and ebook formats through our series: 2LP Explorations in Diversity, 2LP University Books, 2LP Classics, 2LP Translations, Nuyorican World Series, and 2LP Current Affairs, Culture & Politics. Below is a selection of 2Leaf Press' published titles.

2LP EXPLORATIONS IN DIVERSITY

Substance of Fire: Gender and Race in the College Classroom
by Claire Millikin
Foreword by R. Joseph Rodríguez, Afterword by Richard Delgado
Contributors Riley Blanks, Blake Calhoun, Rox Trujillo

Black Lives Have Always Mattered
A Collection of Essays, Poems, and Personal Narratives
Edited by Abiodun Oyewole

The Beiging of America:
Personal Narratives about Being Mixed Race in the 21st Century
Edited by Cathy J. Schlund-Vials, Sean Frederick Forbes, Tara Betts
Afterword by Heidi Durrow

What Does it Mean to be White in America?
Breaking the White Code of Silence, A Collection of Personal Narratives
Edited by Gabrielle David and Sean Frederick Forbes
Introduction by Debby Irving, Afterword by Tara Betts

2LP CLASSICS
Adventures in Black and White
by Philippa Schuyler
Edited and with a critical introduction by Tara Betts

Monsters: Mary Shelley's Frankenstein and Mathilda
by Mary Shelley, edited by Claire Millikin Raymond

2LP TRANSLATIONS
Birds on the Kiswar Tree
by Odi Gonzales, translated by Lynn Levin
Bilingual: English/Spanish

Incessant Beauty, A Bilingual Anthology
by Ana Rossetti, edited and translated by Carmela Ferradáns
Bilingual: English/Spanish

NUYORICAN WORLD SERIES
Entre el sol y la nieve: escritos de fin de siglo / Between the Sun and Snow: Writing at the End of the Century
by Myna Nieves, translated by Christopher Hirschmann Brandt
Bilingual: English/Spanish

Our Nuyorican Thing, The Birth of a Self-Made Identity
by Samuel Carrion Diaz, Introduction by Urayoán Noel

Hey Yo! Yo Soy!, 40 Years of Nuyorican Street Poetry, The Collected Works of Jesús Papoleto Meléndez
Bilingual: English/Spanish

LITERARY NONFICTION
The Emergence of Ecosocialism, Collected Essays by Joel Kovel
Edited by Quincy Saul, with an Introduction by Kanya D'Almeida

No Vacancy; Homeless Women in Paradise
by Michael Reid

The Beauty of Being, A Collection of Fables, Short Stories & Essays
by Abiodun Oyewole, with an Introduction by Felipe Luciano

WHEREABOUTS: Stepping Out of Place, An Outside in Literary & Travel Magazine Anthology
Edited by Brandi Dawn Henderson

ESSAYS
The Emergence of Ecosocialism, Collected Essays by Joel Kovel
Edited by Quincy Saul

PLAYS
Rivers of Women, The Play
by Shirley Bradley LeFlore, photographs by Michael J. Bracey

AUTOBIOGRAPHIES/MEMOIRS/BIOGRAPHIES
An Unintentional Accomplice: A Personal Perspective on White Responsibility
by Carolyn L. Baker

Trailblazers, Black Women Who Helped Make America Great
American Firsts/American Icons, Vols.1 and 2
by Gabrielle David, Edited by Carolina Fung Feng
Introduction by Chandra D. L. Waring,

Mother of Orphans
The True and Curious Story of Irish Alice, A Colored Man's Widow
by Dedria Humphries Barker

Strength of Soul
by Naomi Raquel Enright

Dream of the Water Children:
Memory and Mourning in the Black Pacific
by Fredrick D. Kakinami Cloyd
Foreword by Velina Hasu Houston, Introduction by Gerald Horne
Edited by Karen Chau

The Fourth Moment: Journeys from the Known to the Unknown, A Memoir
by Carole J. Garrison, with an Introduction by Sarah Willis

POETRY
Ransom Street, Poems by Claire Millikin
Introduction by Kathleen Ellis

Wounds Fragments Derelict, Poems by Carlos Gabriel Kelly
Introduction by Sean Frederick Forbes

PAPOLíTICO, Poems of a Political Persuasion
by Jesús Papoleto Meléndez
with an Introduction by Joel Kovel and DeeDee Halleck

Critics of Mystery Marvel, Collected Poems
by Youssef Alaoui, Introduction by Laila Halaby

shrimp
by jason vasser-elong, Introduction by Michael Castro

The Revlon Slough, New and Selected Poems
by Ray DiZazzo, Introduction by Claire Millikin

A Country Without Borders: Poems and Stories of Kashmir
by Lalita Pandit Hogan, Introduction by Frederick Luis Aldama

2Leaf Press is an imprint owned and operated by 2Leaf Press Inc. a Florida-based non-profit organization that publishes and promotes multicultural literature.

FLORIDA ■ NEW YORK
www.2leafpress.org